THE WOMAN QUESTION

THE WOMAN QUESTION
Society and Literature in Britain and America, 1837–1883

Volume 3: Literary Issues

Elizabeth K. Helsinger
Robin Lauterbach Sheets
William Veeder

THE UNIVERSITY OF CHICAGO PRESS
Chicago & London

The University of Chicago Press, Chicago 60637
The University of Chicago Press, Ltd., London

98 97 96 95 94 93 92 91 90 89   5 4 3 2 1

Library of Congress Cataloging in Publication Data

Helsinger, Elizabeth K., 1943–
  The woman question.

  Originally published: New York : Garland, 1983.
  Bibliography: p.
  Includes index.
  Contents: v. 1. Defining voices — v. 2. Social issues
—v. 3. Literary issues.
    1. Women—England—History—19th century. 2. Women—
United States—History—19th century. 3. Women in lit-
erature. 4. Feminism—England—History—19th century.
5. Feminism—United States—History—19th century.
I. Sheets, Robin Ann. II. Veeder, William R. III. Title.
HQ1599.E5H44 1989   305.4′0942   88-27796
ISBN 0-226-32666-7 (pbk.; v. 1)
      0-226-32667-5 (pbk.; v. 2)
      0-226-32668-3 (pbk.; v. 3)

⊗ The paper in this publication meets the minimum requirements
of the American National Standard for Information Sciences—
Permanence of Paper for Printed Library Materials,
ANSI Z39.48-1984.

Acknowledgments

In the eight years since this project was conceived we have accumulated many debts. In particular we would like to thank Nina Auerbach, Edy Cobey, Donald W. Dayton, Michael P. Ditchkofsky, T.J. Edelstein, Clarissa Erwin, Mary Anne Ferguson, Robert Ferguson, Dan Gottlieb, John S. and Robin Haller, Sally Hoffheimer, Randolph Woods Ivy, Robin Jacoby, Elizabeth Janeway, U.C. Knoepflmacher, Margaret Lourie, Ann Matthews, Katharine Rogers, Sue Sayne, Joanne Schlichter, Kitty Von Pabst, George Worth, John Wright, Bonnie Zimmerman, the Humanities Division of the University of Chicago, the Taft Foundation, and the University of Cincinnati Research Council.

We are grateful to the following for permission to reproduce works in their collections: *Forbes Magazine* Collection (illustration 1, Volume I; illustration 2, Volume II); The Tate Gallery, London (illustration 5, Volume III); The Metropolitan Museum of Art, Rogers Fund, 1908 (illustration 7, Volume III). For permission to reprint material from previously published works we wish to thank: Harvard University Press and Manchester University Press for excerpts from *The Letters of Elizabeth Gaskell*, edited by J.A.V. Chapple and Arthur Pollard; University of California Press for a passage quoted in *Christina Rossetti*, by Lona M. Packer; Yale University Library and Yale University Press for a Barbara Bodichon letter included in *The George Eliot Letters*, edited by Gordon Haight. We have made every effort to identify the owners of copyrighted material; we would appreciate having any oversights called to our attention.

Finally, to our spouses, Howard and Jim and Mary, to the three children who have grown up with this project, Aaron and

Sarah and Maisie, and to the three children who were born while it was underway, the two Alex's and Willy, we owe thanks for their respective patience or joyful obliviousness to our long and often perplexed encounter with the Victorian Woman Question.

Contents

Illustrations

Introduction

Discoveries about Victorian women have within the last decade raised serious doubts about our modern understanding of the nineteenth century. What really were the culture's attitudes toward men and women? The question is much less easy to answer now than it once seemed to be. Close study of public opinion between 1837 and 1883 suggests that the traditional model of "a" Victorian attitude—patriarchal domination, expressed publicly as "woman worship"—is inadequate. The predominant form of Victorian writing about women is not pronouncement but debate. Moreover, the arguments in this debate were both more complex and more fluid than the model of a single dominant cultural myth would indicate. For Victorians of "the articulate classes,"[1] the Woman Question, as they themselves called it, really was a question.

Almost any public statement bearing on the Woman Question —whether an essay, a review, a novel, a poem, a lecture, a cartoon, or a painting—was likely to generate a chain of responses, and to be read as a response to prior statements in an ongoing public discussion. To view any of these statements out of context, which as modern readers we often do when we study a novel or a painting, may properly emphasize the integrity of imaginative creation but can only distort our perception of Victorian thinking about women. Charlotte Brontë, Elizabeth Cady Stanton, and John Stuart Mill were not isolated dissenters from a chorus praising one womanly ideal. The controversies in which Brontë, Stanton, and Mill participated form the context for prescriptive writers like Sarah Ellis and Anthony Comstock. Until we understand how these voices of protest and prescription relate to the larger contemporary discussion, the old concept of a single public Victorian attitude toward women will remain largely intact.

For the present study, we have constructed the debate which surrounds prescriptive pronouncements, protests, and imaginative literature about women. Though many of the voices are no longer familiar, most were regular or momentarily prominent contributors to the public discourse of their time. Some are close to the centers of a literate, governing, and opinion-shaping class; others are more eccentric. All, however, were responding to one another in public forums—in books and pamphlets, from pulpits and lecterns, and above all, through the periodicals. For the most part, these exchanges did not take place on a high theoretical plane; they were precipitated by particular political, economic, scientific, religious, or cultural events, and they focused on specific and limited problems. Should married women be granted property rights? What can be done about the high infant mortality rate among mothers working in the mills? What do physiological studies of evolutionary man indicate about women's mental capacities? Does the popularity of sensation novels reveal suppressed anti-social impulses among female readers? Nearly every contemporary topic provoked controversy over women, but the diversity of opinions and issues should not obscure the crucial point: for literate Anglo-American Victorians, woman's nature and place were called into question.

To convey the special qualities of the Victorian debate we have departed in several ways from both the normal format (the anthology or collection of documents) and the prevailing approaches of recent work on the Woman Question. We wish to preserve the polemical immediacy of public controversy by letting the Victorians speak for themselves in the give-and-take of the original debate. At the same time, however, particular voices and controversies need to be placed within their social and cultural context. Our book is thus a critical history of controversies presented directly through Victorian speakers. We have varied the proportions of text and analysis from chapter to chapter. Where the intrinsic interest of the texts is great, especially if they are unfamiliar today, we have quoted generously; in other cases we have excerpted more sparingly and expanded our historical and critical commentary. To include some forgotten writers important in their own day we have omitted sustained analysis of others, like Mary Wollstonecraft, whose work is better known and more accessible today.

We have also departed from prevailing practice by considering British and American discussions together as parts of a single debate. On some issues, of course, the discussions are simply parallel, while others diverge to follow national or local concerns. Nonetheless, Victorian Britain and America formed a single community of letters, within which national variations in the treatment of women provided yet another subject for common discussion. Our writers constantly refer to, quote, and directly respond to statements of conditions from across the Atlantic. Though we have not attempted a comprehensive comparison of British and American views, we have included numerous instances of cross-Atlantic exchanges, and noted parallels and divergences of opinion in particular controversies. Where it became necessary to choose between British and American versions of a debate, we have given the one less familiar today, usually the British—except where the American controversy was notably more heated (as in the case of most religious issues). Our Anglo-American perspective affirms for the Woman Question as a whole what Mary Macarthur observed of the womens' trade union leagues: that the British movement was both the grandmother and the granddaughter of the American.[2]

Finally, our treatment of the Woman Question departs from much recent practice by focusing on middle-class opinions and including male as well as female voices. These choices reflect the nature of the public debate: it was a largely middle-class discussion in which both men and women participated. We have not set out to uncover new examples of the lost views of working class or female sub-cultures. We have, however, made extensive use of the work of feminist critics and social historians who have explored these hidden strains of behavior and opinion. As far as possible, we have tried to indicate the distance between those perceptions of women which shaped the public debate, and evidence which suggests a different Victorian reality. Our aim is to study the nature of that distance and, wherever possible, to examine the reasons for it: personal, social, and cultural. However, this should not suggest that public perception was always at odds with private practice and belief. Conflicting opinions and competing mythologies did find expression within the public debate. Moreover, those who defended "woman's place" and those who sympathized with women's rights were often far more closely linked than we had suspected.

It is, indeed, often difficult to predict where the "conservative" and "dissenting" positions will lie in any particular controversy—or to predict just which assumptions about woman's nature conservatives or dissenters will employ in their arguments. Relatively few Victorians maintained rigidly consistent theoretical positions. Many of the most outspoken, like Elizabeth Cady Stanton, could appeal—with equal conviction and in the same speech—to conflicting cultural myths about women. And even those who were theoretically consistent might still disagree over practical applications: whether, for example, women should be doctors. Conversely, defenders of women doctors might make different assumptions about women's intellectual abilities, rights to professional training, or special feminine characteristics (like patience and solicitude) which fitted them for medicine. Such diversity of both argument and conclusion makes any strict definition of feminist or anti-feminist positions very difficult. We can speak more accurately not of positions but of a set of competing, though not mutually exclusive, myths or models for woman's place in society. Controversialists used these myths to argue for opposing solutions to contemporary problems.

Among such myths we have found four which are especially pervasive. First, the familiar Angel in the House—the wife and mother described in Sarah Ellis' conduct manuals, praised in Felicia Heman's poetry, and embodied in the Agnes Wickfield of Dickens' *David Copperfield*. Her nature is loving and self-sacrificing; her responsibilities, domestic and maternal. Although she is a delicate creature worshipped and protected by husbands and sons, she not only works hard at home but also provides continuity and moral strength in a rapidly changing society. Second, the model of complete equality—women as equal contracting partners with men, legally, sexually, and economically free agents in both domestic and professional matters. Though this model had some famous and articulate advocates—Mill, William Thompson, George Drysdale, Susan B. Anthony—it was so disconcertingly radical and so much at odds with the widespread interest in woman's "special" nature and duties that it seems to have played a smaller role in the public debate than two other competitors to the angelic ideal. One of these might be called the Angel out of the House. Although this model for woman's behavior accepted fundamental differences between men and women, it extended the wife's sphere beyond her home and family. The Angel out of the House did not challenge the leadership of men, but she did define her own distinctive tasks, ministering to the needs of the world at large through philanthropy or social service. The incarnation of this freed Angel, in the popular view, was Florence Nightingale. Finally, there is a radical version of the angelic ideal which combines a belief in woman's distinctive nature with claims for a leadership role in the world—a female saviour leading the way to a fuller humanity and ushering in a new era of community and love. This vision of woman's unique role, which might best be described as apocalyptic feminism, attracted both eccentrics like Eliza Farnham and, to some extent, even staunch conservatives like Sara Josepha Hale, editor of *Godey's Lady's Magazine*. For some, like Farnham, it amounted to an absolute claim to female superiority; for others, like Margaret Fuller, a temporary claim for woman's special role within an overall vision of human equality. Though this view of woman, like the egalitarian view, was held by a minority, it affected surprisingly large numbers of women, especially in America. In the last third of the century it helped fuel the campaigns to abolish contagious diseases acts, hold men to a single sexual standard, promote temperance, improve prisons, and reform corrupt municipal governments. The distinctions between the Angel in the House, the Angel out of the House, and the Female Saviour are often particularly difficult to draw. One or more of these three related but competing myths of woman underlie most of the arguments brought forward in the Woman Question.

These alternative views of woman have, of course, relatives and antecedents before 1837. The Victorian Woman Question is only one chapter in the history of that debate. Both the advocates of an angelic ideal and, particularly, the advocates of equality have important predecessors among late eighteenth and early nineteenth-century writers. Many of the particular issues debated by Victorians had also been discussed before. Yet Victorians themselves, beyond a rare reference to blue stockings or Mary Wollstonecraft, or to early female preachers and writers, did not often trace their views back to the immediate past. To some extent they were right: distinctive emphases, particular myths, even a common set of terms—"woman's mission," "woman's sphere," "woman's influence"—unite the varied controversies between the 1830s and the 1880s.

We have begun our history with six chapters which illustrate the particularly Victorian qualities of the debate. Volume I: *Defining Voices* is exemplary rather than historical; it focuses on representative texts, figures, and controversies for what they reveal about the general character of the Woman Question rather than for their historical connections with earlier and later phases of the debate. The second and third volumes of our study reconstruct and analyze the debate in society and literature as it evolved across the half century from Victoria's accession to the mid-1880s. Volume II: *Social Issues* traces the progress of controversy in law, science, work, and religion. Volume III: *Literary Issues* follows literary debates over the same period, dealing first with public discussion of the woman writer and second with the debate generated by a variety of literary heroines. Chapter 1 discusses the culture's assumptions about sexuality and art, giving particular attention to the traditional roles of muse and mother and to the threats that were perceived in woman's new role of maker. Chapter 2 examines the constraints of the separate sphere implied in the enthusiastic praise for lyric poetry and domestic fiction. The controversy over poets centers on the sense of self, the relation between emotion and art, and the right to speak on social issues; critics of fiction disagree about the kinds of experience appropriate for women's novels, leaving the writers to decide whether to write with women's names or with male pseudonyms. Chapters 3, 4 and 5 trace changing depictions of and critical attitudes toward the angelic heroine (and her strong-minded opposite), the passionate heroine (including fallen, "sensational," and Pre-Raphaelite women), and the American Girl.

One last word. The authors of this history have sometimes found themselves in no more agreement than their Victorian subjects. On most matters our discussions have led to consensus, but we realize that our individual perceptions and myths—like those of the Victorians—run deep, and will be reflected in the selection of voices as well as in the commentary on them. The structure, the format, and the emphases on common themes and arguments are our joint decisions, but each chapter is the work of a single author. Some differences in attitude between them we have not attempted to resolve. Many of the questions debated in the nineteenth century are still very much alive. We can only offer our own differences as testimony to the continuing vitality of the debate.

Notes

[1] So named by G.M. Young, *Victorian England: Portrait of an Age* (London: Oxford Univ. Press, 1936), p. 6.

[2] At the 1919 Convention of the National Women's Trade Union League of America, quoted by Gladys Boone in *The Women's Trade Union League in Great Britain and the United States of America* (New York: Columbia Univ. Press, 1942), p. 20.

The Woman Question
LITERARY ISSUES

1. The Scribbling Woman. Mrs. E.D.E.N. Southworth
Yankee Notions; after George Cruikshank in *The Comic Almanack*

1

Mothers, Muses, and Makers

In England and America, the nineteenth century was hailed as the age of the woman writer. As early as 1835, the *North American Review* observed that "the literary empire, like almost every other, has been divided." Looking forward to reading more books by women, the reviewer entreated them to use their "happy and improving influence" in "all those branches of literature, which are most nearly connected with the welfare of mankind, and tend to exalt and dignify our nature."[1] In 1864 *Sharpe's* also gave enthusiastic encouragement to women writers; the critic believed that women would widen the boundaries of literature by providing access to a new range of human experience.[2] Speaking in 1865, feminist Bessie Rayner Parkes advised women looking for work to enter the literary profession, a field "already conquered by its feminine aspirants," and one which could be easily accommodated to women's lives because "its successful exercise demands little or none of that moral courage which more public avocations require."[3]

With encouragement came cries of alarm, as the Victorians realized that women authors were achieving professional status, financial reward, and literary distinction in varying, but still unprecedented, degrees. Literary women were ridiculed in caricatures and admonished in conduct manuals and major periodicals [see illustrations 1 and 2]. Much of the concern was economic, especially in America, where Sarah Josepha Hale edited *Godey's*, the magazine with the largest national circulation, and where women like Fanny Fern (née Sarah Willis), Susan Warner, E.D.E.N. Southworth, and Harriet Beecher Stowe wrote the most popular novels of the period. Hawthorne denounced the "d—d mob of scribbling women" who were outselling him in America,[4] while in England critic and novelist George Henry Lewes demonstrated considerably more irony by issuing "A Gentle Hint to Writing Women." For the 1850 *Leader*, Lewes assumes a comic mask and laughs at the personal and professional insecurities of his male colleagues.

> It will never do. We are overrun. Women carry all before them. My mother assures me that, in *her* day, women were content to boil dumplings (and what dumplings! no such rotundities of odorous delight smoke upon *our* tables: indeed the dumpling is a myth) and do plain needlework; if they made a dash at the Battle of Prague, *that* was the summit of their accomplishments. But *now*, as the same illustrious author of my days justly remarks, now women study Greek and despise dumplings. If they *only* studied Greek, I should not care; . . . but, from reading books to writing books, the sublime to the ridiculous, you know the distance!
>
> It's a melancholy fact, and against all Political Economy, that the group of female authors is becoming every year more multitudinous and more successful. Women write the best novels, the best travels, the best reviews, the best leaders, and the best cookery-books. . . . They are turning us men into "drugs" (in the market, of course! metaphorically and not apothecarily)—they are ruining our profession. Wherever we carry our skilful pens, we find the place preoccupied by a woman. The time was when my contributions were sought as favours; my graceful phrase was to be seen threading, like a meandering stream, through the rugged mountains of statistics, and the dull plains of matter of fact, in every possible publication. *Then* the pen was a profession. But now I starve. What am I to do—what are my brother-pens to do, when such rivalry is permitted? How many of us can write novels like Currer Bell, Mrs. Gaskell, Geraldine Jewsbury, Mrs. Marsh, Mrs. Crowe, and fifty others, with their shrewd and delicate observation of life? How many of us can place our prose beside the glowing rhetoric and daring utterance of social wrong in the learned romances and powerful articles of Eliza Lynn, or the cutting sarcasm and vigorous protests of Miss Rigby? What chance have we against Miss Martineau, so potent in so many directions? . . .

This is the "march of mind," but where, oh, where are the dumplings! Does it never strike these delightful creatures that their little fingers were made to be kissed not to be inked? Does it never occur to them that they are doing us a serious injury, and that we need "protection?" Woman's proper sphere of activity is elsewhere. Are there no husbands, lovers, brothers, friends to coddle and console? Are there no stockings to darn, no purses to make, no braces to embroider? *My* idea of a perfect woman is of one who can write but won't; who knows all that authors know and a great deal more; who can appreciate my genius and not spoil my market; who can pet me, and flatter me, and flirt with me, and work for me, and sing to me, and love me: I have named Julia. Yes, she is a perfect woman; she never wrote a book. And what shall I say of thee, my stately Harriet, with raven locks and flashing eyes, whom all adore? It is true there *are* rumours of your having poisoned your husband, but *what* could you do less? At any rate you have never written a book; and when I think of that, I really see how the little conjugal episode just alluded to may have many excuses.

Political economists complain of young ladies making purses and embroidering braces as taking work from the industrious classes. But I should like to know what they call writing books and articles but taking work from the industrious authors? To knit a purse or work an ottoman is a graceful and useful devotion of female energies. . . . *That* is what I call something like woman's mission! Women of England! listen to my words: Your path is the path of perdition, your literary impulses are the impulses of Satan. Burn your pens, and purchase wool. Arm chairs are to be made; waistcoats can be embroidered: throw yourselves courageously into *this* department, and you will preserve the deep love, respect, and gratitude (when you work him chairs) of your sorrowful and reproachful VIVIAN

P.S. Since the above went to press I have received a stout packet from Harriet. Opening it with eagerness to find some token of her thoughtful kindness I was aghast at seeing a bulky and illegible M.S. in her own handwriting. It bears this title,—

"CONFESSIONS OF A WASTED HEART."

It is the story of her own domestic life, which Harriet begs me to take to Colburn and negotiate with him respecting its publication; £300 is the lowest sum she will accept. . . . I begin to have modified views respecting that conjugal episode which made Harriet a widow; doubts assail me as to whether Dowding was the domestic tyrant Harriet's mother always declared he was.[5]

"Vivian" prefers the earlier age when women were content to be the mothers of literary men instead of the authors of their own books. Although he would like an intelligent wife who will encourage and appreciate his genius, he realizes that the women of his generation are, by writing, rejecting the role his mother had once fulfilled. "Vivian" regards writing as a dangerous activity for women, not only because it takes them away from needlework, but also because it takes them away from men. He worries that literary women will neglect their husbands, and concludes that Harriet might have murdered hers. Because her novel is based on her unhappy marriage, he associates it with anger and aggression.

Lewes saw that the anxiety about women authors was emotional as well as economic and that their writing was a threat at home as well as in the marketplace. Unlike Lewes, most Victorians did not find the situation amusing. Indeed, many agreed with "Vivian" that women should help men in developing their talents; that a woman's commitment to her own writing would destroy her femininity, threaten her marriage, and disrupt her household; and that literary women were often characterized by strong passions and notorious conduct. To understand these uneasy attitudes toward women writers, it is necessary to consider three issues: the traditional roles of mother or muse which women were asked to take in assisting male artists, and the threats posed by woman as maker: womanly duties in conflict with artistic dedication and the sexual implications of female creativity.

I

During the 1830s and 1840s, writers recommended several ways for women to assist in the transmission of their country's culture: they could serve as the mothers and wives of great men, they could inspire creative activity, and they could use their influence as readers and patrons to improve the taste and tone of society. Three representative speakers insist upon the importance of these functions. Declaring that artists should marry in order to avoid the dangers of celibacy, Isaac Disraeli, a popular writer and the father of the future prime minister, offers sketches of several good wives in *The Literary Characteristics of Men of Genius* (1840). Salomon Gessner, a Swiss writer and painter of the eighteenth century, had a wife who was in Disraeli's opinion "incomparable."

> While Gessner gave himself up entirely to his favourite arts, drawing, painting, etching, and poetry, his wife would often reanimate a genius that was apt to despond in its attempts, and often exciting him to new productions, her sure and delicate taste was attentively consulted by the poet-painter—but she combined the most practical good sense with the most feeling imagination. This forms the rareness of the character; for this same woman, who united with her husband in the education of their children, to relieve him from the interruptions of common business, carried on alone the concerns of his house in *la librairie*. . . . Imagine a woman attending to the domestic economy, and to the commercial details, yet withdrawing out of this business of life into the more elevated pursuits of her husband, and at the same time combining with all this the cares and counsels which she bestowed on her son to form the artist and the man. . . . Such was the incomparable wife and mother of the Gessners! Will it now be a question whether matrimony be incompatible with the cultivation of the arts? A wife who reanimates the drooping genius of her husband, and a mother who is inspired by the ambition of beholding her sons eminent, is she not the real being which the ancients personified in their Muse?[6]

Other writers describe the muse in grander terms.[7] Celebrating woman as the source of poetic inspiration, the 1833 *Fraser's* extolls her personal beauty and the sanctity of her ideals.

> Beauty is to a woman what poetry is to a language, and their similarity accounts for their conjunction; for there never yet existed a female possessed of personal loveliness who was not only poetical in herself but the cause of poetry in others. Were the subject to be properly examined, it would be discovered that the first dawn of poetical genius in a man proceeds, almost invariably, from his acquaintance with the other sex. . . . Without woman, the sweet humanities of existence would be unknown to us, love would be a stranger to our bosoms, and poetry would cease to invest with its hallowed loveliness the kind endearments of social life, and the bright enjoyments of home.[8]

Novelist Edward Bulwer-Lytton believed that women readers could have a refining influence on the nation. In *New Monthly Magazine* (1832) he presses them to commit themselves to serious literature in order to raise the moral and aesthetic standards of the age.

In a country like ours, where active pursuits, commerce, politics, professions, engage so vast a proportion of our men, the women, as every publisher knows, are the great dictating portion of the reading world. And to this, coupled with their education which enables them only to appreciate the lighter and more brilliant order of letters, we owe the great preponderance in point of sale and circulation which novels bear over every other class of composition. . . .

The influence is great—let it be directed nobly: instead of debasing our ambition to the externals of dress, and wealth, and rank—the mere coral and bells of the Baby Fashion—why may it not stimulate us to independence—to a disdain of the selfish Deities we now adore—and make Love, which we at present do right in confusing with Vice, the aliment, the support, the inspiration of Virtue? To be the "Idol of a Drawing-room!" what praise so equivocal?—what distinction can imply qualities so frivolous?— why should it be so? . . . Even in France, there was a time when that phrase was bestowed on the most brilliant wit, on the deepest author, as well as on the wealthiest Peer, or the most accomplished gallant. This was only because women could appreciate wit and genius according to its true dignity; here they do not appreciate— they affront—they make lions, not deities—think of the oddity of talent, not its value, and rather ask a man of genius to be stared at than to be honoured. With women, whose organization renders them so susceptible to new impressions—who are ever prone, when their emotions are deeply roused, to forego and forget self— who, in all great revolutions of mind, from the uprising of a new genius in letters to the promulgation of a new doctrine in religion, are the earliest to catch the inspiration and lead on opinion—with women it will always rest to expedite and advance the career of Social Reform—may they be sensible to the benefits that such reform promises for themselves as for us![9]

Later commentators also find these roles appropriate for women. In 1863 *All the Year Round* complains that Englishwomen do not provide literary men with the personal patronage and intellectual stimulation that Frenchwomen exerted through their salons; in 1864 the *London Review* asks women to abandon their own writing and to return to their proper mission "of keeping alive for men certain ideas, and ideals."[10] It was easier —and far more comfortable—to see woman as the muse instead of the maker.

II

In a well-known letter to essayist and art critic Anna Jameson, Elizabeth Barrett Browning criticized nursing as a mere extension of women's traditional responsibilities and concluded that she and Jameson had made a much more radical decision by embarking upon their careers in art.[11] To become a writer does imply a deviation from prescribed female patterns. The distance between reading and writing is, as "Vivian" realized, immense. Writing represents power, self-assertion, active shaping rather than passive acceptance. In the 1840s and 1850s, the Victorians were not at all sure that it could be accommodated within the code of True Womanhood.

In response to criticism like "Vivian's," the writers were eager to demonstrate that their work was neither a betrayal of their womanly nature nor a rejection of their duties. They deny that they are seeking fame or self-advancement. Instead they ascribe other motives to themselves: a cause, the call of God, the pursuit of an elusive truth or a love of beauty so intense that it transcends personal ambition. While trying to discredit the charges of vanity and pride, women writers also assert their commitment to domestic responsibilities. They were determined, said Harriet Taylor in 1851, not to give men any occasion to say "that learning makes women unfeminine, and that literary ladies are likely to be bad wives."[12] She accused these women of toadying to the established values of a male-dominated press, and John Stuart Mill deplored the fact that household chores and social decorum were draining energy that women should use for their artistic endeavors.[13] But despite such criticism, the great majority of the writers who lived during this period accepted, and indeed endorsed, their domestic responsibilities.[14] As the conditions of their lives became known, some, like Elizabeth Barrett Browning and Harriet Beecher Stowe, were enshrined as loving mothers; others, like Charlotte Brontë and Louisa May Alcott, earned respect as dutiful daughters.

The question of reconciling femininity and art provoked a variety of responses, as suggested by the four texts that follow. An article from *Fraser's* presents an idealized portrait of a poet *and* pretty young mother; novelists Margaret Oliphant and Elizabeth Gaskell provide some qualification of the ideal; and the American writer Fanny Fern advocates a covert rejection of it. Eager to win sympathy and admiration for the woman of genius,

Fraser's depicts a woman writer with enough delicacy, sentiment, and piety to disarm the most misogynistic critic. "Mrs. Verner" has overcome all the dangers of an artist's life. Moreover, her motives are unassailable: needing no money and craving no fame, she is an author "who in innocence of heart and not without enthusiasm, follows literature from pure affection." This extract from the 1846 essay begins with a question from Miss Merton, an older friend who has come to her home for a visit.

"When we parted you were only becoming aware of the powers with which you were gifted, and now you are an authoress. Well I remember the strange new delight you betrayed, and how you seemed to glory in the wealth of mind you had but then known yourself to possess! Have you found all the happiness you expected in your new occupation?"

"All, and more than all," replied Mrs. Verner. "The wild triumphant gladness of the time to which you have referred may have given place to calmer and humbler feelings, but I regret neither the time nor the labour I have bestowed in endeavouring to bring nearer to perfection the faculties wherewith God has endowed me." . . .

"And you," said Miss Merton, "are not one of those poetesses who repine at the comparative solitude of mind consequent on their peculiar talents?"

"No, no! but then I am so happy at home," said the young authoress. "It is true," she added, smiling, "that there are some whimsical inconsistencies in our lives, when we are managers of a household as well as authoresses; and the sudden transitions from the ideal to the actual are often really comic. For instance, I am writing something very tragic. 'What can I do to save you?' cries my hero. 'Would that the sacrifice of . . .' 'Six pound of kitchen candles, ma'am,' exclaims the cook, popping her head into the room. . . . Interruptions of this kind are of course very frequent in my small establishment."

"Now, if you had numbered this among your trials, I should not have been surprised," remarked Miss Merton. "But as to society, have you such as you can like about you here?"

"I suppose society is much the same in every country neighbourhood," replied Mrs. Verner. "It is only by a happy accident that I now and then meet a person of my own tastes and habits,— indeed I speak of them to none but my husband from year's end to year's end, generally. But there is abundant kindness among those who dwell about us, and with some of them, no lack of good sense and information. Few, I believe, are aware of the nature of my pursuits, for I am somewhat careful to conceal them. You know how much I always detested the idea of ever becoming the pet poet of a coterie. Did I ever tell you of my being once at a party in which I found myself treated *professionally?* Never was any thing more ridiculous. The people of the house,—excellent people and old friends,—were whispering my praises, and asking this person and that person whether they had read my compositions. . . ."

"I must confess," observed Miss Merton, "that you have given me a new view of the trials of an authoress. We are accustomed to hear much of the unhappiness of literary women in their domestic life; of the want of sympathetic taste in their husbands, if husbands they have; too often, alas! of their own errors."

However, Mrs. Verner does admit that she, like all gifted women, has found it difficult to deal with the dullness and insipidity of life.

"If I told you all that the experience of my own heart and mind had taught me, I might reveal strange things. Who knows that I have not personally felt the dangerous power of the 'voice of the charmer,'—the voice of sympathy, or what seemed such,—pleading in delicious music amidst the wearisome monotony of common conversation? Who knows that I may not have turned from the vapid dulness of every-day life to the excitement of associating with what we poets call a 'kindred spirit?' . . . The sameness of ordinary existence is a trial to the unquiet spirit of a woman of genius. Even negative happiness is not enough. There is a longing, not merely to *exist*, but to *live*, to experience all varieties of feeling. . . ."

"Where, then, is such a being to turn for happiness?"

"To Him who looks with pity on the weaknesses of humanity. Religion alone can control and guide the wild impulses of a nature so aspiring, yet so weak, so eagerly thirsting for good, yet so prone to be dazzled by evil. But our conversation has again deepened into seriousness. . . . We are interrupted in good time," she continued, as her laughing children bounded into the room, followed by her husband.[15]

Although "Mrs. Verner's" serenity, her economic security, and her seclusion from society were by no means typical, some women writers echo her pleasure at being surrounded by their families. None is more cheerful than Margaret Oliphant. Her *Autobiography*, which was published posthumously in 1899, gives a much more realistic but equally affirmative picture of the writer at home.

I had no table even to myself, much less a room to work in, but sat at the corner of the family table with my writing-book, with everything going on as if I had been making a shirt instead of writing a book. Our rooms in those days were sadly wanting in artistic arrangement. The table was in the middle of the room, the centre round which everybody sat with the candles or lamp upon it. My mother sat always at needle-work of some kind, and talked to whoever might be present, and I took my share in the conversation, going on all the same with my story, the little groups of imaginary persons, these other talks evolving themselves quite undisturbed. . . . But up to this date, 1888, I have never been shut up in a separate room, or hedged off with any observances. My study, all the study I have ever attained to, is the little second drawing-room where all the (feminine) life of the house goes on; and I don't think I have ever had two hours undisturbed (except at night, when everybody is in bed) during my whole literary life. Miss Austen, I believe, wrote in the same way, and very much for the same reason; but at her period the natural flow of life took another form. The family were half ashamed to have it known that she was not just a young lady like the others, doing her embroidery. Mine were quite pleased to magnify me, and to be proud of my work, but always with a hidden sense that it was an admirable joke, and no idea that any special facilities or retirement was necessary.[16]

Elizabeth Gaskell, a minister's wife and spirited mother of four daughters, maintains that women are obligated to discharge domestic chores *and* to exercise their God-given talents, but she sees that the balance is hard to attain. In her 1857 *Life of Charlotte Brontë*, Gaskell observes:

Henceforward Charlotte Brontë's existence becomes divided into two parallel currents—her life as Currer Bell, the author; her life as Charlotte Brontë, the woman. There were separate duties belonging to each character—not opposing each other; not impossible, but difficult to be reconciled. When a man becomes an author, it is probably merely a change of employment to him. He takes a portion of that time which has hitherto been devoted to some other study or pursuit; he gives up something of the legal or medical profession, in which he has hitherto endeavoured to serve others, or relinquishes part of the trade or business by which he has been striving to gain a livelihood; and another merchant or lawyer, or doctor, steps into his vacant place, and probably does as well as he. But no other can take up the quiet, regular duties of the daughter, the wife, or the mother, as well as she whom God has appointed to fill that particular place: a woman's principal work in life is hardly left to her own choice; nor can she drop the domestic charges devolving on her as an individual, for the exercise of the most splendid talents that were ever bestowed. And yet she must not shrink from the extra responsibility implied by the very fact of her possessing such talents. She must not hide her gift in a napkin; it was meant for the use and service of others. In an humble and faithful spirit must she labour to do what is not impossible, or God would not have set her to do it.[17]

While corresponding with the successful painter Eliza Fox, Gaskell discusses the conflict between art and home, self-assertion and service to others. In an 1850 letter written in odd moments eked out of hectic days at home, Gaskell tries two ways of resolving the conflict: first, by seeing the world of the imagination as an anodyne necessary for making everyday life more bearable; second, by regarding her writing as a form of work which has divine sanction.

My dearest Tottie,

Here is Mr Broinett [her children's music teacher] giving his lesson, and I am playing Dragon; so while I dragonize, (I wish you could hear O Salutaris Hostia they are now singing,) I shall write to you. I have a great deal to say; only I don't know if I can ever get the leisure to think and say it out. . . .

One thing is pretty clear, Women, must give up living an artist's life, if home duties are to be paramount. It is different with men, whose home duties are so small a part of their life. However we are talking of women. I am sure it is healthy for them to have the refuge of the hidden world of Art to shelter themselves in when too much pressed upon by daily small Lilliputian arrows of peddling cares; it keeps them from being morbid as you say; and takes them into the land where King Arthur lies hidden, and soothes them with its peace. I have felt this in writing, I see others feel it in music, you in painting, so assuredly a blending of the two is desirable. (Home duties and the development of the Individual I mean), which you will say it takes no Solomon to tell you but the difficulty is where and when to make one set of duties subserve and give place to the other. I have no doubt that the cultivation of each tends to keep the other in a healthy state,—my grammar is all at sixes and sevens I have no doubt but never mind if you can pick out my meaning. I think a great deal of what you have said. Thursday.

I've been reading over yr note, and believe I've only been repeating in different language what you said. If Self is to be the end of exertions, those exertions are unholy, there is no doubt of *that*—and that is part of the danger in cultivating the Individual Life; but I do believe we have all some appointed work to do, whh no one else can do so well; Wh. is *our* work; what *we* have to do in advancing the Kingdom of God; and that first we must find out what we are sent into the world to do, and define it and make it clear to ourselves, (that's *the* hard part) and then forget ourselves in our work, and our work in the End we ought to strive to bring about. I never can either talk or write clearly so I'll ee'n leave it alone. Hearn has been nearly 3 weeks away nursing her mother who is dying, so we are rather at sixes and sevens upstairs. The little ones come down upon us like the Goths on Rome; making inroads and onslaughts into all our plans.[18]

In the 1860s, when her little Goths are grown, Gaskell was still concerned about the place of art in a woman's life. Responding to a young mother who had sought her advice about becoming a novelist, Gaskell suggests that if small children sometimes require women to postpone their writing, the experience of having raised them will eventually enrich it.

The exercise of a talent or power *is* always a great pleasure; but one should weigh well whether this pleasure may not be obtained by the sacrifice of some duty. When I had *little* children I do not think I could have written stories, because I should have become too much absorbed in my *fictitious* people to attend to my *real* ones. I think you would be sorry if you began to feel that your desire to earn money, even for so laudable an object as to help your husband, made you unable to give your tender sympathy to your little ones in their small joys & sorrows; and yet, don't you know how you,— how every one, who tries to write stories *must* become absorbed in them, (fictitious though they be,) if they are to interest their readers in them. Besides viewing the subject from a solely artistic point of view a good writer of fiction must have *lived* an active & sympathetic life if she wishes her books to have strength & vitality in them. When you are forty, and if you have a gift for being an authoress you will write ten times as good a novel as you could do now, just because you will have gone through so much more of the interests of a wife and a mother.[19]

Fanny Fern is much less patient. Although she insists that household chores not be neglected, she knows how tedious they are, especially in homes where husbands disregard the intellectual and emotional needs of their wives. For her, the source of real tension is not the home, but the men who inhabit it. In this extract from *Folly As It Flies* (1868), writing becomes a form of private therapy rather than an act of public service; it does not result from God's inspiration, but from women's anger so intense that it endures after death.

Women can relieve their minds, now-a-days, in one way that was formerly denied them: they can write! a woman who wrote, used to be considered a sort of monster—At this day it is difficult to find one who does not write, or has not written, or who has not, at least, a strong desire to do so. Grid-irons and darning-needles are getting monotonous. A part of their time the women of to-day are content to devote to their consideration when necessary; but you will rarely find one—at least among women who *think*—who does not silently rebel against allowing them a monopoly.

What? you inquire, would you encourage, in the present over-crowded state of the literary market, any more women scribblers? Stop a bit. It does not follow that she should wish or seek to give to the world what she has written. I look around and see innumerable women, to whose barren, loveless life this would be improvement and solace, and I say to them, write! Write, if it will make that life brighter, or happier, or less monotonous. Write! it will be a safe outlet for thoughts and feelings, that maybe the nearest friend you have, has never dreamed had place in your heart and brain. You should have read the letters I have received; you should have talked with the women I have talked with; in short, you should have walked this earth with your eyes open, instead of shut, as far as its women are concerned, to indorse this advice. Nor do I qualify what I have said on account of social position, or age, or even education. It is not *safe* for the women of 1868 to shut down so much that cries out for sympathy and expression, because life is such a maelstrom of business or folly, or both, that those to whom they have bound themselves, body and soul, recognize only the needs of the former. *Let them write* if they will. One of these days, when that diary is found, when the hand that penned it shall be dust, with what amazement and remorse will many a husband, or father, exclaim, I never knew my wife, or my child, till this moment; all these years she has sat by my hearth, and slumbered by my side, and I have been a stranger to her. And you sit there, and you read sentence after sentence, and recall the day, the month, the week, when she moved calmly, and you thought happily, or, at least, contentedly, about the house, all the while her heart was aching, when a kind word from you, or even a touch of your hand upon her head, as you passed out to business, or pleasure, would have cheered her, oh so much! When had you sat down by her side

Mothers, Muses, and Makers   15

after the day's work for both was over, and talked with her just a few moments of something besides the price of groceries, and the number of shoes Tommy had kicked out, all of which, proper and necessary in their place, need not of necessity form the stable of conversation between a married pair; had you done this; had you recognized that she had a *soul* as well as yourself, how much sunshine you might have thrown over her colorless life! . . . You do not see, sir—you will not see—you do not desire to see, how her cheek flushes, and her eye moistens, and her heart sinks like lead as you thus wound her self-respect. You think her "cross and ill-natured," if when, the next morning, you converse with her on the price of butter, she answers you listlessly and with a total want of interest in the treadmill-subject.

I say to such women: Write! Rescue a part of each week at least for reading, and putting down on paper, for your own private benefit, your thoughts and feelings. Not for the *world's* eye, unless you choose, but to lift yourselves out the dead-level of your lives; to keep off inanition; to lesson the number who are yearly added to our lunatic asylums from the ranks of misappreciated, unhappy womanhood, narrowed by lives made up of details. Fight it! oppose it, for your own sakes and your children's! Do not be *mentally* annihilated by it.[20]

III

Fern's essay introduces the most troubling issue of all: the relationship of sexuality and art. In the discussions of women and literature, the sexually-laden language suggests two theories. According to one, female imagination is a volatile and highly erotic force that must be repressed, or at least controlled; according to the other, women's writing is a sign of sexual and emotional frustration. Both must be seen against the prevailing assumption that artistic creation is, like the sexual act, a male activity in which women have only an extremely restricted part. As the *Saturday Review* reminds readers in 1865, "Female nature, mental as well as physical, is essentially receptive and not creative."[21] Women's traditional responsibility is to arouse ideas and nurture them to full development. Defining women's role in the production of art, Mary Ann Stodart, a critic and classical scholar, concludes that "they are found at the commencement, and the close; they frequently inspire the leading sentiment, and they appreciate its expression."[22] In a much more explicit passage, Isaac Disraeli calls the operation of a poet's genius "an orgasm" which the wife patiently endured. "When the burst was over," writes Disraeli, the poet was "charmed by her docility."[23] The making of art, like the instilling of life, is for many Victorians a male prerogative.

The suspicion that female imagination is dangerous assumes that it is plentiful. Despite frequent denials of female creativity, some commentators suspect that women have *greater* artistic abilities than men. In an 1824 *Blackwood's*, American author John Neal advances an ingenious theory of the imagination.

> Imagination, I believe, to be always in proportion to animal sensibility, and to the delicacy of animal organization; women, I believe, to have more animal sensibility, because they are more delicately organized, than men; and, therefore, do I believe that women have *more* imagination than men.
>
> And I contend further, that, if women were educated precisely as men are; and, that, if they had the same opportunities and excitements, that men have—with no more discouragements— they would be more fruitful in works of imagination—in poetry, musick, sculpture, painting, and eloquence, than men are; but altogether less fruitful, in the abstract and profound sciences; in mathematicks, theology, logick, &c. &c. . . .
>
> But, I have promised some endeavour at proof. I have asserted that imagination is always in proportion to animal sensibility.—Is this denied? Look about you, and call to mind those persons, poets, orators, or musicians, who are most remarkable for imagination; and you will find them all, more or less distinguishable from other men, by the delicacy of their organs, or, in others words, by their greater animal sensibility—their more exquisite powers of sensation. Are they not, without one exception, volatile, hasty, capricious, and petulant? Do they ever pursue any one thing, steadily? Are they ever great proficients in science? Have you ever heard of a great mathematician, mechanick, or theologian, who was remarkable for his imagination, or at all remarkable for his animal sensibility,—or very irritable in his temper,—or exceedingly alive to the delicacies of touch, flavour, sound, sight, or smell?—never. For, if he had been so, he would never have been distinguished for abstract, severe, thoughtful science.
>
> Call to mind that man, whom you believe to have the most imagination; and, my life on it, that you find him the most irritable creature alive, for his years and constitution—the most unaccountable in his whims—and the most exquisitely sensible to all that *can* affect the senses. . . . All men, who have been greatly, and *peculiarly* distinguished, for splendour and activity of imagination, so

far as I know anything of them, have been men of inflammable bodily temperaments; great irritability of nerve—with clear, changeable eyes, thin skin, and fine hair, like women. . . . I established my first proposition— . . . My second, that women have more animal sensibility; and are more delicately organized than men, will require no farther proof, that the observation of every human being will furnish, at a glance.

The conclusion, then, is unavoidable, that women have *more* imagination than men.

Although Neal believes that society should encourage the development of women's imagination, a Victorian gentleman who read his description of its activity would very likely disagree.

The faculty of imagination waxes and wanes with our animal sensibility—flourishing precisely in that season, when our animal temperament is most irritable, irritating, and active—(as in youth, or under disease, when the whole atmosphere becomes luminous with beauty, and crowded with a magnificent population; or when we have taken wine, musick, or opium, till our animal nature is inflamed,) and gradually decaying with our animal sensibility.[24]

For parents, educators, and clerics, the imagination remains a source of constant danger. Women's imagination, which is often described as being as lurid and as insatiable as their sexual appetite, is compared to a raging fire; their interest in literature, to an addictive disease, an unhealthy craving. Because their feelings are so easily aroused, women can be overly excited by literature and led into imprudent, even immoral, activities. Men and women who recognize the hazards recommend three ways of overcoming them.

In *Thoughts on Self-Culture,* educators Maria Grey and Emily Shirreff identify the "common defect of the female mind" as a badly regulated imagination.

Could we search the secret annals of many a victim of folly or of vice, how often should we find that the first temptation came rather from *within* than from *without,* rather from the fancy than the heart! How often should we be forced to conclude, that the dangers which finally closed around, and caused her ruin, were at first created by her own disordered mind, and owed all their force to the spell which a vitiated imagination had cast over them. . . . If we examine many a one who is pitied as the victim of passion, we shall find that she never knew the meaning of the word, that her heart was really silent, and she was misled by mere delusions of her own making.

It will, perhaps, be objected, that if the dangers to which imagination may lead are so great, and threaten women so peculiarly, it is rather advisable to repress than to cultivate the natural strength of that faculty. This conclusion, however, seems to us most erroneous. The attempt to repress imagination could only produce . . . [a] chilling effect on the general character . . . without necessarily adding to the strength of the other faculties, since the absence of imagination by no means implies vigor of reason, while the mere neglect of its cultivation would simply allow the natural power to run riot without any of those preservatives against excess which are afforded by careful training, and the supply of worthy objects to excite it. It is *because* women are naturally endowed with lively imagination that the latter particularly needs cultivation to give it a proper tone, and to maintain its due position in the mental economy. . . .

The best means of cultivating the imagination remain now to be considered, and we shall derive considerable help in ascertaining what those are, by examining, . . . how essential the *love of the beautiful* is to the full and perfect development of that faculty. This feeling may be said to preserve the moral balance of the imagination, and where it is wanting, the latter is left to wander wildly without a guide, to follow the chimeras of its own creating instead of the ideals of truth and excellence. It is when severed from this its natural companion that imagination is too justly accused of being the ally of falsehood, and of hindering men in their course towards purity and true knowledge. It is then that it too often loves to revel in the strange, the horrible, the unnatural. . . .

The love of moral beauty and excellence is the highest form which this feeling can take. . . . When we speak of it here, we mean generally that affection of the mind which seeks after and delights in whatever is fair and excellent in the material or spiritual universe,—the loveliness and magnificence of nature, the beauty of art, the grandeur of intellectual achievements, and, above all, the sublimity of virtue. It is this affection which, in its highest development, inspires the poet and the artist; and in its lower degree draws forth, in our daily intercourse, all that is gentle and graceful in character; prompts the taste which adorns our dwellings and pleasure-grounds, refines the tone of society, and beautifies the details of life.[25]

Having separated imagination ("fancy") from passion ("heart"), Grey and Sherriff can argue for its cultivation. For them, as for

"Mrs. Verner," the female imagination escapes from sexuality and self and becomes tender, empathetic, ethereal.

Mary Ann Stodart is much less certain that the imagination can be controlled. In an 1842 book written to dispell prejudice against women writers, she portrays the dangers involved in reading and writing fiction.

> In women, the imagination is commonly too active, the judgment not sufficiently so; and there is no occasion to add fuel to flame, and thus increase the difficulty of bringing into subjection that faculty, which like the fire itself, may be said to be a good servant, but a bad master. . . . If the evils to a woman from novel-reading are not small, those which arise from novel writing are alarmingly great . . . that their attention is too exclusively directed to the tender passions, and this exclusive attention has a tendency to increase the force of those feelings, which in the gentler sex, are generally sufficiently strong. By close attention to any subject, the importance of that subject is magnified. A prominence greater than its relative value authorizes, is thus given to one part of the character, and independently of destroying the moral balance of power, the feelings to which we allude, are precisely those which are most to be guarded against. They are the weak part of woman; the breach in the wall by which the enemy often enters into the city.[26]

Stodart advises women to avoid novels and to work on such other genres as poetry, biography, and letters, but in 1864 the *London Review* goads them to give up authorship entirely. After acknowledging women's innate verbal abilities and recognizing their literary achievements, the author proceeds to argue that writing signifies a loss of purity—spiritually and, in some instances, even physically.

> Literature is not a profession to which English gentlemen are pleased to see their sisters and their daughters turn. There is an indistinct feeling at the bottom of their dislike of feminine authorship, which tells them that literary work has a tendency to wear off some of the delicate bloom which is perhaps the finest part of a woman's natural character. To understand by long experience the meannesses of the world, to comprehend the various ways in which men undergo moral declension and decay, and yet to be able to take a broad and comprehensive view of life after all the destruction of one's ideals and utopias, is part of the necessary qualification for a great writer. The women who attain to it must attain to it by

undergoing a defeminizing process; after which they gain much strength and breadth of view at the sacrifice of that nameless beauty of innocence which is by nature the glory of the woman, and which it is the object of English feminine training to preserve intact. The greatest female author living is certainly George Sand. How much has George Sand given up to gain her literary crown. She has simply abandoned the distinctive characteristics, not to say the distinctive mission, of her sex. She has gratified her genius by immolating to it her instincts and her nature. George Sand is an extreme instance. In this country, it is certain that she would be little admired if she were even tolerated in the world of literature. But though literary women amongst us would be horrified if they were told that George Sand was a type of themselves, she is a beacon that points out the rocks and shoals which literary women seldom reach, but in the direction of which most of them are sailing. Knowledge of life, with all its lights and shadows for a man, is part and a bitter part of his career. For a woman, it is the fruit from off a deadly tree, the taste of which opens to her the wide world, but closes to her the gates of the enchanted gardens of paradise.[27]

While some Victorians associate women's writing with passionate feelings and immoral conduct, others see it as evidence that a woman has failed to find emotional happiness and sexual fulfillment [see Illustration 2]. The latter theory receives its most famous expression in an 1852 essay that George Henry Lewes wrote for the *Westminster Review*.

ALMOST all literature has some remote connexion with suffering. . . . What Shelley says of poets, applies with greater force to women. If they turn their thoughts to literature, it is—when not purely an imitative act—always to solace by some intellectual activity the sorrow that in silence wastes their lives, and by a withdrawal of the intellect from the contemplation of their pain, or by a transmutation of their secret anxieties into types, they escape from the pressure of that burden. If the accidents of her position make her solitary and inactive, or if her thwarted affections shut her somewhat from that sweet domestic and maternal sphere to which her whole being spontaneously moves, she turns to literature as to another sphere. We do not here simply refer to those notorious cases where literature has been taken up with the avowed and conscious purpose of withdrawing thoughts from painful subjects; but to the unconscious unavowed influence of domestic disquiet and unfulfilled expectations, in determining the sufferer to intellectual activity. The happy wife and busy mother are only forced into literature by some hereditary organic tendency, stronger even than the domestic; and hence it is that the cleverest women are not always those who have written books.[28]

Although Fanny Fern agrees that the need to write is rooted in loneliness, frustration, and disappointment, she perceives those qualities not in unmarried women but in wives. The picture of an ugly spinster turning to literature to fulfill her romantic fantasies might elicit laughter,[29] but the married woman provokes a much more disturbing response. If a husband assumes that writing is the product of sexual and emotional tension, is it any wonder that he looks askance at his wife's efforts at authorship? Consider the language that Lydia Sigourney's husband used to express his anger regarding her decision to become a poet. According to Ann Douglas Wood, he "described her career in terms of sexual desire: she evinced a '*lust* of praise, which like the *appetite* of the cormorant is not to be satisfied,' and was guilty of an 'apparently unconquerable *passion* of displaying herself.'"[30] Underneath the frequent warnings that women's writing would eventually undermine the home is often a deeper fear that the marriage had, in its most private areas, already failed.

Three prominent writers—Olive Schreiner, Anna Jameson, and Geraldine Jewsbury—give women's perspective on the relationship between personal frustration and artistic productivity. Olive Schreiner, who published her first novel *The Story of an African Farm* in 1883, dismisses sex as the motivating factor of women's literature. *Woman and Labour*, her 1911 feminist manifesto, declares that women's repression is social rather than sexual.

> It is sometimes stated, that as several women of genius in modern times have sought to find expression for their creative powers in the art of fiction, there must be some inherent connection in the human brain between the ovarian sex function and the art of fiction. The fact is that modern fiction, being merely a description of human life in any of its phases, and being the only art that can be exercised without special training or special appliances, and produced in the moments stolen from the multifarious, brain-destroying occupations which fill the average woman's life, they have been driven to find this outlet for their powers as the only one presenting itself. How far otherwise might have been the directions in which their genius would naturally have expressed itself can be known only to the women themselves; what the world has lost by that compulsory expression of genius, in a form

which may not have been its most natural form of expression, or only one of its forms, no one can ever know. Even in the little third-rate novelist whose works cumber the ground, we see often a pathetic figure when we recognize that beneath that failure in a complex and difficult art, may lie buried a sound legislator, an able architect, an original scientific investigator, or a good judge. Scientifically speaking, it is as unproven that there is any organic relation between the brain of the female and the production of art in the form of fiction, as that there is an organic relation between the hand of woman and the typewriter. Both the creative writer and the typist, in their respective spheres, are merely finding outlets for their powers in the direction of least mental resistance. The tendency of women at the present day to undertake certain forms of labor proves only that in the crabbed, walled-in, and bound conditions surrounding woman at the present day, these are the lines along which action is most possible to her.[31]

Women living during the middle years of the nineteenth century found the matter much more complex. In the journal she kept while she was travelling in Canada and subsequently published as *Winter Studies and Summer Rambles* (1838), Anna Jameson explores the possibility that women turn to literature as a way of compensating for the disappointment of their lives.

Idle to-day, and although I read a good deal, I translated very little, and noted less.

Yet the following passage struck me. The conversation turned on the German poetesses, and Rehbein, Goethe's physician, insisted that the poetical talent in women was "ein Art von geistigem Geschlechtstrieb." "Hear him!" exclaimed Goethe; "hear the physician, with his 'intellectual impulse of sex!'" Rehbein explained himself, by observing "that the women who had distinguished themselves in literature, poetry especially, were almost universally women who had been disappointed in their best affections, and sought in this direction of the intellect a sort of compensation. When women are married, and have children to take care of, they do not often think of writing poetry."

This is not very politely or delicately expressed; but we must not therefore shrink from it, for it involves some important considerations. It is most certain that among the women who have been distinguished in literature, three-fourths have been either by nature, or fate, or the law of society, placed in a painful or a false position; it is also most certain that in these days when society is becoming every day more artificial and more complex, and marriage, as the gentlemen assure us, more and more expensive, hazardous, and inexpedient, women *must* find means to fill up the void of existence. Men, our natural protectors, our lawgivers, our masters, throw us upon our own resources. . . . We have gone away from nature, and we must,—if we can, substitute another nature. Art, literature and science, remain to us. . . . Only in utility, such as is left to us, only in the assiduous employment of such faculties as we are permitted to exercise, can we find health and peace, and compensation for the wasted or repressed impulses and energies more proper to our sex—more natural—perhaps more pleasing to God; but trusting in his mercy, and using the means he has given, we must do the best we can for ourselves and for our sisterhood.[32]

Having experienced a disastrous marriage, Jameson concedes the relevance of the physician's statement. However, she sees that the void in women's existence is not simply sexual, and she maintains that men and society must bear the responsibility for bringing it about.

Novelist Geraldine Jewsbury also discerns the manifold causes of women's dissatisfaction. In an 1851 letter to Jane Welsh Carlyle, she acknowledges that life has thwarted the intellectual energy and maternal instinct of her dearest friend and the most famous literary wife of the period. Unlike Fern, Jewsbury does not advocate writing as an act of anger against men. Instead, she offers it as a bond of affection among women, a way for mothers and daughters to reach one another.

I hope and trust you are writing your tale. I have been thinking of you a great deal, and I am very anxious you should have some employment more stimlulating than mending old clothes, something that will really employ your energy. Writing, as an occupation, has most excellent properties; it not only blunts one's *amour propre*—or, as we politely term it, our sensibilities—so that we not only feel less acutely things that would otherwise irritate beyond endurance, but these things are transformed for us into artistic studies, instructions, experiences, and this goes a long way towards softening their intensely personal application to ourselves. Besides which, one's work is an 'ark of refuge,' into which one flings oneself on all occasions of provocation. . . . It is not, however, altogether for your own sake that I am anxious you should set to work upon a story or a book of any kind that you are moved to do. You have more sense and stronger judgment than any other woman I ever knew, or expect to know; also, you have had such singular life-experiences that it is in your power to say both strengthening and comforting things to other women. . . . If you had had daughters, they would have been educated as few women have the luck to be, and I think you might have enough maternal feeling, sisterly affection, *esprit de corps,* or what you will, to wish to help other women in their very complicated duties and difficulties. Do not go to Mr. Carlyle for sympathy, do not let him dash you with cold water. You must respect your own work and your own motives; if people only did what others thought good and useful, half the work in the world would be left undone. . . . I am just now open to any sort of arrangement you like to make. I will give the staple of my time to this mutual tale if you will begin. . . . So begin, begin! half your loneliness comes from having no outlet for your energies, and no engrossing employment. . . . You ought to have had a dozen daughters—and I am sure they exist somewhere, either 'in the body or out of the body,' or else in some charming 'spiritual translucent element,' as Origen calls it. So let your work be dedicated to your 'unknown daughters.' I am one of your children, after a fashion; I am sure you care for me more as if I were a daughter than as a woman cares for her friend. . . . If ever I am good for you, it is in the way a daughter would be to her mother, for the practical fact that I am nearly as old as you are never interferes with the sentiment. So, finally, my dear love, begin to work. . . . And now good-bye![33]

2

"Poetesses" and "Lady Novelists"

During the 1830s and 1840s, readers delighted in hearing the new voices of "poetesses" and "lady novelists." In England and America, poets earned financial success and critical acceptance by celebrating the affections; novelists prospered by describing the domestic experiences of ordinary life. However, as subsequent analysis will show, the response to both groups of writers helped to establish condescending and confining standards for their successors. Moreover, even the favorable reviews of poems and novels suggest the areas of later disagreement: the woman writer's sense of self, the relationship between emotion and the art of poetry, and the kinds of experiences appropriate for women's fiction.

First, the poetesses.

I

Critics, educators, and authors of advice manuals often agree that poetry is a fit subject for women's study. Educational theorists who fear both the absence of female imagination and its excess see poetry as a way to develop empathy. Reading poetry can take women out of themselves, awaken their feelings for others, and carry them to an ideal realm. In *Thoughts on Self-Culture* (1851), Maria Grey and Emily Shirreff encourage women to disregard fiction and to read a certain kind of poetry.

> In a poem, the wildest language of passion, though it may appeal to the feelings, is generally called forth in circumstances remote from the experience of the reader; but in works which profess to paint real life, a regard to probability is so necessary, that there is nothing to prevent the young reader placing herself in the position of any favorite personage, and should she feel or fancy any resemblance in her own mind and circumstances to those portrayed, she is easily led to expect a similar course of events to draw forth the virtues or the talents, or to give scope to the feelings, of which she is conscious. . . . The grand conceptions of the poet are true in ideal beauty; the novelist's pictures of real life are false, because necessarily covered with an unreal gloss. The object of the poet and artist is to embody their own lofty view of the truly beautiful; that of the novelist, to present us with an imitation of what we see around us, and therefore to mingle with the beautiful all that generally detracts from it in real life, even shrinking from portraying such excellence as we actually *have* known and loved, lest it should appear to border on romance. The one sublimes the soul by lifting it above the present to the contemplation of eternal beauty; the other increases the interest of the actual and the present, already too engrossing, enamoring us of the chain which binds the soul to earth. . . . The poet, in short, elevates the thoughts, while the novelist excites the feelings, and this one difference sufficiently expresses how admirable is the one and how pernicious the other kind of reading for women.[1]

In practice, writers such as Felicia Hemans, Lydia Sigourney, Letitia Landon, and Caroline Norton had demonstrated that it was possible to be a poet and a lady.[2] For example, an 1831 illustration from *Fraser's* shows the beautiful Caroline Norton having tea in her elegantly appointed chambers while her grandfather Richard Brinsley Sheridan smiles down from his portrait on the wall [see Illustration 3]. The sketch, like the accompanying story, implies that Norton is securely ensconced within the home, the upper echelons of society, and the male literary establishment.[3] As a poet she is praised for her life of "elegant retirement"; eight years later when she becomes a polemicist in the

MISS BUNION.

The poetess, author of *Heartstrings, The Deadly Nightshade, Passion Flowers,* &c.
Though her poems breathe only of love, Miss B. has never been married. She is
nearly six feet high; she loves waltzing beyond even poesy; and I think lobster-
salad as much as either. She confesses to twenty-eight; in which case her first
volume, *The Orphan of Gozo,* must have been published when she was three years
old.

    For a woman all soul, she certainly eats as much as any woman I ever saw.
The sufferings she has had to endure are, she says, beyond compare; the poems
which she writes breathe a withering passion, a smouldering despair, an agony of
spirit that would melt the soul of a drayman, were he to read them. Well, it is a
comfort to see that she can dance of nights, and to know (for the habits of
illustrious literary persons are always worth knowing) that she eats a hot
mutton-chop for breakfast every morning of her blighted existence. . . .

      2. Miss Bunion
      William Thackeray, *Mrs. Perkin's Ball,* 1846.

THE AUTHOR OF "THE UNDYING ONE".

Fair Mrs. Norton! Beautiful Bhouddist, as Balaam Bulwer baptizes you, whom can we better choose for a beginning of our illustrious literary portraits, when diverging from the inferior sex, our pencil dares to portray the angels of the craft? . . . . She writes long poems—she is a sprig of nobility—and she is the granddaughter of that right honourable gentleman whose picture is suspended above her head . . . .

We display her as the modest matron making tea in the morning for the comfort and convenience of her husband. . . . Authoresses are liable to many rubs. Mrs. Norton . . . has escaped some. Happy in all the appliances of wealth and fame, there is nothing to alter the beauties of that symmetrical form. . . . She has not passed the night in any sublunary matters; but in the contemplation of that divine philsophy and sublime poetry which is best indulged in without intrusion. . . . She is evidently composing a poem which no doubt will be as fluent, as clear, as lucid, and as warm as the liquid distilling from the urn.

3. Caroline Norton
Daniel Maclise, *Fraser's*, 1831

controversy over child custody laws, she will be reviled as a "monster" and a "she-beast" [see Volume II, Chapter 1].

While Caroline Norton attracted the attention of illustrators Felicia Hemans received the greatest critical acclaim during the early years of Victoria's reign. When Hemans died in 1835, Elizabeth Barrett Browning wrote an elegy for her, and H.F. Chorley, a well-regarded critic for the *Athenaeum*, issued two volumes of *Memorials*. *Blackwood's* proclaimed her to be "the founder of a school" that was having extensive influence on American women writers, and Sarah Josepha Hale, the powerful editor of *Godey's*, saluted Hemans as "a model which perfectly represents what female poetry is and should be." Prominent Unitarian critics Andrews Norton and Andrew Peabody ranked Hemans above Milton and Homer.[4] Hale predicted that "neither her predecessors, or successors, of her own sex, have been, or will be able, to surpass her," but other writers did dislodge Hemans from her prominent position. Although Emily Dickinson's first volume of poems did not appear until 1890, four years after her death, Elizabeth Barrett Browning's *Poems of 1844* forced critics to acknowledge new elements in women's poetry. By 1857 Emily Brontë's highly original lyrics were beginning to get the serious attention that had been denied them at their 1846 publication, and in the 1860s Christina Rossetti's books established her as an accomplished poet.

Today Felicia Hemans' poetry is of little artistic significance, but nineteenth-century responses to her work reveal the climate of thought in which the major women poets defined themselves and sought their audience. In 1840, Lydia Sigourney, Hemans' most successful follower and the first American poet to earn her living by writing, commends Hemans as the selfless bearer of a sacred flame; speaking in the 1847 *Tait's*, the respected Scottish critic George Gilfillan honors her not as the best, but as "the most feminine writer of the age." Their reviews convey the prevailing assumptions about women poets and demonstrate how quickly high praise can become constraint.

> The possessor of this genius evinced both an innate consciousness of its powers, and a determination to devote them to their legitimate purposes. She held on her way, not in self-esteem, but in reverence for the loftiness of her vocation, and with a continually heightening gratitude for the entrusted treasure. She guarded her gift of melody, as the vestal-flame, for whose debasement or

extinction she was bound to give solemn account. So full and entire was she, in this consecration, as to resist the most tempting offers to write prose,—though moved to their acceptance by pecuniary need. She felt that she had a higher and holier calling, and with unwavering confidence pursued its upward promptings. . . .

The genius of Mrs. Hemans was as pure and feminine in its impulses, as in its out-pourings. That ambition which impels the man of genius to "scorn delights, and live laborious days," that he may walk on the high places of the world's renown, and leave a name which shall be as a trumpet-tone to all time, woke no answering echo in her bosom. Sympathy, not fame, was the desire of her being.

> "Fame hath a voice, whose thrilling tone
> Can bid the life-pulse beat,
> As when a trumpet's note hath blown,
> Calling the brave to meet:
> But mine,—let mine,—*a woman's breast,*
> *By words of home-born love be bless'd.*"

All the woman in her shines. . . . Her inspiration always pauses at the feminine point. . . . She is no Sibyl, tossed to and fro in the tempest of furious excitement, but ever a "deep, majestical, and high-souled woman"—the calm mistress of the highest and stormiest of her emotions. . . .

To herself she appears to be uttering oracular deliverances. Alas! "oracles speak," and her poetry, as to all effective utterance of original truth, is silent. It is emotion only that is audible to the sharpest ear that listens to her song. . . . A *maker* she is not. . . .

Mrs. Hemans' poems are strictly effusions. And not a little of their charm springs from their unstudied and extempore character. This, too, is in fine keeping with the sex of the writer. You are saved the ludicrous image of a double-dyed Blue, in papers and morning wrapper, sweating at some stupendous treatise or tragedy from morn to noon, and from noon to dewy eve—you see a graceful and gifted woman, passing from the cares of her family, and the enjoyments of society, to inscribe on her tablets some fine thought or feeling, which had throughout the day existed as a still sunshine upon her countenance, or perhaps as a quiet unshed tear in her eye. In this case, the transition is so natural and graceful, from the duties or delights of the day to the employments of her desk, that there is as little pedantry in writing a poem as in writing a letter, and the authoress appears only the lady in *flower.* . . . After all, the nature of this poetess is more interesting than her genius, or than its finest productions. . . . If not, in the transcendent sense, a poet, her life was a poem.[5]

If a woman writing during the early decades of the nineteenth century did not want to become a "lady in flower," but
attempted instead to define her poetic identity within the context of Romanticism, she would have encountered difficulty.[6]
Neither the public role of prophet nor the private act of self-
definition would have come easily to her. Sheltered at home,
she was supposed to remain a lady, to renounce ambition, to
transcend self by serving others. Even the Romantic emphasis
on emotional spontaneity, which seemed to coincide so nicely
with woman's nature, presented problems. In writing about
their feelings, women had to contend with the limiting and
sometimes contradictory expectations of their audience.

When Gilfillan attributes women's poetry to the primacy of
their emotions, he implies that their work is spontaneous, unstudied—in a word, artless. Neither he nor Sigourney expect to
find the artists in conscious control of their materials; instead,
they assume that the intensity of their feelings will render them
powerless as poets. Moreover, although Gilfillan recognizes the
force of women's emotions, he restricts their range. Valuing
control, he praises Hemans because she is a "calm mistress" of
her passion. In analyzing the relationship between emotion and
art, subsequent critics disagree about the kinds of feelings
women should explore in their poetry; they worry that writers
will center attention on themselves instead of directing their
affection to others; and they question the value of poetry that is
grounded in personal experience.

The debate sometimes concerns the standing of lyric poetry
and the importance of the affections. Can poetry of the heart
ever be as significant as the epic? In *Female Writers* (1842), Mary
Ann Stodart argues that the two sexes inhabit separate but
equal spheres: to the man belongs the epic, with its grand
manner, its sense of history, and its knowledge of good and evil;
to the woman belongs the lyric, with an emphasis on individual
feeling and domestic experience. Asking that the contributions
of the poetesses be taken seriously, she writes:

> O scorn us not! We may not, we cannot 'murmur tales of iron
> wars,' follow the currents of a heady fight; portray with the vivid
> power of Homeric song, the horrid din of war, the rush of con-
> tending warriors, the prancing of the noble steed, the clang, the
> tumult, the stirring interest of the battle-field—no—but we can do
> what mightier man would perhaps disdain—we can follow one
> solitary soldier as he drags his wounded limbs beneath the shel-

tering hedge; and while we mark his glazing eye, we can read with woman's keenness, the thoughts of wife, children, and home, which are playing around his heart. We may not be able to sustain a strain of high and equal majesty like the bard of Mantua, but we can follow out the sorrows of the forsaken Dido, weep over the untimely fate of the warrior-friends, and sympathize with the feminine eagerness of Camilla, as, womanly even in her power, she forgets self-defence and a warrior's duties, in order to seize on the splendid ornaments of an officer in the opposing army. We cannot range through heaven and hell with the fiery wing of our own glorious poet Milton; we cannot ascend to the height of a great argument, and justify the ways of God to man. No woman could have delineated the character of Satan, so evidently 'not less than archangel ruined;' no woman could have tracked the flight of Satan across chaos; or depicted that mysterious assemblage when the rebel angel stood before 'the anarch old;' but we can imagine that some wonderfully endowed woman *might* have pencilled along the peaceful vale; or she will watch the light smoke of the peaceful cottage as it gracefully curls above the surrounding trees, and her heart will ponder on what a true-hearted woman ever loves to portray, the kindly charities of home. . . .[7]

While Stodart ascribes women's choice of lyric in poetry to their sensibility, American writer Caroline May Kirkland relates it to the conditions of their lives. In *The American Female Poets* (1848), she explains:

It must be borne in mind that not many ladies in this country are permitted sufficient leisure from the cares and duties of home to devote themselves, either from choice, or as a means of living, to literary pursuits. Hence, the themes which have suggested the greater part of the following poems have been derived from the incidents and associations of every-day life. And home, with its quiet joys, its deep pure sympathies, and its secret sorrows, with which a stranger must not intermeddle, is a sphere by no means limited for woman, whose inspiration lies more in her heart than her head. Deep emotions make a good foundation for lofty and pure thoughts. The deeper the foundation, the more elevated may be the superstructure. . . . And where should women lavish most unreservedly and receive most largely, the warmest, purest, and most changeless, affection, but in the sacred retirement of home.[8]

Like Stodart, Kirkland believes that poetry about women's emotions and experiences should be respected. But an 1868 *Saturday Review* suggests that the separate spheres were no more equal in art than in politics. The essay does record a significant shift in taste: the critical demise of Felicia Hemans, Lydia Sigourney, and their generation, and the recognition of a "triad of genuine poetesses" in Elizabeth Barrett Browning, Christina Rossetti, and Emily Brontë. Yet this reviewer, who finds their work limited by its emphasis on feeling, decries the absence of "largeness and universality."

> And as Emily Brontë is by far the least known of the three, and indeed scarcely known at all except as the wild and uncultured sister of a woman of genius, it may be as well to begin with her. . . . Her strength was her weakness. She entrenched herself so resolutely in her isolation from mankind, that her communication with them was cut off. She said so emphatically, "I will be myself," that her sympathies were narrowed, and her knowledge of the language and tone of the world almost destroyed. If, either by gradual influences in her youth, or by some sudden blow when older, she had been forced out of the circle in which she was confined, so that her great feeling and originality could have flowed out upon the outer world, it is difficult to say what eminence she might not have attained. . . .
>
> Let us turn to Miss Rossetti. . . . Feeling, with her, is absolutely predominant; there are no symptoms of any struggles of thought, of any intellectual range; and though these latter qualities are not absolutely essential to poetry, they endow it with a far greater power. Hence we do not think her naturally so strong a genius as Emily Brontë; but her imaginative power is decidedly greater. Their most prominent characteristic, intense personal feeling, is the same in both. . . .
>
> Mrs. Browning is too considerable a person to be dealt with fully in the space that is left to us. We can therefore here only make a few observations on her. That which distinguishes her from Emily Brontë and Christina Rossetti is the intense effort after objectivity, after downright portraiture, narration, description, which in the other two is entirely wanting. The poetry of women (unlike the novels written by women) has, from Sappho downwards, been almost entirely subjective and personal. Nor perhaps can any instance be given, besides Mrs. Browning, of a poetess who even attempted to escape from these limits. Was she successful in the endeavour? Not more than partially, we think. . . .
>
> Why is it that, while the novels written by women approach so nearly in excellence to those written by men, the poetry of women should be so inferior? Miss Austen, Charlotte Brontë, and "George Eliot" almost, if not quite, equal any men who can be set

against them. . . . We presume, women, in writing poetry, draw their style from other women, and thus miss that largeness and universality which alone compels attention, and preserves a work through all changes of sentiment and opinion.[9]

Readers who accept the importance of lyric poetry and the experience on which it was based do not encourage women to give free rein to their emotions. Rather, they prescribe the kinds of emotions that women should depict and assume that those emotions will be directed toward others. The 1864 *Fraser's* advises women to write lyric poetry because it is "like a modest rustic maiden, who turns away her head, nor looks you full in the face."[10] Reticence, shyness, and modesty—these were the qualities valued in women's poetry. In *The Female Poets of America* (1848), popular American critic Rufus Griswold maintains that women poets have a special responsibility to control their emotions.

> The conditions of aesthetic ability in the two sexes are probably distinct, or even opposite. Among men, we recognise his nature as the most thoroughly artist-like, whose most abstract thoughts still retain a sensuous cast, whose mind is the most completely transfused and incorporated into his feelings. Perhaps the reverse should be considered the test of true art in woman, and we should deem her the truest poet, whose emotions are most refined by reason, whose force of passion is most expanded and controlled into lofty and impersonal forms of imagination.[11]

Reviewers who chastize Elizabeth Barrett Browning for "fits of frenzy," "unrestrained expression," and "oracular ravings" are more comfortable with the emotional quality of Christina Rossetti's poems. Although twentieth-century critics see a dark side to Rossetti—a restless and assertive self operating behind the mask of genteel composure and protesting against woman's dependence on man—nineteenth-century reviewers extol her sweetness, simplicity, happiness, and serenity.[12] In 1869, H.B. Forman applauds Rossetti as an accomplished poet, but the control he admires is psychological as well as technical.

> As little tripped up by feminine dress as any lady who ever trimmed a verse is Miss Christina Rossetti; and although she has not produced any one work of great dimensions, or even of great

scope in small dimensions, her two little volumes yet constitute not only a very choice contribution to real poetry, but also a significant fact in the history of female literature. Miss Rossetti shows before all things that a woman of esthetic genius is not necessarily a wayward *fabricante* of whatever matter comes to her hand for artistic manipulation, but that a woman may train herself to a special manner of workmanship, and become amenable to the influences of a movement just as advantageously as a man may. The first thing that strikes us on going through this lady's works is that she is a poet: this impression is the earliest, because we *feel* it; and the second thing which comes forward prominently—second, because we find it out by *thinking*, not *feeling*—is that she is a Preraphaelite poet, profoundly influenced by the Preraphaelite movement in literature, and perfectly conscious of certain principles in workmanship. To say that she has attained a uniform perfection in this matter of workmanship would be rash; but it may be fearlessly said that her works exhibit, in a greater degree than those of any other woman-poet of her country, the sense of execution, the sense that the words in which a thought first suggests itself are not of necessity the fittest words in which to put that thought before the world,—and this notwithstanding the Preraphaelite aim of approximating the 'actualities' of language more nearly than is usual with poets. . . .

Mrs. Browning *was* a poet to the very depth of her nature; and no one ever had a higher or holier sense of the responsibilities of a poet. Nevertheless she has not shown, with all her impassioned bursts and sweet outpourings, which attain perfection by force of passion or sweetness, the *sense* that careful and dextrous manipulation is a requisite of poetic art; and Miss Christina Rossetti, without this sweeping force of passion, with a more limited emotional range, and with a narrower area of subject, has unquestionably shown this sense. . . .

Take rather, as an instance, the little song called *A Birthday*, in the volume styled *Goblin Market and other Poems*: it is only two verses, and those are not freighted with any weighty thought or strained to the pitch of reasonance by any volubility or fire-blast of passion; but the whole sixteen lines are full of healthy happiness and the ringing melody of a joyful young heart:

> 'My heart is like a singing bird,
>   Whose nest is in a watered shoot;
> My heart is like an appletree,
>   Whose boughs are bent with thickset fruit;
> My heart is like a rainbow shell,
>   That paddles in a halcyon sea;

> My heart is gladder than all these
> Because my love is come to me.
>
> Raise me a dais of silk and down;
>   Hang it with vair and purple dyes;
> Carve it in doves, and pomegranates,
>   And peacocks with a hundred eyes;
> Work it in gold and silver grapes,
>   In leaves, and silver fleurs-de-lys;
> Because the birthday of my life
>   Is come, my love is come to me.'

. . . This is the very essence of maiden delicacy: the exuberance of joy breaks forth in no unmeasured and uncomely burst, but is poured simply, fluently, heartily, and, with a masterly selection of expression. . . . This song must be called perfect; and to attain this perfection in treating an exuberantly joyful subject could have been no easy matter even for one of Miss Rossetti's delicacy and acute sensibility—seeing that all expansive passion has a natural proneness to run in the direction of over-intensity, suggestive of personality—a tendency to become distasteful to the reader of average delicacy through excessive openness of expression. Reticence in songs of the affections is a gift of great price; and here we have it.[13]

Rossetti's emotions seemed to be centered on others: here, her lover; in other poems, her God. Emphasis on self was an affront to Victorian aesthetics, but readers seem to have found it particularly disagreeable in works by women because the exploration of one's own feelings and intentions could easily become an act of assertion. Thus when Rufus Griswold said that Lydia Sigourney lacked the "consciousness of subjective ability," he was paying her a compliment.[14] Consciously or not, most women poets developed strategies for self-effacement. In *Maude,* the semi-autobiographical work of Christina Rossetti that was published posthumously in 1897, the poetess-heroine fears that her mind has "an undercurrent of thought intent upon itself."[15] When Maude dies and wills the destruction of her poems, it seems as if Christina Rossetti is trying to kill the dangerous part of herself.[16]

At a time when the "aesthetics of renunciation" were pervasive, Elizabeth Barrett Browning made a uniquely public commitment to the poetry of self-definition. As a young girl, Browning had been "much affected" by a Hemans poem[17]; as a fledgling poet, she published in the same annuals as Hemans, Landon, Sigourney, and Norton. However, the publication of the *Poems of 1844* immediately set her apart from her predecessors. Acclaiming her "very extraordinary powers of mind," *Blackwood's* asserted that her powers extended over "a wider and profounder range of thought and feeling, than ever before fell within the intellectual compass of any of the softer sex." From America, Margaret Fuller ranked her "in vigour and nobleness of conception, depth of spiritual experience, and command of classic allusion, above any female writer the world has yet known."[18]

Despite such praise for the writer's learning, many reviewers emphasized the maudlin poems: "The Mournful Mother," a lament for a blind child's death, and "Bertha in the Lane," the story of a woman who dies of grief after making her sister a wedding gown so that she can marry the man she herself had loved. In 1861, journalist William Stigand still regarded "Bertha in the Lane" as "the sweetest and most affecting of Browning's poems. . . . It is the most simple and most true in its quiet and resigned tone of pathos, to the tale of self-abnegation which it portrays."[19] Other poems, like the daring sonnets to George Sand and *The Drama of Exile*, an epic account of Eve's part in the fall which the poet regarded as her "most important work," suggested that Browning might develop in less conventional directions.

In the preface, she declared her aspirations:

In any case, while my poems are full of faults,—as I go forward to my critics and confess,—they have my heart and life in them,— they are not empty shells. If it must be said of me that I have contributed immemorable verses to the many rejected by the age, it cannot at least be said that I have done so in a light and irresponsible spirit. Poetry has been as serious a thing to me as life itself; and life has been a very serious thing: there has been no playing at skittles for me in either. I never mistook pleasure for the final cause of poetry; nor leisure, for the hour of the poet. I have done my work, so far, as work,—not as mere hand and head work, apart from the personal being,—but as the completest expression of that being to which I could attain,—and as work I offer it to the public,—feeling its shortcomings more deeply than any of my readers, because measured from the height of my aspiration,—but feeling also that the reverence and sincerity with which the work was done should give it some protection with the reverent and sincere.[20]

Stigand objected to this very passage:

> But notwithstanding the apparent modesty of this preface, we
> cannot avoid observing that the humility is more professed than
> real. The writer assumes that her Being alone is sufficient to make
> good poetry, if she can find the due expression of it—and this
> assumption accompanied her through life. She studied only to give
> due expression to what she imagined to be her own nature; not to
> become acquainted with human nature generally, to find materials
> for the exercise of her art and to discover the necessary relation
> between her own powers and the subjects adapted to them, in
> order to produce works which should embody, in an artistic form,
> the real life and the best aspirations of the age. A poet can no more
> spin poems out of his own brain, unassisted by the thoughts and
> feelings which he should draw from humanity around him, than a
> weaver can make tissues out of the tips of his fingers. The origi-
> nality of the poet is shown in the creations he is able to make out
> of the solid stuff of human life. And this requires not only careful
> study of human nature generally, but also a power of passing out
> of self, forgetting self altogether, in the sentiments and feelings of
> others, so as to invest them with artistic concreteness; or of
> drawing into one's own nature the general aspirations and emo-
> tions of the time, and finding an echo for them in the individual
> soul of the poet. But to regard the Poet's Being as the primary
> cause and motive power of poetry—as at once subject and object—
> is a fundamental mistake. Originality, doubtless, is much; but true
> originality will never be attained by a self-conscious, morbid, rest-
> less assertion of the value of a man's own individuality. This was
> the prime error of Mrs. Browning's artistic theories. (519)

Elizabeth Barrett Browning continued to take herself as
subject in two later works which have female poets as speakers:
"Sonnets from the Portuguese" (1850) and *Aurora Leigh* (1856).
In the sonnet sequence, the speaker describes herself as "an out-
of-tune worn viol" and honors the sexual and artistic energy of
her husband; compared with his voice, hers is only a cricket's
chirping against a mandolin.[21] In *Aurora Leigh*, which Browning
regarded as the most mature of her works and the one into
which her "highest convictions upon Life and Art have entered,"
the speaker regards herself more seriously. The long "verse-
novel," as she called it, is an epic and an autobiography, an
indictment of the age and an account of her poetic development.
Browning told Anna Jameson that she expected to be "put in the
stocks . . . as a disorderly woman and free-thinking poet."

With its panoramic description of society, its depiction of good and evil, its epic manner and classical allusions, its "coarse" diction and irregular versification, *Aurora Leigh* violated all the rules for women's poetry. As the *Athenaeum* said, "The effect of this remarkable production, remarkable by whatever standard it may be tried, was without precedent in the annals of poetry by women." *Aurora Leigh* quickly became a test case for women's poetry. George Eliot described it as an androgynous work, a sign that a woman could succeed as a poet *and* as a poetess; *Saturday Review* said the poem was so badly flawed that it proved no woman could ever achieve greatness.[22] As a "strong-minded woman," the heroine received mixed reviews [see Chapter 3]. As a poet upholding imaginative vision against utilitarian ethos and vindicating the achievements of female artists in a male culture, she elicited a great deal of criticism.

In one particularly controversial passage, Aurora declares that she and other poets have a responsibility to their age.

> Nay, if there's room for poets in this world
> A little overgrown (I think there is).
> Their sole work is to represent the age,
> Their age, not Charlemagne's,—this live, throbbing age,
> That brawls, cheats, maddens, calculates, aspires,
> And spends more passion, more heroic heat,
> Betwixt the mirrors of its drawing-rooms,
> Than Roland with his knights at Roncesvalles.
> To flinch from modern varnish, coat, or flounce,
> Cry out for togas and the picturesque,
> Is fatal,—foolish, too. King Arthur's self
> Was commonplace to Lady Guinevere;
> And Camelot to minstrels seemed as flat
> As Fleet Street to our poets.
>   Never flinch,
> But still, unscrupulously epic, catch
> Upon the burning lava of a song
> The full-veined, heaving, double-breasted age,
> That, when the next shall come, the men of that
> May touch the impress with reverent hand, and say,
> "Behold, behold, the paps we all have sucked!
> This bosom seems to beat still, or at least
> It sets ours beating: this is living art,
> Which thus presents and thus records true life.[23]

Aurora's dedication to art is even more disconcerting than her immersion in life. The 1856 *Tablet* is angered by the hero's humiliation ("a great feature in the works of modern literary ladies"), by Aurora's assertiveness in proposing to him, and by the "artist-workwoman."

> The *femme incomprise*, the artist-workwoman, the high-souled female with "a mission," is a terrible companion in a journey of twelve thousand lines, and ever since the genius of Thackeray introduced us to honest Miss Bunion, we chose her as the pink and flower of her class, and would admit no rivalry. But Miss Aurora Leigh is a bad specimen even of her very unattractive class. She tells us her own story in the first person singular, and though never woman thought more highly of herself, nor was at more pains to describe her supereminent gifts, she is a very ridiculous person, and what is worse than ridiculous, she is intolerably tedious.[24]

After finding fault with the poem's implausible events and oracular language, *Saturday Review* also comments on Aurora's sense of herself as a writer and reaffirms the difference between a poet and a poetess.

> The negative experience of centuries seems to prove that a woman cannot be a great poet. Those who are curious in intellectual physiology may find, in *Aurora Leigh*, some materials for the explanation of feminine misadventures in art. It was natural that, in the exceptional position of a poet's wife, herself possessing undoubted genius, Mrs. Browning should enter on an ambitious enterprise; but it is not surprising that she should have failed in the attempt to achieve several simultaneous impossibilities. A novel in blank verse, containing twelve thousand lines, is in itself alarming to an ordinary reader. . . . The characters are few and unreal—the incidents, though scanty, are almost inconceivable—and the heroine and autobiographer, as a professed poetess, has tastes and occupations which are, beyond all others, incapable of poetical treatment. With all nature and life at its command, Art is only precluded from selecting its own mechanism as its subject. But, of late, the poet's eye, instead of glancing from earth to heaven, seems, by some strange inversion, to be exclusively fixed on the process of writing verses. . . .
>
> Notwithstanding the defects of the poem, Mrs. Browning has more fully than ever proved that she is a poetess. . . . Mrs. Browning has a fine ear, and an observant mind. Her partial

failure is far less attributable to a want of poetical instinct than to the erroneous theory that art is the proper subject for itself. When Aurora forgets that she is a poetess—or, still better, when she is herself forgotten—the troublesome machinery which had been interposed between the writer and reality is effectually removed. If Mrs. Browning would trust her first thoughts, and condescend to be simple, she would be almost always picturesque and forcible.[25]

The essay does not, to be sure, identify artistic self-consciousness as a peculiarly feminine failing. Yet when the reviewer asks that Browning "condescend to be simple," we hear echoes of those earlier critics who eulogized the poetess for her artless simplicity. As William Stigand says, "It is very questionable taste for a poetess to be continually declaiming on the superiority of her own craft" (524).

Because responses to *Aurora Leigh* demonstrate the risks of moving from the ideal to the real, from the shelter of home to the turmoil of the city, they introduce the final issue for debate: the poet's right to speak on public matters. Occasionally poets did involve themselves in social problems. Caroline Norton decried factory conditions in England; Edna Proctor and Helen Hunt Jackson protested against the treatment of American Indians. Frances Ellen Watkins Harper, a black writer and highly regarded lecturer on the abolitionist circuit, wrote popular propagandist poems on racial themes, women's rights, and temperance—and achieved moderate success.[26] But such examples do not constitute the norm; to engage in social protest was to challenge Victorian aesthetics and conventional ideas about women.

For instance, when Christina Rossetti wrote "The Iniquity of the Fathers Upon the Children," her brother Gabriel advised against including it in her 1866 collection. In the poem, a young girl ruminates about her own illegitimacy, expressing bewildered pain at her mother's refusal to acknowledge their relationship and anger at her father's treachery; she is determined to remove herself from the marriage market and remain alone. Gabriel seems to have felt that women should remain ignorant of sexual intrigue and social evil. Christina, who did social work at the St. Mary Magdalen Home for Fallen Women during the 1860s, agreed that the subject matter was unpleasant, but argued against the limitations her brother wanted to place on her imagination.

. . . whilst I endorse your opinion of the unavoidable and indeed much-to-be-desired unreality of women's work on many social matters, I yet incline to include within the female range such an attempt as this. . . . Moreover, the sketch only gives the girl's own deductions, feelings and semi-resolutions; granted such premises as hers, and right or wrong it seems to me she might easily arrive at such conclusions: and whilst it may truly be urged that unless white could be black and Heaven Hell my experience (thank God) precludes me from hers, I yet don't see why "the Poet mind" should be less able to construct her from its own inner consciousness than a hundred other unknown qualities.[27]

In that particular case, Rossetti disregarded her brother's advice. More typically, though, she approached women's issues obliquely. Such poets as Rossetti, Dickinson, and Emily Brontë resorted to masks and various forms of rhetorical subterfuge to write poems on sisterhood, the search for freedom, and the inviolability of the self—often with profoundly radical implications. But the most important poet to write explicitly about child labor, slavery, and prostitution was Elizabeth Barrett Browning.[28]

Her reading of *Uncle Tom's Cabin* (1852) helped her understand her obligations as a woman poet. Urging Anna Jameson to read the novel, Browning exclaimed:

Not read Mrs. Stowe's book! But you *must.* Her book is quite a sign of the times, and has otherwise and intrinsically considerable power. For myself, I rejoice in the success, both as a woman and a human being. Oh, and is it possible that you think a woman has no business with questions like the question of slavery? Then she had better use a pen no more. She had better subside into slavery and concubinage herself, I think, as in the times of old, shut herself up with the Penelopes in the "women's apartment," and take no rank among thinkers and speakers.

As the decade progressed, Browning became increasingly concerned with women's problems. Tennyson's treatment of the Crimean War in *Maud* (1855) prompted her to think of the hordes of nameless women suffering silently in the city of London. In an 1855 letter, she said:

War, war! It is terrible certainly. But there are worse plagues, deeper griefs, dreader wounds than the physical. What of the forty thousand wretched wretched women in this city? The silent writhing of them is to me more appalling than the roar of the cannons. Then this war is *necessary* on our sides. Is *that* wrong necessary? It is not so clear to me.

When *Aurora Leigh* appeared, some reviewers castigated the author for being coarse and sordid in her depiction of the fallen woman, Marian Erle. Analyzing the readers' anger in an 1857 letter, she wrote:

> In respect to certain objections, I am quite sure you do me the justice to believe that I do not willingly give cause for offence. Without going as far as Robert, who holds that I "couldn't be coarse if I tried," (only that!) you will grant that I don't habitually dabble in the dirt; it's not the way of my mind or life. If, therefore, I move certain subjects in this work, it is because my conscience was first moved in me not to ignore them. What has given most offence in the book, more than the story of Marian—far more!— has been the reference to the condition of women in our cities, which a woman oughtn't to refer to, by any manner of means, says the conventional tradition. Now I have thought deeply otherwise. If a woman ignores these wrongs, then may women as a sex continue to suffer them; there is no help for any of us—let us be dumb and die. I have spoken therefore, and in speaking have used plain words—words which look like blots, and which you yourself would put away—words which, if blurred or softened, would imperil perhaps the force and righteousness of the moral influence.[29]

Three years later, Elizabeth Barrett Browning went even further away from her proper sphere with *Poems Before Congress.* By celebrating Italian nationalism and denouncing slavery in "A Curse for a Nation," she antagonized English and American readers. Women speakers against slavery had been the center of controversy since the 1830s. In this poem's prologue, however, the speaker abandons the abolitionist appeal for pity and accepts the legitimacy of anger.

> I heard an angel speak last night,
>   And he said 'Write!
> Write a Nation's curse for me,
> And send it over the Western Sea.'
>
> I faltered, taking up the word:
>   'Not so, my lord!

If curses must be, choose another
To send thy curse against my brother.

'For I am bound by gratitude,
    By love and blood,
To brothers of mine across the sea,
Who stretch out kindly hands to me.'

'Therefore,' the voice said, 'shalt thou write
    My curse to-night.
From the summits of love a curse is driven,
As lightning is from the tops of heaven.'

'Not so,' I answered. 'Evermore
    My heart is sore
For my own land's sins: for little feet
Of children bleeding along the street:

'For parked-up honors that gainsay
    The right of way:
For almsgiving through a door that is
Not open enough for two friends to kiss:

'For love of freedom which abates
    Beyond the Straits:
For patriot virtue starved to vice on
Self-praise, self-interest, and suspicion:

'For an oligarchic parliament,
    And bribes well-meant.
What curse to another land assign,
When heavy-souled for the sins of mine?'

'Therefore,' the voice said, 'shalt thou write
    My curse to-night.
Because thou hast strength to see and hate
A foul thing done *within* thy gate.'

'Not so,' I answered once again.
    'To curse, choose men.
For I, a woman, have only known
How the heart melts and the tears run down.'

'Therefore,' the voice said, 'shalt thou write
    My curse to-night.
Some women weep and curse, I say
(And no one marvels), night and day.

'And thou shalt take their part to-night,
    Weep and write.

A curse from the depths of womanhood
Is very salt, and bitter, and good.'

So thus I wrote, and mourned indeed,
   What all may read.
And thus, as was enjoined on me,
I send it over the Western Sea.

W.E. Aytoun, poet and professor of rhetoric at Edinburgh University, responds by saying that women should not interfere with politics. He concludes his 1860 *Blackwood's* review with these comments on "A Curse for a Nation":

> Mrs. Browning avers that she heard an angel speak, and he said, Write!—
> We are always sorry to be under the necessity of contradicting a lady, but we are decidedly of opinion that no angel desired the gifted authoress to do anything of the kind. The communication came directly from a pernicious little imp who had been turned out of Pandemonium for profanity. Angels, we firmly believe, have a decided objection to all kinds of cursing and swearing; and had Mrs. Browning's good angel been beside her when she penned this very objectionable production, we do think he would have entered his most solemn protest against its publication. . . .
> We are glad, however, to be able to state that Mrs. Browning does not shine in imprecation. She merely scolds, and that neither forcibly nor coherently, which is a great comfort to us, because we should be sorry to see our poetess transformed into a *poissarde*. But let us ask Mrs. Browning in all seriousness whether she considers it her duty to curse any one? To bless and not to curse is woman's function; and if Mrs. Browning, in her calmer moments, will but contrast the spirit which has prompted her to such melancholy aberrations with that which animated Florence Nightingale, she can hardly fail to derive a profitable lesson for the future. We abstain from making any quotation from this preposterous malison, and lay aside the little volume with profound regret that it ever was proffered to the public.[30]

Interestingly, "The Cry of the Children," an 1843 poem depicting the wretched conditions of children in the mines, had been exceedingly popular—perhaps because the 1840s were more eager for reform than the 1860s, perhaps because it was easier for readers to respond to the cry of children than to the curse of an adult woman.   .

In the spring of 1861, a few months before she died, Elizabeth Barrett Browning tried to publish "Lord Walter's Wife," a poem which shows a wife exposing her husband's friend as a would-be seducer. Browning was by then enshrined in English and American hearts as "the wife, mother, and poet, three in one, and such an earthly trinity as God had never before blessed the world with."[31] As editor of *Cornhill*, the novelist William Makepeace Thackeray awkwardly explained why he was unable to publish the poem.

36 Onslow Sq^r April 2. 1861.

My dear kind Mrs. Browning

Has Browning ever had an aching tooth w^h must come out (I don't say Mrs Browning, for women are much more courageous) —a tooth w^h must come out and which he has kept for months and months away from the dentist? I have had such a tooth a long time, and have sate down in this chair, and never had the courage to undergo the pull.

This tooth is an allegory (I mean *this* one). Its your poem that you sent me months ago—and who am I to refuse the poems of Elizabeth Browning, and set myself up as a judge over her? I cant tell you how often I have been going to write, and have failed.

You see that our Magazine is written not only for men and women, but for boys, girls, infants, sucklings almost, and one of the best wives, mothers, women in the world, writes some verses, w^h I feel certain would be objected to by many of our readers— Not that the writer is not pure, and the moral most pure chaste and right—but there are things my squeamish public will not hear on Mondays though on Sundays they listen to them without scruple. In your poem you know there is an account of unlawful passion felt by a man for a woman—and though you write pure doctrine and real modesty and pure ethics, I am sure our readers would make an outcry, and so I have not published this poem.

To have to say no to my betters is one of the hardest duties I have—but I'm sure we must not publish your verses—and I go down on my knees before cutting my victim's head off, and say 'Madam you know how I respect and regard you, Browning's wife and Peniny's mother: and for what I am going to do I most humbly ask your pardon.'

My girls send their very best regards and remembrances: and I am, dear Mrs. Browning

Always yours

W M Thackeray

In response, Browning sent him back what she called a piece of "supererogatory virtue": a dreadful poem about a dying child. "Little Mattie" was worthy of Felicia Hemans. But the letter which accompanied it shows that Browning, like Lord Walter's wife and so many activists of the nineteenth century, wanted to use her authority as wife and mother to demand the moral reform of a patriarchal society.

April 21. Rome.
126 Via Felicè.

Dear M.ʳ Thackeray Pray consider the famous "tooth" (a wise tooth!) as extracted under chloroform, and no pain suffered by anybody.

To prove that I am not sulky I send another contribution—which may prove too much perhaps,—and, if you think so, dispose of the supererogatory virtue by burning the ms, as I am sure I may rely on your having done with the last.

I confess it, dear M.ʳ Thackeray, never was anyone turned out of a room for indecent behaviour in a more gracious and conciliatory manner! Also I confess that from your Cornhill stand:point, (paterfamilias looking on) your are probably right ten times over. From mine, however I may not be wrong—and I appeal to you as the deep man you are, whether it is not the higher mood which on Sunday bears with the 'plain word', so offensive on monday during the cheating across the counter—? I am not a 'fast woman'—I dont like coarse subjects, or the coarse treatment of any subject—But I am deeply convinced that the corruption of our society requires, not shut doors and windows, but light and air—and that it is exactly because pure & prosperous women choose to *ignore* vice, that miserable women suffer wrong by it everywhere. Has paterfamilias, with his Oriental traditions and veiled female faces, very successfully dealt with a certain class of evil? What if materfamilias, with her quick pure instincts and honest innocent eyes, do more towards their expulsion by simply looking at them & calling them by their names—

See what insolence you put me up to by your kind way of naming my dignities,—"Browning's wife, and Penini's mother"—And I, being vain, (turn some people out of a room and you dont humble them properly) retort with—"materfamilias"!— . . .

My husband bids me give you his kind regards, and I shall send Pen's love with mine to your dear girls—

most truly yours
Elizabeth Barrett Browning.[32]

While Elizabeth Barrett Browning took an active part in the artistic and moral arguments of her age—turning poetry from the ideal to the real, pursuing personal feelings and artistic self-consciousness, and using her tremendous popularity to articulate women's problems—one of her most astute readers removed herself from the fray. Although Emily Dickinson was interested in Browning, Sand, Eliot, and the Brontës, she never allowed herself to be identified as a woman poet. In 1862, she asked Thomas Wentworth Higginson to read her poems. Failing to understand them, he advised against publication, not because she was a woman, but because he found her works formless and her grammar fractured. Disturbed because editors altered the syntax and punctuation of the few pieces which did appear in print, Dickinson decided to keep her poems for herself and a few close friends. Unpublished, with neither the audience's expectations nor the critics' judgment to contend with, the century's greatest woman poet was free to define her own place in the literary tradition.[33]

II

Discussions of women's poetry occurred sporadically, usually in response to an event—the publication of a new volume or a writer's death. Analysis of fiction was more sustained, with a far greater number of participants evaluating individual novels and generalizing about the strengths and weaknesses of all women novelists.[34] A burst of important articles appeared at mid-century, when women's achievements were particularly evident. With the astounding sales of *The Wide, Wide World* (1851) by Susan Warner and *Uncle Tom's Cabin* (1852) by Harriet Beecher Stowe, women's fiction manifested itself as America's favorite reading material. In 1853 publisher G.P. Putnam sent Hawthorne $144 for the year's royalties on *Mosses from an Old Manse*; he sent Susan Warner $4,500 for six month's sales of *The Wide, Wide World*. During that same year, *Uncle Tom's Cabin* sold 305,000 copies in America and 1,500,000 in England and the colonies.[35]

English novelists produced their shares of best-sellers, like Charlotte Yonge's *Heir of Redclyffe* (1853), but the tension between popular and serious fiction was less marked than in America. Until the 1860s, when improvements in the literacy rate and innovations in publishing made the development of mass literature financially advantageous, it was possible to assume that literature very successful with the novel-reading public was probably worth reading.[36] Unlike the great majority of their American counterparts, English women novelists often earned good sales *and* lengthy consideration in the leading periodicals. When *Jane Eyre* (1847) was followed by so many significant novels in such a short period of time—*Wuthering Heights* (1848), *Mary Barton* (1848), *Ruth* (1853), *Villette* (1853), *Adam Bede* (1859), and *The Mill on the Floss* (1860)—scores of prominent reviewers set out to explain the motives and methods of the lady novelists. In following the controversy from the late 1840s to the early 1860s, we will survey attitudes toward three groups of novelists: "angels in the house," who published as women and seemed to conform to prevailing beliefs about women's roles and duties, including Anne Marsh and Susan Warner; "angels out of the house," such as Elizabeth Gaskell and Harriet Beecher Stowe, who identified themselves as women but enlarged their sphere of responsibility by attacking society's major problems; and "seekers of critical equality," who adopted male pseudonyms to conceal their identity and escape bias, especially Charlotte Brontë and George Eliot.

Most novelists publishing under women's names were pursuing a tradition of domestic realism that was already established when Victoria came to the throne. Since the late eighteenth century, commentators like Hannah More had argued that women had a particular gift for writing about the everyday experiences of heart and home. The domestic novel, with its realistic setting, its interest in the emotional life, and its attention to social conduct seemed to be an appropriate genre for women. Epic poems and historical novels were beyond women's reach. But as Elizabeth Strutt said in 1857, "familiar and sentimental fiction" was like "lyric and elegiac poetry"—a field where women might excel with "felicity of tact," "acuteness of perception and apprehension," and "depth and warmth of feeling."[37]

England had a number of domestic novelists, including Catherine Gore, Anne Marsh, Harriet Martineau, and Charlotte Yonge.[38] Although they helped the novel earn respectability by articulating solid middle-class values, they remained relatively minor figures. In America, the domestic novelists constituted such a large block of the successful writers that they seemed to dominate the culture between 1820 and 1870.[39] Writing out of economic necessity, they saw themselves as hard workers and their fiction as a marketable commodity intended for a primarily female audience. Although a few of the sentimentalists, as they are sometimes called, issued their early works anonymously, like Maria McIntosh and Maria Cummins, most wrote under their own names, like E.D.E.N. Southworth, Caroline Hentz, Ann Stephens, and Augusta Wilson Evans. If modesty demanded a pseudonym, it was female: Susan Warner published *The Wide, Wide World* and *Queechy* (1852) as Elizabeth Wetherell, while her sister Anna used the name of Amy Lathrop for *Dollars and Cents* (1852).[40]

In the domestic novels, modern readers often find a criticism of patriarchy, perhaps even a subversion of its values; Victorian critics saw an affirmation of conventional beliefs. In 1855, for example, Margaret Oliphant complimented three popular British novelists—Anne Marsh, Catherine Gore, and Frances Trollope —for being "orthodox and proper beyond criticism." They were the "respectable elder sisters of the literary corporation," whose ideal of chivalrous love was shattered by "the younger sisterhood" of Charlotte Brontë and Elizabeth Gaskell.[41] Favorable reviews of *Emilia Wyndham* (1846) by Anne Marsh and *The Wide, Wide World* (1851) by Susan Warner will show the qualities that critics valued in domestic fiction.

When the financially distressed Anne Marsh began publishing in 1834, her husband insisted that she remain anonymous to avoid embarrassing their daughters. But by 1849, she was so respectable that *Dublin University Magazine* saw the popularity of her novels as evidence of England's moral integrity.[42] The 1846 *Examiner* commends the moral of *Emilia Wyndham*; James Lorimer's 1849 article from the *North British Review* compliments its author.

> *Emilia Wyndham* is a masterpiece.
> The characters are few, the incidents those of every day, and the philosophy homely enough. The book has no lofty flights. But we can never cease to know the people in it, or to be better for having known them. Their tale is of suffering and trial surmounted by duty and affection. It deals with the extremes of passion and of self-control.
> The mere story is so slight, and depending so much on the subtler developments of feeling and character, that a bare outline would do it no sort of justice. But it turns upon the life-struggle of

a highminded, devoted girl, whose noble performance of what she sees to be her duty, conducts her at last through the saddest sacrifices, through the most affecting patience and self-denial, to a solid and sacred happiness.

. . . All ends happily: with the lesson that husbands and wives have much to correct in each other, that duty is a better thing than pleasure, and that there is no apparently evil fortune which a cheerful heart, and an honest patience, and a humble reliance in good, may not help us to endure.

[Mrs. Marsh] writes as an English gentlewoman should write; and what is better still, she writes what English gentlewomen should read. Her pages are absolutely like green pastures, when we come to them from the barren and terrible scenery of the more ambitious female writers of the day—Madame du Devant, for example [Mme. Dudevant was the married name of George Sand]. . . . We are in no danger with her of falling over a metaphysical precipice into an abyss of unbelief; we feel that her verdure is not indebted for its luxuriance to the heat of a moral volcano. Neither does she belong to those who depend for the interest of their fictions on that which in real life is offensive and disgusting. She seldom paints vicious and degraded characters, or scenes of abject misery; and whilst we remain with her we are pretty safe from having our olfactory nerves regaled by the odours of the workhouse and the dock. Even the "crimes célèbres" have little charm for her; the dagger and the bowl are not among her favourite implements; and she has but one adultery that we remember.[43]

Extolling Marsh for writing novels with "a decided and intentional feminine aspect," American author Caroline Kirkland complains in the *North American Review* that the progeny of most women writers "raise the suspicion of a maternal beard." Fortunately, in Susan and Anna Warner, Kirkland finds a revival of "the novel feminine," and a continuation of the domestic genre. In 1879, when M.G. Van Rensselaer hails the "developed manhood" of American literature in Hawthorne, Cooper, James, and Howells, he will dismiss the Warners and other women novelists because their books are "not properly literature."[44] In 1853, when Kirkland seeks to define the new class of novels that mark the beginning of an "indigenous tradition," she centers on *Queechy* and *The Wide, Wide World.*

Where, then, let us ask, in conclusion, shall we class these American novels of ours? There is very little romance about them;

they have nothing of the . . . didactic tone; they are not devoted to showing up the vices and weaknesses of society; nor do they take up any particular grievance, in order to probe the sluggish consciences of those who practise or tolerate it. . . . They paint human nature in its American type; they appeal to universal human sympathy. . . . They recognize the heart as the strong-hold of character, and religion as the ruling element of life. . . .

Such a spontaneous popularity is interesting as an index of national character. . . . The interest of both [novels] lies in a most life-like picture of the character and fate of a little girl. . . . This little figure, set in a frame-work of homely circumstances, coarse dress, domestic drudgery, and uncongenial companionship, is the light of the book. . . . It is of the little heart, beating at once with timidity and courage, that we think. The sweet childish face and loving ways make "a sunshine in the shady place," under the most humiliating circumstances. (121–23)

Even these sympathetic reviews express the tension between prescription and practice. In praising Marsh and Warner for being proper novelists, journalists reveal their uneasiness about less conventional female authors. From the 1820s well into the 1860s, commentators urge the novelists to create noble, self-sacrificing female characters; to affirm the truth of the affections, the sanctity of the home, and the importance of religion; and to provide detailed descriptions of everyday life. Like educators and politicians, literary critics apply the spur and the rein, encouraging writers to develop in one direction, and restraining them from another.

That the association of women writers with domestic realism had profound implications is clear from this 1865 review by Henry James. In the *Nation*, James commends Susan Warner, Charlotte Yonge, and other women for producing a more acceptable kind of realism than Flaubert. Yet he sees women and children as semi-developed creatures satisfied with a semi-developed form. Like other Victorian critics, he regards women's mimetic skills ("painting") as evidence that other, more fundamental abilities are lacking ("drawing"). Moreover, by aligning realism with rectitude, he excludes from the novel vast areas of human experience.

The foremost property of the school to which these works belong is an attempted, and, to a certain degree, successful, compromise between the interests of youth and those of maturity, between the serious and the trivial. This, indeed, is the mark of a vast proportion of the efforts of modern bookmaking—efforts which in their aggregate may be regarded as an attempt to provide books which grown women may read aloud to children without either party being bored. Books of this class never aim at anything so simple as merely to entertain. . . . They in all cases embody a moral lesson. This latter fact is held to render them incompetent as novels; and doubtless after all, it does, for of a genuine novel the meaning and the lesson are infinite; and here they are carefully narrowed down to a special precept.

It would be unjust to deny that these semi-developed novels are often very charming. Occasionally, like the "Heir of Redclyffe," they almost legitimate themselves by the force of genius. But this only when a first-rate mind takes the matter in hand. By a first-rate mind we here mean a mind which (since its action is restricted beforehand to the shortest gait, the smallest manners possible this side of the ridiculous) is the master and not the slave of its material. It is just now very much the fashion to discuss the so-called principle of realism, and we all know that there exists in France a school of art in which it is associated with great brilliancy and great immorality. The disciples of the school pursue with an assiduity worthy of a better cause the research of local colors with which they have produced a number of curious effects. We believe, however, that the greater successes in this line are reserved for that branch of the school which contains the most female writers; for if women are unable to draw, they notoriously can at all events paint, and this is what realism requires. For an exhibition of the true realistic *chique* we would accordingly refer that body of artists who are represented in France by MM. Flaubert and Gérome to that class of works which, in our own literature are represented by the "Daisy Chain" and "The Wide, Wide World." . . . Until the value of *chique* can be finally established, we should doubtless be thankful that in our literature it lends its vivifying force only to subjects and situations of the most unquestioned propriety.[45]

In discussing women's use of realism, other critics are more explicit about their innate limitations. According to journalist and theologian R.H. Hutton, the novelists' predilection for realism and their reliance on their own experience results from their lack of imagination. In an 1858 essay for *North British Review*, he explains:

It may seem a harsh and arbitrary dictum, that our lady novelists do not usually succeed in the field of imagination, properly so called—the creation of the unseen side of character in conformity with the traits delineated as representing it to society. Yet we are fully convinced that this is the main deficiency of feminine genius. It can observe, it can recombine, it can delineate, but it cannot trust itself farther; it cannot leave the world of characteristic traits and expressive manner, so as to imagine and paint successfully the distinguishable, but not easily distinguished, world out of which these characteristics grew. Women's fancy deals directly with *expression*, with the actual visible effects of mental and moral qualities, and seems unequal to go apart, as it were, with their conception, and work it out firmly in fields of experience somewhat different from those from which they have directly gathered it. Thus no woman, we believe, has ever painted men as they are amongst men. Their imagination takes no grasp of a masculine character that is sufficiently strong to enable them to follow it in imagination into the society of men.[46]

If the novel is an accurate depiction of ordinary reality peculiarly adapted to women because they have the aptitude to observe and transcribe without the ability to abstract and imagine, then the boundaries of their lives will become the limitations of their art. Critics direct women to the areas they presumably know best—the manners of society and the affairs of the heart; however, authors who follow their advice often discover that novels on the first subject are considered trivial, while novels on the second are dangerous. Five speakers present different views on women's experience and its relationship to their fiction: a contributor to the *London Review*, W.R. Greg, J.M. Ludlow, George Henry Lewes, and George Eliot. The first two critics show how the restricted quality of women's social and sexual experiences could lead to a devaluation of their novels. In an 1860 article about domestic fiction, *London Review* applauds women's attention to everyday events *and* undercuts their significance.

> The most successful female novelists are those who have drawn upon the topics that lay closest at hand, and submitted them to the investigation of the microscope. There is no generalisation, or reasoning, of a practical kind in these works, but they contain abundance of quiet and vivid surface observation, acute guesses at profounder things, and heaps of conventional commonplaces which men generally overlook, or are incapable of appreciating. . . . The female novelist who keeps strictly to the region within which she acquires her knowledge may never produce a fiction of the highest order, but she will be in the right path to produce the best fiction of the class in which she is most likely to excel.[47]

The use of domestic materials is correct but commonplace; the treatment of love is a consistently vexing issue. "No writer can depict the passion as to touch others, who has not experienced its influence or closely observed its operation, and who does not draw upon the sources of actual knowledge, instead of taking the inspiration as second-hand from books," says *Fraser's* in 1856.[48] Do women have enough "actual knowledge" to write truthfully about passion? Should they acquire it? No, declares W.R. Greg in the 1859 *National Review*.

The number of youthful novelists, and of young-lady novelists, extant at this moment passes calculation, and was unparalleled at any former epoch. . . . But it is in the nature of things impossible that productions of such a character, from such a source, however able or captivating, should not be radically and inherently defective. . . . If the writer be a young man, his experience of life must be brief, imperfect, and inadequate. If the writer be a young lady, her experience must be not only all this, but must be partial in addition. Whole spheres of observation, whole branches of character and conduct, are almost inevitably closed to her. Nay, even with respect to the one topic which forms the staple of most novels, and a main ingredient in all, viz. love, and its various phases, varieties, and developments,—her means of judgment and of delineation must be always scanty and generally superficial. She may have felt the passion, it is true; but she will have felt it only in one form,—the form congenial to her own nature;—she will be able, therefore, in all likelihood, to depict it only under one aspect, and will estimate its character and consequences from a personal point of view. She may possibly have enjoyed (or suffered) opportunities of observing the workings of the sentiment in some one of her friends; but its wilder issues and its fiercer crises are necessarily and righteously hidden from her sight. She may, by dint of that marvellous faculty of sympathy and intuition which is given to those who have felt profoundly and suffered long, be able to divine much which she cannot discover, and to conceive much which she has never seen or heard; and the pure and God-given instincts which some women possess in so rare a measure may enable her to distinguish between the genuine and the false, the noble and the low;—but many of the saddest and deepest truths in the strange science of sexual affection are to her mysteriously and mercifully veiled; and the knowledge of them can only be purchased at such a fearful cost, that we cannot wish it otherwise. The inevitable consequence, however, is, that in treating of that science she labours under all the disadvantages of partial study and superficial insight.[49]

Writing for the 1853 *North British Review,* social reformer J.M. Ludlow argues that the novel should be based on the fullness of "wifely and motherly experience." Assuming that unmarried women can never feel all the emotions necessary to write a good novel, he urges them to forsake their art altogether.

> But now a question arises, not to be flinched from. *What* women ought to write novels, that novels may be such as really ought to be written? . . . When we look at female writers, we cannot help observing that *the* woman's book of the age—"Uncle Tom's Cabin"—is that of a wife and mother; and even if we contrast the two names more immediately before us, those of the authoresses of "Jane Eyre" and "Mary Barton," many of us at least can hardly repress the feeling, that the works of the former, however more striking in point of intellect, have in them a something harsh, rough, unsatisfying, some say all but unwomanly, as compared with the full, and wholesome, and most womanly perfection of the other.
>
> Is there anything strange in this? . . . If the novel addresses itself to the heart, what more natural than that it should then reach it most usefully and perfectly, when coming from the heart of a woman ripe with all the dignity of her sex, full of all wifely and motherly experience? . . .
>
> But still, what is to become of the women who remain unmarried, and yet have gifts such as fully qualify them to do good service in literature? Gently, and with all reverence must we tell them—Endeavour to find for your gifts other employments. Precisely because your lot is a solitary one, do not make it more so by literary labours. . . . Because you have leisure, which the wife and mother has not, spend that leisure upon others. . . . To you belongs the daily working, the drudgery of all charitable institutions. The adoptive motherhood of the schools may be yours, yours the adoptive sisterhood of the Nurses' Institution, of the Penitentiary, of the simple district-visitor. Here, together with the household of your parents, or your own brothers or sisters, is the sphere within which your heart may preserve itself fresh and lovely, and mellow every year more and more. Who does not know some one old maid who is the blessing of a whole circle?[50]

G.H. Lewes takes a different position, asserting that happy wives and mothers do not normally involve themselves in literature. According to Lewes, art originates in suffering: a solitary life, frustrated maternal instincts, thwarted affections [see Chapter 1]. He values women's fiction because it conveys a new quality of experience. Like his contemporaries, Lewes believes that most of women's experiences will be emotional and domestic, but he is unique in extending their range into the sexual realm. Arguing that previous women writers had erred by imitating men, Lewes advises them to take a new direction in "The Lady Novelists," an 1852 essay for the *Westminster Review*. Lewes is the only major Victorian critic to recognize the importance of Jane Austen and George Sand; he is also the first to assign them a high place in the history of women's fiction.

> What does the literature of women mean? It means this: while it is impossible for men to express life otherwise than as they know it—and they can only know it profoundly according to their own experience—the advent of female literature promises woman's view of life, woman's experience: in other words, a new element. Make what distinctions you please in the social world, it still remains true that men and women have different organizations, consequently different experiences. To know life you must have both sides depicted. . . . And if you limit woman's sphere to the domestic circle, you must still recognise the concurrent necessity of domestic life finding its homeliest and truest expression in the woman who lives it.
>
> Keeping to the abstract heights we have chosen, too abstract and general to be affected by exceptions, we may further say that the Masculine mind is characterized by the predominance of the intellect, and the Feminine by the predominance of the emotions. According to this rough division the regions of philosophy would be assigned to men, those of literature to women. . . .
>
> Woman, by her greater affectionateness, her greater range and depth of emotional experience, is well fitted to give expression to the emotional facts of life, and demands a place in literature corresponding with that she occupies in society; and that literature must be greatly benefited thereby, follows from the definition we have given of literature.
>
> But hitherto, in spite of splendid illustrations, the literature of women has fallen short of its function, owing to a very natural and very explicable weakness—it has been too much a literature of imitation. To write as men write, is the aim and besetting sin of women; to write as women, is the real office they have to perform. Our definition of literature includes this necessity. If writers are bound to express what they have really known, felt, and suffered, that very obligation imperiously declares they shall not quit their own point of view for the point of view of others. To imitate is to abdicate. We are in no need of more male writers; we are in need of

genuine female experience. The prejudices, notions, passions, and conventionalisms of men are amply illustrated; let us have the same fulness with respect to women. . . .

Of all departments of literature, Fiction is the one to which, by nature and by circumstance, women are best adapted. Exceptional women will of course be found competent to the highest success in other departments; but speaking generally, novels are their forte. The domestic experiences which form the bulk of woman's knowledge find an appropriate form in novels; while the very nature of fiction calls for that predominance of Sentiment which we have already attributed to the feminine mind. Love is the staple of fiction, for it "forms the story of a woman's life." The joys and sorrows of affection, the incidents of domestic life, the aspirations and fluctuations of emotional life, assume typical forms in the novel. Hence we may be prepared to find women succeeding better in *finesse* of detail, in pathos and sentiment, while men generally succeed better in the construction of plots and the delineation of character. Such a novel as "Tom Jones" or "Vanity Fair," we shall not get from a woman; nor such an effort of imaginative history as "Ivanhoe" or "Old Mortality;" but Fielding, Thackeray, and Scott are equally excluded from such perfection in its kind as "Pride and Prejudice," "Indiana," or "Jane Eyre:" as an artist, Miss Austen surpasses all the male novelists that ever lived; and for eloquence and depth of feeling, no man approaches George Sand. . . .

First and foremost let Jane Austen be named, the greatest artist that has ever written, using the term to signify the most perfect mastery over the means to her end. There are heights and depths in human nature Miss Austen has never scaled nor fathomed, there are worlds of passionate existence into which she has never set foot; but although this is obvious to every reader, it is equally obvious that she has risked no failures by attempting to delineate that which she had not seen. Her circle may be restricted, but it is complete. Her world is a perfect orb, and vital. Life, as it presents itself to an English gentlewoman peacefully yet actively engaged in her quiet village, is mirrored in her works with a purity and fidelity that must endow them with interest for all time. To read one of her books is like an actual experience of life: you know the people as if you had lived with them, and you feel something of personal affection towards them. . . . Of all imaginative writers she is the most *real*. Never does she transcend her own actual experience, never does her pen trace a line that does not touch the experience of others. Herein we recognise the first quality of literature. We recognise the second and more special quality of womanliness in the tone and point of view: they are novels written by a woman, an Englishwoman, a gentlewoman; no signature could disguise that fact; and because she has so faithfully (although unconsciously) kept to her own womanly point of view, her works are durable. There is nothing of the *doctrinaire* in Jane Austen; not a trace of woman's "mission;" but as the most truthful, charming, humorous, pure-minded, quick-witted, and unexaggerated of writers, female literature has reason to be proud of her.

Of greater genius, and incomparably deeper experience, George Sand represents woman's literature more illustriously and more obviously. In her, quite apart from the magnificent gifts of Nature, we see the influence of Sorrow, as a determining impulse to write, and the abiding consciousness of the womanly point of view as the subject matter of her writings. In vain has she chosen the mask of a man, the features of a woman are everywhere visible. Since Goethe no one has been able to say with so much truth, "My writings are my confessions." Her biography lies there, presented, indeed, in a fragmentary shape, and under wayward disguises, but nevertheless giving to the motley groups the strange and unmistakeable charm of reality. Her grandmother, by whom she was brought up, disgusted at her not being a boy, resolved to remedy the misfortune as far as possible by educating her like a boy. We may say of this, as of all the other irregularities of her strange and exceptional life, that whatever unhappiness and error may be traceable thereto, its influence on her writings has been beneficial, by giving a greater range to her experience. . . . In the matter of eloquence, she surpasses everything France has yet produced. . . .

But deeper than all eloquence, grander than all grandeur of phrase, is that forlorn splendour of a life of passionate experience painted in her works. There is no man so wise but he may learn from them, for they are the utterances of a soul in pain, a soul that has been tried. No man could have written her books, for no man could have had her experience, even with a genius equal to her own. The philosopher may smile sometimes at her philosophy, for *that* is only a reflex of some man whose ideas she has adopted; the critic may smile sometimes at her failure in delineating men; but both philosopher and critic must perceive that those writings of hers are *original*, are genuine, are transcripts of experience, and as such fulfil the primary condition of all literature.[51]

George Eliot agrees that women's literature should differ from men's, but while Lewes offers women a literary tradition, she asks for them a greater share of reality. In "Woman in France," an 1854 *Westminster* article written before she became a novelist, Eliot gives particular attention to the cultural conditions that would stimulate women to express themselves and to make a unique contribution to their country's literature.

With a few remarkable exceptions, our own feminine literature is made up of books which could have been better written by men; books which have the same relation to literature in general, as academic prize poems have to poetry: when not a feeble imitation, they are usually an absurd exaggeration of the masculine style, like the swaggering gait of a bad actress in male attire. . . .

In France alone woman has had a vital influence on the development of literature; in France alone the mind of woman has passed like an electric current through the langauge, making crisp and definite what is elsewhere heavy and blurred; in France alone, if the writings of women were swept away, a serious gap would be made in the national history. . . .

[One] cause was probably the laxity of opinion and practice with regard to the marriage-tie. Heaven forbid that we should enter on a defence of French morals, most of all in relation to marriage! But it is undeniable, that unions formed in the maturity of thought and feeling, and grounded only on inherent fitness and mutual attraction, tended to bring women into more intelligent sympathy with men, and to heighten and complicate their share in the political drama. . . . Gallantry and intrigue are sorry enough things in themselves, but they certainly serve better to arouse the dormant faculties of woman, than embroidery and domestic drudgery. . . . The dreamy and fantastic girl was awakened to reality by the experience of wifehood and maternity, and became capable of loving, not a mere phantom of her own imagination, but a living man, struggling with the hatreds and rivalries of the political arena; she espoused his quarrels, she made herself, her fortune, and her influence, the stepping-stones of his ambition; and the languid beauty, who had formerly seemed ready to "die of a rose," was seen to become the heroine of an insurrection. . . .

But the most indisputable source of feminine culture and development in France was the influence of the *salons*; which, as all the world knows, were *réunions* of both sexes, where conversation ran along the whole gamut of subjects, from the frothiest *vers de société* to the philosophy of Descartes. . . . Those famous *habitués* of the Hôtel de Rambouillet did not, apparently, first lay themselves out to entertain the ladies with grimacing "small-talk," and then take each other by the sword-knot to discuss matters of real interest in a corner; they rather sought to present their best ideas in the guise most acceptable to intelligent and accomplished women. And the conversation was not of literature only; war, politics, religion, the lightest details of daily news—everything was admissible, if only it were treated with refinement and intelligence. The Hôtel de Rambouillet was no mere literary *réunion*; it included *hommes d'affaires* and soldiers as well as authors, and in such a circle women would not become *bas bleus* or dreamy moralizers, ignorant of the world and of human nature, but intelligent observers of character and events. . . .

Women become superior in France by being admitted to a common fund of ideas, to common objects of interest with men; and this must ever be the essential condition at once of true womanly culture and of true social well-being. We have no faith in feminine conversazioni, where ladies are eloquent on Apollo and Mars; though we sympathize with the yearning activity of faculties which, deprived of their proper material, waste themselves in weaving fabrics out of cobwebs. Let the whole field of reality be laid open to woman as well as to man, and then that which is peculiar in her mental modification, instead of being, as it is now, a source of discord and repulsion between the sexes, will be found to be a necessary complement to the truth and beauty of life. Then we shall have that marriage of minds which alone can blend all the hues of thought and feeling in one lovely rainbow of promise for the harvest of human happiness.[52]

Although mature sexual relationships, political turmoil, and the sophisticated interchange of the salons might have awakened the intellectual and artistic energies of French women, such prospects did not appeal to an Anglo-American audience. The argument for a greater breadth of experiences was heard only occasionally, and it had no practical consequences for the novelists.

Rather than enlarge the range of women's activities, many writers kept the home as the basis of their fiction and attempted to extend its influence into the public sphere. In literature, as in politics, education, and religion, writers could use the seemingly restrictive assumptions about woman's sphere to argue for individual and social reform. Although the sentimentalists did not usually attack specific abuses, they did assert the power of women's emotions. According to Caroline Kirkland, childish innocence and womanly affection could overcome the hardened resistance of paterfamilias and the publishing industry. In commenting on the public reception of *The Wide, Wide World*, Kirkland discloses a good deal about the way a woman writer might see herself: like the book, the writer is a seemingly insignificant entity operating outside the system and eventually breaking down bastions of male power.

> As far as we know the early history of the Wide, Wide World, it was, for some time, bought to be presented to nice little girls, by parents and friends who desired to set a pleasant example of docility and self-command before those happy beginners. Elder sisters were soon found poring over the volumes, and it was very natural that mothers next should try the spell which could so enchain the more volatile spirits of the household. After this, papas were not very difficult to convert, for papas like to feel their eyes moisten, sometimes, with emotions more generous than those usually excited at the stock exchange or in the counting-room. Whether any elder brothers read, we must doubt, in the absence of direct testimony; for that class proverbially despises any thing so "slow" as pictures of domestic life; but we are much mistaken if the Wide, Wide World, and Queechy, have not been found under the pillows of sober bachelors,—pillows not un-sprinkled with the sympathetic tears of those who, in broad day, manfully exult in "freedom" from the effeminate fetters of wife and children.
> All this while nobody talked very loud about these simple stories. They were found on everybody's table, and lent from house to house, but they made no great figure in the newspapers or show-bills. By and by, the deliberate people who look at title-pages, noticed the magic words, "Tenth Thousand," "Twelfth Thousand," and so on; and as the publishing house was not one of those who think politic fibs profitable, inevitable conclusions began to be drawn as to the popularity of the books—conclusions to which the publisher had come long before, perhaps not without a certain surprise. (112–13)

While Susan Warner and the sentimentalists emphasized women's capacity for affection, Harriet Beecher Stowe and Elizabeth Gaskell reminded them of their obligation to act upon their feelings. They considered the social and moral problems of a nation well within their realm. Against an oppressive society that sanctioned slavery and prostitution, they invoked the power of maternal love in *Uncle Tom's Cabin* (1852) and *Ruth* (1853). The cult of domesticity provided some protection from criticism: both Stowe and Gaskell were recognized as authors of domestic tales, and their position as wives and mothers merited personal respect.[53] (Indeed, Ludlow's argument that mothers make the best novelists resulted from his analysis of *Ruth*.) Writing to one of her children, Stowe explained how her experiences as a mother had motivated her to write *Uncle Tom's Cabin*.

> I well remember the winter you were a baby and I was writing 'Uncle Tom's Cabin.' My heart was bursting with the anguish excited by the cruelty and injustice our nation was showing to the slave, and praying God to let me do a little and to cause my cry for them to be heard. I remember many a night weeping over you as you lay sleeping beside me, and I thought of the slave mothers whose babes were torn from them.[54]

Stowe stated her determination to reform a patriarchal society in an 1851 letter to Gamaliel Bailey, editor of the abolitionist newspaper that published the novel in serial form.

> Mr. Bailey, Dear Sir:
>   I am at present occupied upon a story which will be a much longer one than any I have ever written, embracing a series of sketches which give the lights and shadows of the "patriarchal institution," written either from observation, incidents which have occurred in the sphere of my personal knowledge, or in the knowledge of my friends. I shall show the *best side* of the thing, and something *faintly approaching the worst*.
>   Up to this year I have always felt that I had no particular call to meddle with this subject, and I dreaded to expose even my own mind to the full force of its exciting power. But I feel now that the time is come when even a woman or a child who can speak a word for freedom and humanity is bound to speak. The Carthagenian [sic] women in the last peril of their state cut off their hair for bow-strings to give to the defenders of their country; and such peril and shame as now hangs over this country is worse than Roman slavery, and I hope every woman who can write will not be silent. I have admired and sympathized with the fearless and free spirit of Grace Greenwood, and her letters have done my heart good. My vocation is simply that of *painter*, and my object will be to hold up in the most lifelike and graphic manner possible slavery, its reverses, changes, and the Negro character, which I have had ample opportunities for studying. There is no arguing with *pictures*, and everybody is impressed by them, whether they mean to be or not.
>   I wrote beforehand, because I know that you have much matter to arrange, and thought it might not be amiss to give you a

hint. The thing may extend through three or four numbers. It will
be ready in two or three weeks. . . .

Yours with sincere esteem,
H. Stowe[55]

Although some readers, especially in the southeastern United
States, denounced Stowe for stepping outside her sphere and
betraying her sex, most believed that she embodied desirable
womanly attributes.[56] In 1852, three reviewers find different
reasons to defend *Uncle Tom's Cabin* as a woman's novel. Charles
Beard, Unitarian divine and editor of the *Theological Review*,
claims that Stowe represents the strengths and weaknesses of
the domestic novelists, while British novelist Anna Maria Hall
hails Stowe as a new type of woman writer—despite her lack of
imaginative ability.[57] From France, novelist George Sand suggests that Stowe's alleged deficiencies are the true source of her
greatness. In *La Presse*, George Sand reports that the novel is
triumphing "in the discussion it causes in domestic circles."

For this book is essentially domestic and of the family,—this
book, with its long discussions, its minute details, its portraits
carefully studied. Mothers of families, young girls, little children,
servants even, can read and understand them, and men themselves, even the most superior, cannot disdain them. We do not say
that the success of the book is because its great merits redeem its
faults; we say its success is because of these very alleged faults. . . .
Mrs. Stowe is all instinct; it is the very reason that she appears
to some not to have talent. Has she not talent? What is talent?
Nothing, doubtless, compared to genius; but has she genius? I
cannot say that she has talent as one understands it in the world of
letters, but she has genius, as humanity feels the need of genius,—
the genius of goodness, not that of the man of letters, but of the
saint. Yes,—a saint! Thrice holy the soul which thus loves, blesses,
and consoles the martyrs. Pure, penetrating, and profound the
spirit which thus fathoms the recesses of the human soul. Noble,
generous, and great the heart which embraces in her pity, in her
love, an entire race, trodden down in blood and mire under the
whip of ruffians and the maledictions of the impious. . . .
The saints also have their claw! it is that of the lion. She buries
it deep in the conscience, and a little of burning indignation and of
terrible sarcasm does not, after all, misbecome this Harriet Stowe,
this woman so gentle, so humane, so religious, and full of evangelical unction. Ah! yes, she is a very good woman, but not what we

derisively call "goody good." Hers is a heart strong and courageous, which in blessing the unhappy and applauding the faithful, tending the feeble and succoring the irresolute, does not hesitate to bind to the pillory the hardened tyrant, to show to the world his deformity.

She is, in the true spirit of the word, consecrated. Her fervent Christianity sings the praise of the martyr, but permits no man the right to perpetuate the wrong. She denounces that strange perversion of Scripture which tolerates the iniquity of the oppressor because it gives opportunity for the virtues of the victims. She calls on God himself, and threatens in his name; she shows us human law on one side, and God on the other!

Let no one say that, because she exhorts to patient endurance of wrong, she justifies those who do the wrong. Read the beautiful page where George Harris, the white slave, embraces for the first time the shores of a free territory, and presses to his heart wife and child, who at last are *his own*. What a beautiful picture, that! What a large heart-throb! what a triumphant protest of the eternal and inalienable right of man to liberty!

Honor and respect to you, Mrs. Stowe! Some day your recompense, which is already recorded in heaven, will come also in this world.[58]

Sand's essay, which she called an act of homage rather than a review, is a remarkable instance of one woman honoring the moral and artistic force of another. Unfortunately, reviewers' attempts to formulate a critical vocabulary for women's fiction usually had a limiting effect on the writers' achievements and often drove them to assume male pseudonyms in the hope of receiving more respect.[59]

In 1861, when the male pseudonym had become prevalent in England, *Dublin University Magazine* urged the novelists to cast off their masculine attire and become as "womanly" as Felicia Hemans and Elizabeth Barrett Browning. The promise of fair treatment is undercut by the clichés of True Womanhood, the animal imagery, and the male critic's pleasure at his superior insight.

Why are female novelists so prone to masquerade in garments borrowed from the sterner sex? is the question likeliest to be raised by those critics who see no wisdom in the act of an ostrich hiding her head in the sand. A disguise which any reader of average shrewdness can pierce in a few minutes seems, to our simple fancy, an elaborate mistake. It is a poor compliment to male critics to suppose that the putting of a man's name in the first page of a new novel will therefore blind them to the real authorship of that novel. . . .

But the murder will soon out, even to the contentment of the least discerning, while the more experienced will, from the first, have laughed to themselves at the affectation of a mystery which was neither needed nor well done. . . . None but shallow or one-sided dogmatists would speak of women's books with an air of conscious patronage or affected reserve. . . .

A true woman's book will reveal its own special charm, whether of strength or weakness; will speak to his heart in tones more or less different from those uttered by his fellowmen. Like woman herself, it is nothing unless it be "pure womanly." A good female writer, in her own way, has no rival among the brethren of her craft; only in laying aside the garb or the graces of her sex does she lay herself open to the charge of failure in a character which she had no business to undertake. Striving to copy the man's free carriage, deep tones, and hard reasonings, she can only succeed in behaving like a better sort of monkey.[60]

In America, women occasionally gave up their names when they tried to move beyond their proper fictive sphere. Rebecca Harding Davis chose anonymity for her 1865 story depicting the squalor and degradation of life in the iron mills of West Virginia, and when Louisa May Alcott sold her lurid tales of mystery and intrigue, she steadfastly refused the publisher's offer of additional money if she would use her own name. She resorted instead to anonymity or to the neutral pen name of A.M. Barnard. But in England, the choice of a male pseudonym characterized an entire age: the "feminine phase" began with the appearance of the male pseudonym during the 1840s and lasted until the death of George Eliot in 1880. The Brontës and George Eliot are only the most famous of the English writers to have assumed male pseudonyms. Holme Lee, Ennis Graham, F.G. Trafford, Allen Raine, Lucas Malet, John Strange Winter, Lanoe Falconer, George Egerton, Lawrence Hope, Vernon Lee, Claude Lake, Ross Neil, John Oliver Hobbes, Martin Ross, and Michael Fairless were also women. In public terms, the pen name reflects the novelists' desire to protect themselves from personal attack and to win the serious respect of reviewers. In private terms, the masculine name suggests the fantasy of ac-quiring a more exciting identity and the guilt of choosing a vocation in direct conflict with woman's status.[61]

The emphasis on the male pseudonym may mean that the English novelists experienced greater ambition and more intense conflict than the Americans. They certainly encountered more forceful opposition in the male-dominated press. At mid-century, the journals with serious interest in fiction were more numerous, more sophisticated, and more influential in England than in America. Determined to overcome the allegations of female inferiority and to earn the approval of the press, British novelists insisted on high standards; they regarded the reviewers soberly, and they made sharp judgments of one another's work.[62]

The problems associated with the male pseudonym are illustrated in practical rather than theoretical terms by Charlotte Brontë's correspondence with G.H. Lewes and by the angry response to Eliot's 1860 novel *The Mill on the Floss*. Of course, Eliot and Brontë cannot be considered typical women writers: extraordinarily talented and eventually successful in gaining widespread respect, they loomed larger than life and had a somewhat daunting effect on their successors.[63] Yet the controversies they provoked will show the commonly held critical biases that drove women to adopt a pseudonym and illustrate the painful consequences of losing its protection.

Brontë was anxious about *Jane Eyre's* reception. "It has no learning, no research, it discusses no subject of public interest," she wrote to W.S. Williams in 1847. "A mere domestic novel will, I fear, seem trivial to men of large views, and solid attainments."[64] After the novel's publication, Brontë was pleased to receive a congratulatory letter from G.H. Lewes. Lewes knew nothing about the conditions of "Currer Bell's" life, but he was certain that *Jane Eyre* had been written by a woman. Lewes' letters have not survived, but their contents can be deduced from Brontë's responses and from the reviews he wrote of her novels. His emphasis on experience raised disturbing questions for Charlotte Brontë. How was she, a clergyman's daughter living at a country parsonage, going to find additional material for subsequent novels? Why should fiction be based on life instead of imagination? The terms of their first disagreement are indicated by three documents: Brontë's first letter to Lewes, Lewes' 1847 *Fraser's* review of *Jane Eyre*, and Brontë's reply.

November 6th, 1847.
Dear Sir,—Your letter reached me yesterday. I beg to assure you that I appreciate fully the intention with which is was written, and I thank you sincerely both for its cheering commendation and valuable advice.

You warn me to beware of melodrama, and you exhort me to adhere to the real. . . . You advise me, too, not to stray far from the ground of experience, as I become weak when I enter the region of fiction; and you say 'real experience is perennially interesting, and to all men.'

I feel that this also is true; but, dear sir, is not the real experience of each individual very limited? And, if a writer dwells upon that solely or principally, is he not in danger of repeating himself, and also of becoming an egotist? Then, too, imagination is a strong, restless faculty, which claims to be heard and exercised: are we to be quite deaf to her cry, and insensate to her struggles? When she shows us bright pictures, are we never to look at them, and try to reproduce them? And when she is eloquent, and speaks rapidly and urgently in our ear, are we not to write to her dictation?

I shall anxiously search the next number of *Fraser* for your opinions on these points.—Believe me, dear sir, yours gratefully,

C. BELL.

Reality—deep, significant reality—is the great characteristic of the book. It is an autobiography,—not, perhaps, in the naked facts and circumstances, but in the actual suffering and experience. The form may be changed, and here and there some incidents invented; but the spirit remains such as it was. . . . This gives the book its charm: it is soul speaking to soul; it is an utterance from the depths of a struggling, suffering, much-enduring spirit: *suspiria de profundis!*

When we see a young writer exhibiting such remarkable power as there is in *Jane Eyre*, it is natural that we should ask, Is this experience drawn from an abundant source, or is it only the artistic mastery over small materials? Because, according as this question is answered, there are two suggestions to be made. Has the author seen much more and felt much more than what is here communicated? Then let new works continue to draw from that rich storehouse. Has the author led a quiet secluded life, uninvolved in the great vortex of the world, undisturbed by varied passions, untried by strange calamities? Then let new works be planned and executed with excessive circumspection; for, unless a novel be built out of real experience, it can have no real success. . . .

HAWORTH, January 12th, 1848.
DEAR SIR,—I thank you, then, sincerely for your generous review. . . . I mean to observe your warning about being careful how I undertake new works; my stock of materials is not abundant, but very slender; and besides, neither my experience, my acquirements, nor my powers are sufficiently varied to justify my ever becoming a frequent writer. I tell you this because your article in 'Fraser' left in me an uneasy impression that you were disposed to think better of

"Poetesses" and "Lady Novelists"

the author of 'Jane Eyre' than that individual deserved; and I would rather you had a correct than a flattering opinion of me, even though I should never see you. If I ever *do* write another book, I think I will have nothing of what you call 'melodrama'; I *think* so, but I am not sure. I *think*, too, I will endeavour to follow the counsel which shines out of Miss Austen's 'mild eyes,' 'to finish more and be more subdued'; but neither am I sure of that. When authors write best, or, at least, when they write most fluently, an influence seems to waken in them, which becomes their master—which will have its own way—putting out of view all behests but its own, dictating certain words, and insisting on their being used, whether vehement or measured in their nature; new-moulding characters, giving unthought-of turns to incidents, rejecting carefully elaborated old ideas, and suddenly creating and adopting new ones.

Is it not so? And should we try to counteract this influence? Can we indeed counteract it?[65]

Despite her belief in the imagination, Brontë kept Lewes' comments in mind when she was writing her next novel. In the first chapter of *Shirley* (1849), she warned the readers not to expect "passion, and stimulus, and melodrama." "Calm your expectations," she said. "Something real, cool, and solid lies before you." The choice of an omniscient narrator and the emphasis on homey prosaic details very likely reflect Brontë's desire to avoid the excesses Lewes had warned her against.[66] The exchange of letters surrounding *Shirley* concern her identity rather than her imagination. When Lewes told her he had discovered that "Currer Bell" was Charlotte Brontë, she asked him to preserve her pseudonym. In his 1850 analysis of the book for *Edinburgh Review,* Lewes praises the boldness of Brontë's imagery and the sharpness of certain character sketches; he also identifies the book's central weakness—the abandonment of the individual perspective that had given life to *Jane Eyre.* However, in the sections excerpted here, Lewes does what Brontë feared most: he identifies her as a woman and attributes some of the flaws in the novel to the circumstances of her life. Included here are Brontë's letter, Lewes' review, and Brontë's immediate reply.

November 1st, 1849.

MY DEAR SIR,—It is about a year and a half since you wrote to me; but it seems a longer period, because since then it has been my lot to pass some black milestones in the journey of life [the deaths of

Branwell, Emily, and Anne]. Since then there have been intervals when I have ceased to care about literature and critics and fame; when I have lost sight of whatever was prominent in my thoughts at the first publication of 'Jane Eyre'; but now I want these things to come back vividly, if possible: consequently it was a pleasure to receive your note. I wish you did not think me a woman. I wish all reviewers believed 'Currer Bell' to be a man; they would be more just to him. You will, I know, keep measuring me by some standard of what you deem becoming to my sex; where I am not what you consider graceful you will condemn me. All mouths will be open against that first chapter, and that first chapter is as true as the Bible, nor is it exceptionable. Come what will, I cannot, when I write, think always of myself and of what is elegant and charming in femininity; it is not on those terms, or with such ideas, I ever took pen in hand: and if it is only on such terms my writing will be tolerated, I shall pass away from the public and trouble it no more. Out of obscurity I came, to obscurity I can easily return. . . . Wishing you all success in your Scottish expedition,—I am, dear sir, yours sincerely,

C. Bell.

Currer Bell's 'Shirley.'

. . . We must confess our doubts whether women will ever rival men in *some* departments of intellectual exertion; and especially in those which demand either a long preparation, or a protracted effort of pure thought. But we do not, by this, prejudge the question of superiority. We assume no general organic inferiority; we simply assert an organic *difference*. . . . The grand function of woman, it must always be recollected, is, and ever must be, *Maternity*: and this we regard not only as her distinctive characteristic, and most endearing charm, but as a high and holy office—the prolific source, not only of the best affections and virtues of which our nature is capable, but also of the wisest thoughtfulness, and most useful habits of observation, by which that nature can be elevated and adorned. But with all this, we think it impossible to deny, that it must essentially interfere both with that steady and unbroken application, without which no proud eminence in science can be gained—and with the discharge of all official or professional functions that do not admit of long or frequent postponement. . . .

If it be said that these considerations only apply to wives and mothers, and ought not to carry along with them any disqualification of virgins or childless widows, the answer is, that as Nature qualifies and apparently designs *all* women to be mothers, it is impossible to know who are to escape that destiny, till it is too late to begin the training necessary for artists, scholars, or politicians. . . .

But we must pursue this topic no further; and fear our readers may have been wondering how we have wandered away to it, from the theme which seemed to be suggested by the title of the work now before us. The explanation and apology is, that we take Currer Bell to be one of the most remarkable of *female* writers; and believe it is now scarcely a secret that Currer Bell is the pseudonyme of a woman. An eminent contemporary, indeed, has employed the sharp vivacity of a female pen to prove 'upon irresistible evidence' that 'Jane Eyre' *must be* the work of a man! But all that 'irresistible evidence' is set aside by the simple fact that Currer Bell *is* a woman. . . .

Currer Bell is exceedingly scornful on the chapter of heroines drawn by men. The cleverest and acutest of our sex, she says, are often under the strangest illusions about women—we do not read them in their true light; we constantly misapprehend them, both for good and evil. Very possibly. But we suspect that female artists are by no means exempt from mistakes quite as egregious when *they* delineate their sex; nay, we venture to say, that Mrs. Pryor and Caroline Helstone are as untrue to the universal laws of our common nature as if they had been drawn by the clumsy hand of a male: though we willingly admit that in both there are little touches which at once betray the more exquisite workmanship of a woman's lighter pencil.

Mrs. Pryor, in the capital event of her life—at least as far as regards this story—belies the most indisputable laws of our nature, in becoming an unnatural mother,—from some absurd prepossession that her child *must* be bad, wicked, and the cause of anguish to her, because it is pretty! . . . Currer Bell! if under your heart had ever stirred a child, if to your bosom a babe had ever been pressed,—that mysterious part of your being, towards which all the rest of it was drawn, in which your whole soul was transported and absorbed,—never could you have *imagined* such a falsehood as that! It is indeed conceivable—under some peculiar circumstances, and with peculiar dispositions—that the loathing of the wife for the husband, might extend to the child, because it was the husband's child; the horror and hate being so intense as to turn back the natural current of maternal instincts; but to suppose that the mere beauty and 'aristocratic' air of an infant could so wrest out of its place a woman's heart,—supposing her not irretrievably insane,— and for eighteen years keep a mother from her child, is to outrage all that we know of human nature. . . .

This, however, is but one point in the faulty treatment of the character. A graver error,—one implying greater forgetfulness of dramatic reality and probability,—is the conduct of Caroline in her love for Moore. The mystery kept up between the two girls is the trick of a vulgar novelist. . . . But what is more incredible still, Caroline—who believes that Moore loves Shirley and will marry her—never once feels the sharp and terrible pang of jealousy! Now, unless we are to be put out of court as men, and consequently incompetent to apprehend the true nature of woman, we should say that this entire absence of jealous feelings on Caroline's part, is an omission, which, conscious or unconscious, we cannot reconcile with any thing we have ever seen, heard, or read of about the sex. That a girl like Caroline might be willing to resign her claims, might be willing even to submit in silence to the torture of her disappointment, is conceivable enough; and a fine theme might this have afforded for some profound psychological probings, laying open the terrible conflict of irrepressible instincts with more generous feelings,—the conflict of jealousy with reason. But Caroline Helstone merely bows her head in meekness, and loves and clings to Shirley all the more; never has even a moment's rebellion against her, and behaves like pattern young ladies in 'good' books! . . .

Schiller, writing to Goethe about Madame de Stael's 'Corinne,' says, 'This person wants every thing that is graceful in a woman; and, nevertheless, the faults of her book are altogether womanly faults. She steps out of her sex—without elevating herself above it.' This brief and pregnant criticism is quite as applicable to Currer Bell: For she, too, has genius enough to create a great name for herself; and if we seem to have insisted too gravely on her faults, it is only because we are ourselves sufficiently her admirers to be most desirous to see her remove these blemishes from her writings, and take the rank within her reach.

[January, 1850].

I can be on my guard against my enemies, but God deliver me from my friends!

CURRER BELL.[67]

A grating exchange, but one from which both novelist and critic seem to have benefited. In *Villette* (1853) Brontë returned to the immediacy and intensity of a first-person narrator whose situation at a school in Belgium bore many resemblances to her own; in Lewes' later reviews he demonstrated more willingness to accept the validity of experiences which had been felt as well as lived, and greater respect for the imagination's ability to make from a drab life an emotionally rich work of art.[68]

Through his own experiences, Lewes also learned why women novelists might need to conceal their identity. George

Henry Lewes and George Eliot began their life-long liaison in 1854. He was a highly regarded intellectual unable to obtain a divorce from his wife; she was still Marian Evans, writer and editor for the *Westminster Review* and translator of biblical criticism which threatened Victorian faith. Lewes encouraged his brilliant companion to write fiction, and for the rest of his life acted as a kind of literary husband, discussing her projects, criticizing preliminary drafts, negotiating with publishers, and supporting her in moods of depression.

In 1856, shortly before she began work on her first story for *Scenes from Clerical Life*, Eliot published "Silly Novels by Lady Novelists" in the *Westminister Review*. Writing anonymously, she repudiates many of her predecessors, aligns herself with the major women writers of the age, and issues an admonition to the rest. Her sternness is reminiscent of the women educators as they goaded their students to meet requirements set by men's schools and warned them against the far-reaching consequences of their failure.

"Be not a baker if your head be made of butter," says a homely proverb, which, being interpreted, may mean, let no woman rush into print who is not prepared for the consequences. We are aware that our remarks are in a very different tone from that of the reviewers who, with a perennial recurrence of precisely similar emotions, only paralleled, we imagine, in the experience of monthly nurses, tell one lady novelist after another that they "hail" her productions "with delight." We are aware that the ladies at whom our criticism is pointed are accustomed to be told, in the choicest phraseology of puffery, that their pictures of life are brilliant, their characters well drawn, their style fascinating, and their sentiments lofty. . . . Harriet Martineau, Currer Bell, and Mrs. Gaskell have been treated as cavalierly as if they had been men. And every critic who forms a high estimate of the share women may ultimately take in literature, will, on principle, abstain from any exceptional indulgence towards the productions of literary women. For it must be plain to every one who looks impartially and extensively into feminine literature, that its greatest deficiencies are due hardly more to the want of intellectual power than to the want of those moral qualities that contribute to literary excellence—patient diligence, a sense of the responsibility involved in publication, and an appreciation of the sacredness of the writer's art. In the majority of women's books you see that kind of facility which springs from the absence of any high standard; that fertility in imbecile combination or feeble imitation which a little self-criticism would check and reduce to barrenness; just as with a total want of musical ear people will sing out of tune, while a degree more melodic sensibility would suffice to render them silent. The foolish vanity of wishing to appear in print, instead of being counterbalanced by any consciousness of the intellectual or moral derogation implied in futile authorship, seems to be encouraged by the extremely false impression that to write *at all* is a proof of superiority in a woman. On this ground, we believe that the average intellect of women is unfairly represented by the mass of feminine literature, and that while the few women who write well are very far above the ordinary intellectual level of their sex, the many women who write ill are very far below it. So that, after all, the severer critics are fulfilling a chivalrous duty in depriving the mere fact of feminine authorship of any false prestige which may give it a delusive attraction, and in recommending women of mediocre faculties—as at least a negative service they can render their sex—to abstain from writing. . . .

No educational restrictions can shut women out from the materials of fiction, and there is no species of art which is so free from rigid requirements. Like crystalline masses, it may take any form, and yet be beautiful; we have only to pour in the right elements—genuine observation, humour, and passion. But it is precisely this absence of rigid requirement which consitutes the fatal seduction of novel-writing to incompetent women. . . . In novel-writing there are no barriers for incapacity to stumble against, no external criteria to prevent a writer from mistaking foolish facility for mastery. And so we have again and again the old story of La Fontaine's ass, who puts his nose to the flute, and, finding that he elicits some sound, exclaims, "Moi, aussi, je joue de la flute;"—a fable which we commend, at parting, to the consideration of any feminine reader who is in danger of adding to the number of "silly novels by lady novelists."[69]

Eliot's stories were published anonymously, but when her first novel was ready, she and Lewes were convinced a pseudonym would be necessary. "When *Jane Eyre* was finally known to be a woman's book," observed Lewes with no discernible irony, "the tone noticeably changed." He was determined to get *Adam Bede* judged "on its own merits, and not prejudged as the work of a woman, or of a particular woman." Marian Evans later explained her choice of name: "George was Mr. Lewes's Christian name, and Eliot was a good mouth-filling easily-pronounced word."[70] The pseudonym was so successful that many readers believed George Eliot to be a rural minister.

But when a clergyman named Liggins claimed authorship of *Adam Bede*, Eliot revealed her identity in order to protect her artistic reputation.

As a result, when *The Mill on the Floss* appeared in 1860, most reviewers knew who the author was. Readers were stunned to discover that George Eliot was not a clergyman—she was a religious skeptic living with a married man. While a few journals remarked favorably upon Eliot's treatment of love and her analysis of moral complexities, most denounced Maggie and Stephen's love as dangerous and reproached Eliot for failing to embody absolute laws of conduct in the narrative.[71] Brontë was criticized because she had too little experience of life and love; Eliot, because she had too much. *Dublin University Magazine* and *London Quarterly Review* are among the most virulent of the reviewers: the former accuses Eliot of giving too much leeway to passion; the latter implies that she is using the novel to defend her relationship with Lewes.

> The lengthened treatment of a mystery so full of doubt and danger, by an Englishwoman writing for readers of both sexes, speaks as poorly for her good taste as the readiness wherewith a large-hearted girl yields up all her noblest scruples, her tenderest sympathies, to the paltry fear of seeming cruel in the eyes of a weak, unworthy tempter, speaks, in our opinion, for her knowledge of human character. Surely, no woman of Maggie's sort would have let herself be wholly drawn away from her love for the deformed and suffering Philip by a mere outside fancy for the good-looking, sweet-voiced coxcomb, Stephen Guest. Nor could any moral or artistic end be furthered by a close relation of the circumstances which made her so unaccountably false both to her old lover and the cousin with whom she had been staying. . . . The development of a gross passion much more akin to lust than love, takes up far too many pages. . . . Englishmen have not yet come to believe in the triumph—speaking vulgarly—of matter over mind. With all due allowance for the power of circumstances, they cling the more reverently to their old faith in a sound heart and a steady will. In the love passages between Stephen and Maggie, they find only a detailed unlikely picture of animal feelings. . . .
>
> [The author] puts guilt and responsibility out of sight, raises from circumstance an extenuating plea, invests natural character with excusing force, makes the consequences of wrongdoing more prominent than wrongdoing, the sufferings of sin more prominent than sin, and then demands lenience for offenders, not

because we too have fallen, but because they could scarcely choose but fall. Well may they hope for leniency in judgment who drag down the standard that alone condemns them: their religion is the religion of 'I could not help it,' and the plea that excuses others excuses themselves. . . .

Everything is done to throw around Maggie the excusing plea of helplessness. She is said to be honourable and upright, yet she meets her lover for a whole year clandestinely; she is a good daughter, yet she secretly outrages her father's strongest wishes; she is a loving cousin, yet she steals from Lucy her affianced lover's heart. . . . Maggie's conduct is most base; but how is it we are not allowed to see the baseness? Why are we told so often that she is truthful and upright, except to suggest the idea of her helplessness to resist temptation? . . . Why is right principle made so odious in Tom Tulliver, and no principle at all so attractive in Maggie? Was the book written, as we doubt not it has been often read, with a comforting sense of excusability in many a past crisis of our lives, when good and evil, life and death, were set before us, and we did *not* choose life, that we might live?[72]

Never again did Eliot write so freely about sex, even when she was well established as one of England's greatest novelists. The travel, the learning, the years of intelligent conversation are reflected in her novels, but her experience of passion is not. Love was supposed to be the subject of women's fiction as well as the center of their lives, but they did not have the artistic freedom to explore it.

Given the hostile and wrong-headed reaction of the press, friendship among women authors became particularly important. In their private correspondence, women's support for one another also balances the severity of their own public pronouncements, like "Silly Novels by Lady Novelists." Letters written after the publication of *Adam Bede* illustrated these points: one from Barbara Bodichon conveys the exaltation women had in meeting the expectations of the critical establishment; an exchange between Gaskell and Eliot conveys the affectionate respect that women writers often gave to each other. Bodichon was living in Algiers when she received good reviews of Eliot's first novel. Despite the pseudonym, she knew immediately that *Adam Bede* had been written by Marian Evans and that it represented an achievement for women as important as her own work for legal and educational reform.

26 April [1859]

My darling Marian!

Forgive me for being so very affectionate but I am so intensely delighted at your success. I have just got the "Times" of April 12th with the glorious review of "Adam Bede" and a few days ago I read the "Westminster Review" article. I can't tell you how I triumphed in the triumph you have made. It is so great a one. Now you see I have not yet got the book but I *know* that it is you. There are some weeks passed since in an obscure paper I saw the 1st review and read one long extract which . . . instantly made me internally exclaim that is written by Marian Evans, there is her great big head and heart and her wise wide views.

Now the more I get of the book the more certain I am, not because it is like what you have written before but because it is like what I see in you. "It is an opinion which fire cannot melt out of me. I would die in it at the stake." I have not breathed a word to a soul except to the Doctor who is like the tomb for a secret.

Here an Archdeacon of the Church of England, one of our friends, is eloquent in praise of the Scenes of Clerical Life and sent me all the "Times" notice of "A.B." I can't tell you, my dear George Eliot how enchanted I am. Very few things could have given me so much pleasure.

1st. That a woman should write a wise and *humourous* book which should take a place by Thackeray.

2nd. That YOU *that you* whom they spit at should do it!

I am so enchanted so glad with the good and bad of me! both glad—angel and devil both triumph!

Although Elizabeth Gaskell was troubled by Eliot's relationship with Lewes, she too wrote to express her admiration.

1 Abbey Terrace [Whitby.] Thursday, November 10th.

My dear Madam,

Since I heard, from authority, that you were the author of Scenes from "Clerical Life" and "Adam Bede," I have read them again; and I must, once more, tell you how earnestly fully, and humbly I admire them. I never read anything so complete, and beautiful in fiction, in my whole life before. I said "humbly" in speaking of my admiration, because I remembered Dr. Johnson's words. . . . I should not be quite true in my ending, if I did not say before I concluded that I wish you *were* Mrs. Lewes. However that can't be helped, as far as I can see, and one must not judge others.

Once more, thanking you most gratefully for having written all—Janet's Repentance perhaps most especially of all,—and may I tell you how I singled out the 2nd number of Amos Barton in Blackwood, and went plodging through our Manchester streets to get every number, as soon as it was accessible from the Porters reading table. Believe me to remain,

Yours respectfully
E.C. Gaskell.

Holly Lodge, South Fields | Wandsworth.| November 11. 59.

My dear Madam

Only yesterday I was wondering that artists, knowing each other's pains so well, did not help each other more, and, as usual, when I have been talking complainingly or suspiciously, something has come which serves me as a reproof.

That "something" is your letter, which has brought me the only sort of help I care to have—an assurance of fellow-feeling, of thorough truthful recognition from one of the minds which are capable of judging as well as of being moved. You know, without my telling you, how much the help is heightened by its coming to me afresh, now that I have ceased to be a mystery and am known as a mere daylight fact. I shall always love to think that one woman wrote to another such sweet encouraging words—still more to think that you were the writer and I the receiver.

I had indulged the idea that if my books turned out to be worth much, you would be among my willing readers; for I was conscious, while the question of my power was still undecided for me, that my feeling towards Life and Art had some affinity with the feeling which had inspired "Cranford" and the earlier chapters of "Mary Barton." That idea was brought the nearer to me, because I had the pleasure of reading Cranford for the first time in 1857, when I was writing the "Scenes of Clerical Life," and going up the Rhine one dim wet day in the spring of the next year, when I was writing "Adam Bede," I satisfied myself for the lack of a prospect by reading over again those earlier chapters of "Mary Barton." I like to tell you these slight details because they will prove to you that your letter must have a peculiar value for me, and that I am not expressing vague gratitude towards a writer whom I only remember vaguely as one who charmed me in the past. And I cannot believe such details are indifferent to you, even after we have been so long used to hear them: I fancy, as long as we live, we all need to know as much as we can of the good our life has been to others. Ever, my dear Madam,

Yours with high regard
Marian Evans Lewes.[73]

The furor over *The Mill on the Floss* and the revelation of Eliot's identity mark a turning point in the discussion of women novelists. Eliot's personal reserve and the obvious moral intent of her later fiction so thoroughly dissipated the initial scandal that by 1885 Margaret Oliphant could raise a quizzical eyebrow at the "duller sorts" of readers so swayed by the conditions of George Eliot's life that they found her "superlative tale of duty" to be "improper."[74] Moreover, Eliot's continuing artistic achievements helped to refute the critical clichés regarding women novelists. After *Middlemarch*, it was more difficult to talk about woman's failure at abstraction, her inability to depict psychological struggles other than her own, or her refusal to deal with large social and intellectual issues.

In the 1860s and 1870s, journals were not featuring as many articles about lady novelists as they had during the 1850s. Charlotte Brontë died in 1855, Gaskell in 1865. Although numbers of women were writing, English history did not, unfortunately, repeat itself by producing—almost simultaneously and with such startling effect—another generation of major writers. In America, the Civil War had a devastating effect on the sentimentalists. Despite its phenomenal success, the 1867 publication of Augusta Evans Wilson's *St. Elmo* marked the end of a female tradition.[75] In both countries people interested in the Woman Question had new areas for concern, like the suffrage campaign and the plans to found women's colleges. Literary critics turned their attention to the disturbing rise of sensation fiction and the shocking appearance of the "fleshly" school of poetry. By 1866, the prominent English critic E.S. Dallas observed that "the women have been having it all their way in the realm of fiction." Reasserting the belief that women are either saints or sirens, Dallas describes two effects of feminine influence: the triumph of domestic fiction and its angelic new heroine, who is discussed in the next chapter, and the development of sensation fiction with its dangerously seductive protagonists, who are analyzed in Chapter 4.[76]

3

The Angel and the Strong-minded Woman

Victorian discussion of literary heroines employs its own vocabulary of feminine types. It names phenomena easily recognized by contemporary audiences but elusive for modern readers. Although a literary heroine rarely embodies a cultural type completely, such types provide criteria for both aesthetic and moral judgments. Contemporary responses to the nineteenth century's most famous literary heroines measure them against the "true English woman," the angel, or the womanly woman; invoke the specter of the strong-minded or emancipated woman; or point with disapproval at heroines who resemble the up-to-date young lady whom Linton later named the "Girl of the Period" (see Volume I, Chapter 6). Other female characters are discussed in terms of special situations—the Fallen Woman and the American Girl—with, again, comparisons between their behavior and conventional expectations. A third group of heroines seem to critics to be primarily literary creations—"sensation" and "fleshly" women, for example—but they are understood to be literary phenomena which may have subterranean connections with or influence on contemporary culture. These images of women, whether created by literature or simply reflected in discussions of literary heroines, are seldom static, even after they receive labels which preclude the need for extensive description. The comparison of imaginative creations and cultural stereotypes is a constant feature of Victorian discussions of books by or about women, shaping aesthetic judgments of such works as *Jane Eyre*, *Ruth*, *Lady Audley's Secret*, D.G. Rossetti's *Poems*, and *Daisy Miller*. These critical discussions are one of the best places to find out what was happening to Victorian images of woman during the course of the century's great debate over her nature and fate.

I

Most readers today, like most Victorians, think of the Angel in the House as the nineteenth-century ideal. In 1863, *Fraser's* responded to Coventry Patmore's domestic epic *The Angel in the House* (1854–62) as many reviews did to "good" heroines of fiction and verse throughout the Victorian period.

> . . . the great charm of Petrarch, as well as of Mr. Patmore, is, to our minds, the pure and graceful type of woman hood that he holds forth as a call on man's respect for the fair sex, and on woman's comely behaviour with our own. . . . It cannot, we think, be too often repeated in song or prose, that it is highly worth our care to give women a fair chance of becoming true women. We should treat woman with the finest respect, not only for that she is pure, but for that she might become more rather than less so. . . . The objective mind of woman is a mirror to show man his uncomeliness, for his refinement. . . . The majesty of pure-minded beauty as a refiner of man, is well shown by Mr. Patmore, as it ought to be shown, even to woman herself, as a call to the fulfilling of her mission. . . . Mr. Patmore's writings are good wisdom as well as good poetry; and we think his Angel in the House would be a good wedding gift to a bridegroom from his friends; though, wherever it is read with a right view of its high aim, we believe it will be found itself . . . an angel in the house, offering to woman herself a high pattern of gentle purity, and helping man to a knowledge and feeling of the excellent in the true woman's mind. . . .[1]

Critics had been measuring more or less angelic heroines against an ideal figure since at least the mid-1840s. Thackeray's Amelia in *Vanity Fair* (1847-48) and Dickens' Agnes Wickfield and Esther Summerson in *David Copperfield* (1849-50) and *Bleak House* (1852-53) are held up to judgment by this standard. During these decades the angelic image is rarely questioned as a guide for the attitudes of men toward women. The angel is the model for hundreds of good little girls in American popular fiction. Husbands, sons, and brothers should expect to find in woman an inspiring figure of purity and selflessness—ministering within the family sphere—and should feel toward her the reverence which her other-worldly perfection demands. Very few critics publicly dispute the obligation to worship the ideal woman in her domestic role. But reviewers of heroines like Amelia, Agnes, Esther, and Patmore's Honoria do debate what personal and intellectual qualities the family angel should possess. And at the same time, less orthodox heroines like Jane Eyre, Princess Ida, Aurora Leigh, and Dorothea Brooke (from works by Charlotte Brontë, Alfred, Lord Tennyson, Elizabeth Barrett Browning, and George Eliot) provide reviewers with fictional examples of unusual minds and tempers challenging— or struggling to conform to—the angelic role. These unorthodox heroines are rejected by some readers as too strong-minded, but critical response to literary heroines, both angelic and strong-minded, suggests that in the middle decades of the century the feminine ideal was changing.

Woman's angelic function is fully set forth in the books of Sarah Ellis and Sarah Lewis in the late 1830s (see Volume I, Chapter 1). As Lewis writes, "Let every mother then engrave upon the heart of her son such an image of feminine virtue and loveliness, as may make it sufficient for him to turn his eyes inward in order to draw thence a power sufficient to combat evil, and to preserve him from wretchedness." Wives and mothers are the "guardian angels of man's infancy" and manhood. Loveliness, feminine purity, and unselfishness are essential to the image of woman which protects men from evil.[2] But to these qualities—possessed by the angel in the house in all of her real and fictional guises—Lewis and Ellis add others which were not always included by the novelists and poets. Besides devotion, Ellis stresses thoughtful competence and useful domestic activity—a kind of practical intelligence—as "what is most striking in the characteristics" of the ideal woman.[3] Lewis warns that angels must have minds for another reason:

> High moral principle and devoted maternal love will make mothers safe and efficient guides for childhood, but they will possibly have to be the guides of early manhood—and here intelligence must aid devotedness. . . . The combination of high mental power with feminine purity and unselfishness gives a dignity to intellectual maternity which really overawes the youthful mind, and unless it be totally corrupt, has a great tendency to stamp it indelibly with virtuous sentiments, and with those high views of feminine character which are so essential to man's happiness and goodness.[4]

For critics discussing literary heroines in the following decades, the issue of mind is central. How much practical energy of thought or overawing high mental power should the ideal woman have to fulfill her angelic role—before she oversteps its bounds and becomes a strong-minded woman?

Readers of Thackeray's *Vanity Fair* evidently had no difficulty recognizing Amelia as the domestic angel, but whether she was intended to embody an ideal or to satirize it was (and still is) much debated. A crucial issue in the 1840s was the reviewer's own opinion about how much intelligence a woman should have, for no one missed the fact that Amelia did not have much. *Edinburgh Review* in 1848 refers to her as

> a gentle, amiable, sweet-tempered girl, who cannot be better described than in the oft-quoted lines of Wordsworth—
> A creature not too bright or good
> For human nature's daily food,
> For transient sorrows, simple wiles,
> Praise, blame, love, kisses, tears, and smiles.[5]

But most contemporary critics, while not challenging the role Amelia plays as wife and mother, are disturbed by the portrait of her. Comments range from the moderate "good and amiable but somewhat selfish and insipid" to the caustic "thoroughly selfish as well as silly," "the silliest of angels," a "milk-and water heroine," "that mean-minded whimpering little woman whose loving temperament never inspires her with one noble sentiment," and "a fool."[6] David Masson, in an extensive comparison of Dickens and Thackeray for the *North British Review* in 1851, defends Thackeray's unflattering presentation of his "good" heroine as the technique of the realist. "True, as is frequently said, his amiable characters are often sadly silly, and not half so interesting as his bad ones—his Becky, for example, being a much more attractive person than his Amelia. . . . Even here, however, we fear he is not quite unnatural."[7] Henry F. Chorley in the *Athenaeum* for 1847 regrets that Thackeray has tempered the angelic ideal in the interest of realism: "in the chapter of Womankind, where—to speak sentimentally—we are used to seek our repose and solace, he has been somewhat too niggardly."[8]

Critics in the 1850s and 1860s continue to reflect a consensus that the ideal woman ought to be her family's angel, but they also continue to find fault with insipid heroines. An 1850 review in the *Examiner* praises *David Copperfield* especially for the relationship between David and his "good angel" Agnes:

> The mutual relations of man and woman, their alternating superiority and inferiority, their incompleteness apart from each other, are nicely evolved in the story of Agnes and David. Her gentle equable strength at first places her above him; but latent in his nature there is a range of power which, when thoroughly awakened by her influence, carries him to flights beyond her. If she points the way, and imps his wings, he carries her upward with him when he soars. Imogen, Desdemona, or Sophia Western are not truer or more loveable women than many of Mr. Dickens' heroines. His Agnes is the finishing grace of Copperfield, a sunshine in the shady place, an abiding light in the darkest hours, a magic influence softening even sorrow with pleasure, a full-hearted, earnest, enduring woman, whose very silence is eloquent.[9]

And Patmore's poem, while often attacked as uninspired verse, is praised by writers as diverse as Hawthorne, Tennyson, and Caroline Norton for its elevating attitude toward woman.[10] Like Amelia, however, even the "good" heroines of Patmore and Dickens leave many critics disappointed. Honoria draws no one's special praise. The *North British Review* (1858) finds her "prudish" and "petty," remarking that "Mr. Patmore seems to us to take at once an exaggerated view of woman's natural graces, and a very depreciating view of their capacities for growth."[11] Dickens' Esther Summerson, for all her angelic qualities, is also disliked by many reviewers. Though *Putnam's*, in 1853, calls her "a gentle, loving, true-hearted creation [who] possesses all the good points of the feminine character,"[12] Henry Chorley of the *Athenaeum* finds her "over-perfect."[13] *Bentley's Miscellany* remarks, "A little more strength of character would not be objectionable—even in a wife."[14] That one so good should tell her own story, as Esther does, seems to most reviewers to be an uncharacteristic act of assertion, which only serves to call attention to Esther's usual blandness. "Such a girl would not write her memoirs," remarks the *Spectator*, "and certainly would not bore one with her goodness till a wicked wish arises that she would either do something very 'spicy' or confine herself to superintending the jampots at Bleak House."[15] The responses to Amelia, Honoria, and Esther suggest the difficulties writers experienced when they cast the domestic angel as heroine. Where she shows strength of mind, character, or spirit—like Esther writing her memoirs— she may cease to be angelic, and where she does not, she is a small-minded bore.

Occasionally, literary criticism extends to social criticism, and the attitude of woman worship is itself called into question. In Britain the *Edinburgh Review* writes of Amelia in 1854:

> It is her nature to love all those with whom she comes in contact, just as it is the nature of a spaniel to caress every visitor. But her love, being founded on propinquity, not on judgment, is, like that of the spaniel, indiscriminating. . . . [Thackeray] keeps repeating that Amelia was adorable; that she was the idol of all who approached her, and deserved to be so; in short, that she was the perfection of womanhood. Now we will not deny that she had qualities which would make her agreeable as a plaything, and useful as a slave; but playthings and slaves are not what men look for in wives. They want partners of their cares, counsellors in their perplexities, aids in their enterprises, and companions in their pursuits. To represent a pretty face, an affectionate disposition, and a weak intellect as together constituting the most attractive of women, is a libel on both sexes.[16]

The British reviewer suggests that a partner with intellect and judgment should replace the angel as wifely ideal. The American reaction is distinctly different. Three 1853 reviews of Thackeray's novels insist that women not only can but do act as domestic angels while exhibiting mental and moral strength superior to that of ordinary men. *Putnam's* attacks Thackeray for his inability to imagine a woman who is both "good" and "strong."

Mr. Thackeray, with infinite fertility of invention, and with the acutest perception of the varieties of mankind, and a power and unity in their demonstration which an anatomical entomologist might envy, gives us but two varieties—two phases of woman-kind—his Becky, Blanche, and Beatrix; women with all the weaknesses, and without a particle of the affection, of their sex . . . [and] his Amelia, Mrs. Pendennis, and that insipid, homeopathic dilution of womanhood, Lady Esmond. . . . We do not so much object to Becky, Blanche, and Beatrix. (Is the alliteration accidental?) They show for what they are worth; they are beacons on the great highway of life, buoys to warn the mariner from hidden rocks; but it is Mr. Thackeray's pattern woman that we disclaim—his ideal—a woman doomed and content "to dwell in decencies for ever," a woman with the instincts of maternity (common to her sex), "jealous as a Barbary cock-sparrow," gentle without calmness, generous without discernment, self-sacrificing, not from strength, but weakness; loving, but never wisely, and spoiling all she loves. We freely confess that these are not portraits from lay figures. They are lifelike, painted from originals—there are plenty of them; but there are also exceptions. You may find them in every household, and every where, where women most do congregate. . . . We wish . . . to show how a woman can be a heroine in domestic life, without ever overstepping its modest boundary; how she may combine strength and wisdom with love, gentleness with courage, delicacy with intrepidity, cheerfulness and tolerance with an all-pervading, all-informing piety, and the greatest good to others with self-renunciation.[17]

The *Knickerbocker's* version of the argument for stronger angels blames men for turning women into Amelias by refusing to acknowledge the moral laws on which the True Woman's influence depends.

. . . and if authors *write down* to the level that has compelled Thackeray, in spite of his better nature, to make his heroines the heartless, insipid beings they are, yet it is the adoption and carrying out of such views and principles in regard to women by men, whom they are born to serve, to please, to love, and to endeavor to delight, that makes so many of them seemingly what they are, 'humble, flattering, tea-making, piano-playing deceivers'. . . .

The whole error exists and has arisen from defective moral training in men for untold ages; lowering the standard of excellence at which they are to aim, and lessening their responsibility, and the force of moral perceptions of right. Here lies the evil. Let but a Decalogue be acknowledged for men as well as women; let but both sexes be trained to clear and earnest views of right, truth, and duty, and there need be no clashing or collision of interests, or jealous claims for superiority. Men will have manliness enough to see, to feel, to admire, to allow and acknowledge the beauty, purity, refining and beneficial influence of clear, high-minded, right-principled women; will know that bread and puddings can be as well concocted, and buttons and braids as neatly put on, by a woman of such qualifications, as by one who has striven earnestly to be a wheedling, fondling, lying one through life; and woman will look up with delighted reverence and proper homage to her lord, her governor, her king, in the broad place of rightful head and superior, where GOD and nature placed him.[18]

What is striking in this critic's position, however, is that the angelic *role* is never rejected, despite the vigorous attack on men for denying women their mental and moral strength. From this position, articulated well before the Civil War, we can trace the roots of apocalyptic feminism, and of the postwar Purity Reform Movement led by feminists who believed that women were not only different from but in some respects stronger than men—and that the reverence accorded the domestic angel was indeed woman's natural due, when she ministered to society as well (see Volume I, Chapter 3 and Volume II, Chapter 3).

The *North American Review* defends the realism of Thackeray's polarized female types but points to a combination of angel and strong woman which had already occurred, in literature as well as in life.

Ambition,—aspirations for self—by which the angels fell, is also the deadliest sin of our terrestrial angels; while in man, it is a virtue that leads to honor and reward. Hence women are divided by a strong barrier into two classes: women who submit and women who rebel; women who are tender, loving, devoted, who sacrifice self, and think only of their husbands and their children; and women who are ambitious, independent, indignant at their trammels, who seek for a career, who cannot sink their own aspirations in those of another, and who think and strive only for themselves; women whom society smiles upon and approves, and women whom society suspects, and in extreme cases disowns. Whether all the restrictions from which this great breach originates, are necessary and natural, or whether the victims only are to blame, it is not our province to inquire. Thackeray, who paints the world as he finds it, reproduces again and again these two contrasted classes of women. His Becky and Amelia, his Beatrix and Lady Castlewood, are the magnetic poles of repulsion and attraction. If the former class display intellect superior to that of the latter, this we think is entirely natural. It is the active and original mind that is most likely to stray beyond the limits which a law, not altogether free from an arbitrary character, has assigned to it; and the experience that it thus gains, sharpens powers which might have rusted from want of exercise. After all, the qualities of Becky Sharp are just those by which men commonly attain success in life, especially in political life; her maxim was the same as that which every obscure man adopts who looks forward to fame; "she had her own way to make in the world; there was no one to take care of her." And if she sometimes makes use of methods not quite legitimate, consider the difficulties of one who had no beaten track to walk on, but was forced to make the ladder by which she was to climb. Had she been placed in a position which afforded free play to her talents, mankind would have applauded the very character which it now condemns. . . .

The picture, therefore, which Thackeray gives us of the female mind, is a correct, but, as we have already said, not a complete picture. The struggle that ends in resignation, the impatience that at length folds its wings in despair—the mind, in short, of which we obtain a glimpse in "Jane Eyre" and "Villette," that, with intellect and imagination chafing beneath their trammels, is yet curbed by the pious consciousness that abnegation is the highest act of the free will—Thackeray does not attempt to exhibit. On one side, is the woman who triumphs over the prejudice of education, because she has never known the restraint of principle; and on the other, the willing slave who never questions the righteousness of her destiny, whose heart may sometimes beat a little against the bars, but whose intellect is always quiescent.

To the emergence of a third possible heroine we will turn in a moment. The *North American* reviewer closes his discussion, however, with a final testimony to the power of the angelic image over even those Victorian men sympathetic to the struggles of a rebellious mind.

Thackeray's aim is not to cultivate our taste for what is rare, but to quicken our appreciation of what is common; and we cannot but think that the ordinary effect of the existing constitution of society, is to divorce the intellect from the affections. Where there is no weakness there will be no submission; where there is no folly, there will be no blindness; where there is no blindness there will be precious little love. Amelia is a fool, you say, to make an idol of

Osborne, and bring her daily offering to his selfish shrine; a fool to let that boy who succeeds to his father's place in her heart, grasp its tender fibres with the same rude and heedless hand, and thus prodigally to sow where she could reap no harvest but bitter tears. We grant the folly. But ask your own heart what is its sweetest yet most painful memory. Do you never dream that you are back again in those old years, when thoughtless love was thus squandered upon you? Do you never wake with a remorseful pang, sharper than any that the ambiguous deed of the hardened present can inflict, and think what a blessed thing it would be if you could stanch the wounds which your barbed arrow made, and expiate that ignorance and self-engrossment by watchful, tender care? And if this be so, can you now criticize the extravagant love which you abused, and sneer at it as folly, and blame the indulgence which spoilt you, and made you selfish, and tell how you would have been a wiser and a better man, if you had been more wisely trained?[19]

This critic's momentary longing is not only to recall the extravagant love of his mother, but also to meet it with his own watchful, tender care—the angel's special virtue. Such a passage suggests that one reason for the persistent attraction of the angel for Victorian men, despite their extensive criticism of particular literary angels, may have been their own discomfort with the "ambiguous deeds of the hardened present"—the aggressive activity and sexuality expected of adult men.[20]

II

Despite the continuing power of the angelic ideal, some of the period's most successful fictional women are clearly not "good" heroines. Reviewers compare an unorthodox character like Amelia's opposite, Becky Sharp, with both the angel whom she does not resemble and the *un*womanly woman her bold actions suggest. Most Victorians recognize that unwomanly woman in the caricatured figure of the strong-minded female (see Illustration 4).

In Victorian Britain and America, only women are ever called strong-minded—and the epithet is rarely meant to praise. Frances Willard, the founder of the Woman's Christian Temperance Union, remembers in 1876 how as a girl of sixteen (in

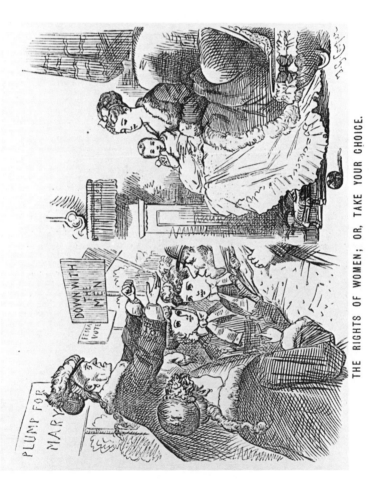

THE RIGHTS OF WOMEN; OR, TAKE YOUR CHOICE.

4. The Rights of Women; or, Take Your Choice

July, 1869

1855) she watched her father and twenty-one-year-old brother
go off to vote.

> Turning to my sister Mary, who stood beside me, I saw that the
> dear innocent seemed wonderfully sober, too. I said: "Don't you
> wish we could go with them when we are old enough? Don't we
> love our country just as well as they do?" and her frightened little
> voice piped out: "Yes, of course we ought. Don't I know that? but
> you mustn't tell a soul—not mother, even; we should be called
> strong-minded."[21]

And the *London Quarterly Review* critic who, in 1861, denounces
Amelia as "mean-minded" can nonetheless go on to warn against

> that hard intellectual type of woman-kind which is commonly
> stigmatized as "strong-minded" [who] is frightening authors from
> the study of qualities essentially womanly. It is woman's vocation to
> be strong, not in mind, but in noble and generous impulses; that,
> while her husband and sons know best what is expedient, logical, or
> wise, she should know best what is true, gallant, and right.[22]

From the late 1840s until the end of the high Victorian period,
the real threat to the womanly woman is usually perceived—
Linton and the *Saturday Review* excepted—not as the frivolous Girl
of the Period but as her serious sister, the strong-minded female.
It is the strong-minded woman whom the Victorians accuse of
first raising the issue of Woman's Rights; it is also she who
takes part in the great but often male-dominated debate that
follows, the Woman Question. The woman author is as likely
to be branded "strong-minded" as her subversive heroines.[23]
She is the stereotype of the unnatural woman: mind rules heart
in man, but heart should dominate mind, even to total unself-
consciousness, in woman. As the *Saturday Review*, which made
light of strong-minded women, quips "A strong-minded woman
is like a pretty man; the merit is unnatural to both, and both
are certain to be ridiculously vain of it."[24] The strong-minded
woman is too much a caricature to figure as a heroine herself,
but she profoundly influences both characters and critics, from
Tennyson's *The Princess* (1847) and Charlotte Brontë's *Jane Eyre*
(1847) through Elizabeth Barrett Browning's *Aurora Leigh* (1856)
to George Eliot's *Middlemarch* (1872).

The term "strong-minded" had not always been pejorative,
nor applied exclusively to women. At the beginning of the cen-

tury, when Jane Austen's Captain Wentworth, in *Persuasion* (1818), describes the kind of woman he is looking for, "'A strong mind, with sweetness of manner,' made the first and the last of the description." Before the end of the novel, "he had learnt to distinguish between the steadiness of principle and the obstinacy of self-will, between the darings of heedlessness and the resolution of a collected mind." Strength of mind, "like all other qualities of the mind, . . . should have its proportions and limits."[25] Steadiness of principle and the resolution of a collected mind are as important for Austen's characters, male and female, as the capacity to be persuaded. The limits which Austen sets on strength of mind are defined by human relationships, not settled by woman's nature. Her heroines' intelligence is a moral quality and a human possession.

Americans adopted "strong-minded" to derogate outspoken women several years before the English discovered the term in the early 1850s. *North American Review* in 1848 finds *Jane Eyre* displaying some unconscious feminine touches "which the strongest-minded woman that ever aspired after manhood cannot suppress."[26] But in England, as late as 1851, when Coventry Patmore describes in the *North British Review* exactly the sort of man-rivalling woman later called strong-minded, he can find no name for her:

> It is more to our purpose, in a paper occasioned by the modern agitation of the question of "Woman's Rights and Duties," to consider the generic character of those ladies who endeavour to exceed their commission. "Emancipated women," or "women of the nineteenth century," or "femmes d'esprit," as the kind of ladies in point are self-designated in Germany, America, and France, do not as yet constitute so considerable a fraction of the "female sect" in Great Britain as to have merited a distinctive appellation. Probably, however, there are few of our readers who have never met with an individual of the species. In speaking of her we will call her the "emancipated woman," that being the most expressive phrase of the three. Our English word "Blue-stocking" is nearly obsolete, and not much to the purpose, since it assumes that the bearer of it writes books, which is by no means an invariable, though a lamentably frequent characteristic of the "emancipated woman." These, then, are some of the principal features in virtue of which she claims, and is very often by others considered to hold a position above and in advance of the rest of her race. Of course her leading feature is her emancipation from the Christian faith, or at least

from all that ordinary persons understand by the Christian faith. It is the fashion, in our days, to be "earnest," "serious," "supersensuous," and so forth; she is, therefore, no vulgar sceptic of the Voltaire cut; she has read our modern prophets well enough to have obtained a general notion that "faith" is quite essential to her position in the vanguard of intellect; but she is unbounded in her liberality with regard to the objects of faith; indeed, she has not any very positive conception that faith demands an object at all. If you are rude or foolish enough to compare together her assertions upon this matter, with the inevitable result of breaking their heads, one against the other, she will let you know that she scorns dialectics and dialecticians, and that her order of mind is "affirmative," or "intuitional," or something of some sort which dispenses with and transcends reasoning. . . . With respect to herself, she has an acute aesthetic perception of the beauty of charitableness. If she gives five shillings to a poor dependent, her loving heart fails within her, from the rapture of being beneficent; and a consciousness of the noble struggle to seem to think lightly of the action, and so to preserve its excellence unblemished, is the crown to her self-complacency. She loves sympathy, and professes to sympathize with you; but by sympathizing with, she means anatomizing you; and when she seems to be full of interest in your affairs, she is doing her best to "find you out," à la Goethe. . . .

She has often many attractive qualities; but whatever good she possesses, she remembers so well herself that she is apt to make others forget it. She believes those men and women only to be truly noble who, in the end, will perhaps be counted with the "filthy dreamers" who "despise dominion, and speak evil of dignities;" and, on the other hand, commonly attaches the notion of mediocrity and goody-ness to the thoughtfulness and disciplined moderation of spirits who are "after God's own heart." She has not thought the peculiar virtues of women worth cultivating; but unfortunately she has not made up for this neglect by the subjugation of their peculiar failings; indeed, with many other faults to boot, the "emancipated woman" has most of the weaknesses of her sex in excess; for example, the arrantest tuft-huntresses are known to be among those ladies who deal the most profusely in ultra-radicalism by profession; she talks an immense deal about, and immensely admires art and poetry, artists and poets, but in her heart she believes them all to be lies and liars, and that there are no such things in the universe as are thereby rumoured of; if a man appreciates her at her own standard, he certainly is, or will be, the light of the age. She has not learnt that "c'est plus par leurs défautes que par leurs bonnes qualités que les femmes plaisent aux gens du monde;" and is lamentably deficient in the wisdom which dictated the following passage:—"She who discovers to us her intention to govern by her power, or by her haughty temper, produces a disgust which all our efforts can never conquer. Such conduct in a woman is the same thing as it would be in a lion to fight with his hinder legs, or for a hare to face about and defy the teeth of the pursuing pack; it is neglecting to make use of what nature has furnished, and endeavouring to use what she has thought proper to deny." She makes one of the prodigious multitude self-styled "the judicious few;" her husband is not only not the head of his house, he is not even his lady's peer in prerogatives of government; his servants respectfully indicate that they "will ask their mistress" whether any order that he may give can be obeyed; and the visitors to the house are, for the most part, unknown and uncared for, by their host. She is commonly "emancipated" from all real modesty, and from all pretence to it, beyond what may be absolutely needful to the maintenance of a place in a very tolerant society. Her conversation often owes not a little of its piquancy to an undercurrent of allusion, which would shock and humiliate an unenlightened woman, if she understood it. In this, and in many other ways, she would prove to men that she is as good as a man, by shewing them that she is as bad. She is seldom handsome, and seems to think that she retaliates Nature's injuries by injuries to Nature, not knowing that it is in the power of every well-conditioned woman to fulfil the duty of being *lovely*. Finally, she hates, and affects to despise most of her own sex, for, in spite of her emancipation from womanhood, she secretly remembers, and with envy, that the sweetness of love which abounds towards the meek and simple-minded, is better than the sound of praise which is without an echo in the conscience, but which is the only compensation for the loss of that which cannot be bought though one should give all the substance of his house for it, and which is inevitably starved to death in the lofty intellectual regions wherein she delights to have her habitation.[27]

By 1854, however, the term "strong-minded" is everywhere. When George Lewes writes in that year to explain to a disapproving Carlyle his reasons for leaving England with Marian Evans [George Eliot], Carlyle, unappeased, marks the envelope "G.H. Lewes and 'Strong-minded Woman.'"[28] Lewes himself began his famous essay on lady novelists (1852) by remarking that "it is easy to be supercilious and sarcastic on Blue Stockings and literary ladies. . . . one may admit that such sarcasms have frequently their extenuation in the offensive pretensions of what are called 'strong-minded' women."[29] Already the term is pejorative and any defense of the intellectual or literary woman—be she Jane Austen, George Sand, or George Eliot herself—must begin by dissociating her from the offensive and unwomanly ambitions of the strong-minded stereotype.

In the following decades, "strong-minded" is applied to women with political, religious, or intellectual ambitions allegedly incompatible with True Womanhood. But a woman can be offensively strong-minded without becoming politically or intellectually active. The term is expanded to apply to any temperament exhibiting not only intelligence, but also will, passion, resolution, self-consciousness, and independence of judgment. What Victorians find most intolerable about the strong-minded woman is her "self-assertion," her "aspiring after manhood," her "pushing of [herself] forward," her failure to keep whatever mind and will of her own she may in fact possess out of sight. "In nine cases out of ten," *Cassell's* reminds readers in 1878, "a quiet, womanly woman, wise enough not to seem too clever, is twice as successful in bringing about what she desires, whether for the private or the public good."[30] As Lewis and Ellis insisted years before, the fundamental requirement of the ideal wife and mother is selflessness; the strong-minded woman's real threat to manhood lies in her discovery of self, and in her expression, in words or acts, of her new self-consciousness.

There are, however, a few Victorians who use the term "strong-minded" with approval. As early as 1855 a character in Elizabeth Gaskell's *North and South* remarks, "'And then, what with Sholto playing with the fire, and the baby crying, you'll begin to wish for a strong-minded woman, equal to any emergency.'"[31] Gaskell recognizes that self-possession is necessary for just the kind of practical competency which the strong-minded woman is supposed to lack (see Dickens' Mrs. Jellyby in *Bleak House*). The same truth is echoed later in the century by other women novelists such as Caroline Norton and Charlotte Yonge. "The feeble silly woman who was Gertrude's mother, said her few words of protection and defense as sensibly as if she had been the most strong-minded of females . . . ," writes Norton in *Old Sir Douglas* (1868).[32] "'That's the value of a strong-minded wife . . . she is not given to making a fuss about small matters,'" according to Yonge in *The Clever Woman of the Family* (1865).[33] By 1862, Frances Power Cobbe proclaims in *Fraser's* a new admiration, at least by women, of strength in female writers, painters, and their heroines. "*Now*, women who possess any real genius, apply it to the creation of what they (and not society for them) really admire. A woman naturally admires power, force, grandeur. It is these qualities, then, which we shall see more and more appearing as the spontaneous genius of woman asserts itself." Cobbe speaks for the major women writers when she insists that "as God means a woman to *be* a woman, and not a man, every faculty he has given her is a woman's faculty, and the more each of them can be drawn out, trained, and perfected, the more *womanly* she will become."[34]

The era of strong, self-conscious heroines began for the Victorians as early as 1847, when two very different works took as their central figures discontented articulate women. The strength of mind, passion, and spirit displayed by Tennyson's Princess Ida and Charlotte Brontë's Jane Eyre were disturbing to most critics when they first appeared. The unreformed Ida is the intellectual strong-minded woman; Jane Eyre possesses a strong-minded temperament. Tennyson's Princess was ultimately less controversial, partly because her attempt to put mind over heart is defeated by the power of maternal feeling. She founds a college for women; she rejects the angelic roles of wife and mother; conscious of her superiority, she asserts herself among both men and most women. She is also physically impressive: tall, dark, full-voiced, and frequently linked imagistically with lone trees and eagles and mountain heights. But the tone of Tennyson's presentation of Ida is notoriously difficult to determine. In some passages, she is magnificent; in others, she verges on the caricature which, as a cultural type, the strong-minded woman was quickly to become. Critical response to Ida, however, took very seriously her departures from the womanly ideal.

For most critics, Ida is readily recognizable as a contemporary phenomenon. Initially reviewers find Tennyson's treatment of her unambiguous, and they support wholeheartedly his apparent condemnation of unnatural aspirations. They find little to admire in the unwomanly type embodied in Ida before her reformation. The *Gentleman's Magazine* (1848) calls her "a *frozen* woman," and remarks that even "when she *thaws* at last, we should have liked a little more heat and more water."[35] *Howitt's* sees her as a contemporary type, the "she-man": "she-philosophers and politicians who would be in Parliament instead of the domestic circle, who smoke cigars and hookahs; who do coarse men's work in coarse mannish attire, [and who] are neither the persons to win the crown of true womanhood for themselves or for the sex in general."[36] Charles Kingsley, writing for *Fraser's* in 1850, finds Ida's assertion of self-will not only unnatural but a serious moral failure to live up to the selfless ideal prescribed for women.

> In every age women have been tempted . . . to deny their own womanhood, and attempt to stand alone as men. . . . in *The Princess* Mr. Tennyson has embodied the ideal of that nobler, wider, purer, yet equally fallacious, because equally unnatural analogue, which we may meet too often up and down England now. He shows us the woman, when she takes her stand on the false masculine ground of the intellect, working out her own moral punishment, by destroying in herself the tender heart of flesh: not even her vast purposes of philanthropy can preserve her, for they are built up, not on the womanhood which God has given her, but on her own self-will; they change, they fall, they become inconsistent, even as she does herself, till, at last, she loses all feminine sensibility; scornfully and stupidly she rejects and misunderstands the heart of man; and then falling from pride to sternness, from sternness to sheer inhumanity, she punishes sisterly love as a crime, robs the mother of her child, and becomes all but a vengeful fury, with all the peculiar faults of woman and none of the peculiar excellencies of man.[37]

Tennyson's Prince finally defends the equal, complementary importance of male and female natures, though he insists on the traditional hierarchy of roles in family and society. While several critics praise Tennyson for defending women in the Prince's concluding speech, only one reviewer praises him for the rebellious Ida's feminist eloquence before her reformation. Linking Ida with Mary Wollstonecraft, the reviewer for the *Eclectic* hails *The Princess* for dwelling "upon *her* cherished subject, 'the rights of women,' and pleading those rights with a force and an eloquence which the world has scarcely witnessed before."[38]

The contradictory message of Tennyson's poem—its admiration for both feminist and feminine women—became clearer to Victorians over the next several decades. *The Princess* is widely quoted in the 1850s and 1860s in support of *both* ideals of womanhood. Anna Jameson and Caroline Dall use the following passage to support feminist views, Jameson as the epigraph for her *Communion of Labour* (1856), Dall to illustrate her argument for *Woman's Right to Labor* (1860).

                    At last
She rose upon a wind of prophecy
Dilating on the future; "everywhere
Two heads in council, two beside the hearth,
Two in the tangled business of the world,
Two in the liberal offices of life,
Two plummets dropt for one to sound the abyss
Of science, and the secrets of the mind:
Musician, painter, sculptor, critic, more:
And everywhere the broad and bounteous Earth
Should bear a double growth of those rare souls,
Poets, whose thoughts enrich the blood of the world."[39]

Conservatives on the woman's-sphere issue like Dora Greenwell and the American minister R. Heber Newton, on the other hand, turn to these famous lines from the Prince's closing speech:

The woman's cause is man's: they rise or sink
Together, dwarfed or godlike, bond or free: . . .
We two will serve them both in aiding her—
Will clear away the parasitic forms
That seem to keep her up but drag her down—
Will leave her space to burgeon out of all
Within her—let her make herself her own
To give or keep, to live and learn and be
All that not harms distinctive womanhood.
For woman is not undevelopt man,
But diverse: could we make her as the man,
Sweet Love were slain: his dearest bond is this,
Not like to like, but like in difference.
Yet in the long years liker must they grow;
The man be more of woman, she of man;
He gain in sweetness and in moral height,
Nor lose the wrestling thews that throw the world;
She mental breadth, nor fail in childward care,
Till at the last she set herself to man,
Like perfect music unto noble words. . . .[40]

To Tennyson's suggestion that in the future the sexes may achieve a different partnership—that men may become more feminine and women more masculine—few critics respond. Where reviewers notice the Prince at all, they find him unpleasantly effeminate.

Charlotte Brontë's Jane Eyre appears "dangerous"[41] where Tennyson's Ida does not. Not only is Ida at times too close to caricature to be threatening, but Tennyson's poem ultimately rejects the strong-minded for the womanly woman. The Prince's final speech is taken by most readers to reflect the poet's position, but Brontë's attitude toward Jane Eyre seems less clear. Jane herself, temperamentally independent though she has fewer intellectual aspirations, is in many ways a more radically subversive character than Ida.

Jane Eyre was popular. The *North American Review* speaks in 1848 of "the Jane Eyre fever" sweeping New England;[42] the *North British Review* (1849) notes the emergence of a "class of young ladies, of which she has been recognized as the type, and which consequently is now beginning to be known by the epithet of 'Jane Eyrish.'"[43] George Henry Lewes in the *Westminster Review* (1853) expresses the reaction to Brontë's unorthodox men and women at its most positive:

> Indeed, one may say of Currer Bell, what a contemporary has already said, that her genius finds its fittest illustration in her 'Rochesters' and 'Jane Eyres'; they are men and women of deep feeling, clear intellects, vehement tempers, bad manners, ungraceful, yet loveable persons. Their address is *brusque*, perhaps unpleasant, but, at any rate, individual, direct, free from 'shams' and conventions of all kinds. They outrage good taste, yet they fascinate. You dislike them at first, yet you learn to love them. The power that is in them makes its vehement way right to your heart. Propriety, ideal outline, good features, good manners, ordinary thought, ordinary speech, are not to be demanded of them.[44]

More typically, the *North British Review* recognizes Jane's fascination but feels compelled to note her "graver faults" as woman. Trying to pin down her peculiar attraction, the *Review* compares her at length with the conventional (angelic) heroine of a contemporary novel by the popular Anne Caldwell Marsh (*Emilia Wyndham*, 1846)—and discovers a preference for Jane, precisely because of her strong-minded qualities of ingenuity and spirit.

> Which is the favourite? That Emilia is the prettier girl cannot be questioned. That she is far more graceful and agreeable, in the ordinary sense, is also probably true; and when their characters are developed, in their subsequent stories, we are not astonished when we find that it is she whom we ought to love, for, from the first, we

had a presentiment that to her our approval must be given; but do we do so instinctively? We believe that we do not; and though we have some difficulty in accounting for the partiality, and still more in justifying it, we plead guilty, for our own part, to a peculiar *penchant* for the wicked looking "pug" with the pale face and the smoothed hair; and we believe that to the majority of men she is the more attractive character of the two.

. . . Like her author, good, excellent Mrs. Marsh, she [Emilia] is a *wee, wee* bit prosy—the least possible thing "slow." Sometimes she will linger a little on the obvious—she will perversely demonstrate what nobody can deny; and this is an impatient age! Now, Jane, be her faults what they may, is never tedious; her worst enemy cannot say that she wearies him, and this probably is the reason why she comes in for rather more than her fair share of our love and favour. She never disputes with you except when she is in the wrong, and then there is at least some field for ingenuity, there is something to contend with, and the tools are not likely to lie quite ready to hand. . . .

There is another fault, of a kindred nature, at which we would gently hint in referring in the outset, thus generally, to the character of Mrs. Marsh as a novelist—a slight deficiency, namely, of spirit.[45]

Most critics, however, cannot forgive Jane Eyre for her independence of judgment, her passion, and, above all, her self-consciousness. As more than one reviewer speculates, a heroine with these qualities must be the work of a masculine author or, if not, of an unwomanly or strong-minded woman.[46] The first objection to Brontë's heroines, from Jane Eyre through Lucy Snowe in *Villette* (1853), is their unfitness as potential wives and mothers. To the *Christian Remembrancer* (1853) the independent mind, like the caricatured strong mind, seems incompatible with the role of domestic angel.

The moral purpose of this work seems to be to demand for a certain class of minds a degree of sympathy not hitherto accorded to them; a class of which Lucy Snowe is the type, who must be supposed to embody much of the authoress's own feelings and experience, all going one way to express a character which finds itself unworthily represented by person and manner, conscious of power, equally and painfully conscious of certain drawbacks, which throw this superiority into shade and almost hopeless disadvantage. For such she demands room to expand, love, tenderness, and a place in happy domestic life. But in truth she draws a character unfit for this home which she yearns for. We want a woman at our hearth; and her impersonations are without the feminine element, infringers of modest restraints, despisers of bashful fears, self-reliant, contemptuous of prescriptive decorum; their own unaided reason, their individual opinion of right and wrong, discreet or imprudent, sole guides of conduct and rules of manners,—the whole hedge of immemorial scruple and habit broken down and trampled upon. We will sympathize with Lucy Snowe as being fatherless and penniless, and are ready, if this were all, to wish her a husband and a fireside less trying than M. Paul's must be, unless reformed out of all identity; but we cannot offer even the affections of our fancy (the right and due of every legitimate heroine) to her unscrupulous, and self-dependent intellect—to that whole habit of mind which, because it feels no reverence, can never inspire for itself that one important, we may say, indispensable element of man's true love.[47]

Besides her self-dependent intellect, Jane's surprising strength of mind displays itself in her capacity for, and knowledge of, passion. The *Christian Remembrancer* (1848) was taken aback. "The love-scenes glow with a fire as fierce as that of Sappho, and somewhat more fuliginous. There is an intimate acquaintance with the worst parts of human nature, a practised sagacity in discovering the latent ulcer, and a ruthless rigour in exposing it, which must command our admiration, but are almost startling in one of the softer sex."[48]

A more serious objection is raised by Elizabeth Rigby, Lady Eastlake, writing for the *Quarterly* in 1848 what is perhaps the most famous review of *Jane Eyre* besides Lewes' laudatory one. Lady Eastlake acknowledges the book's power and sympathizes with Jane's difficult position as governess, but she is primarily concerned with Jane's failure to accept the selfless role thrust upon her, however unfairly (see Volume II, Chapter 3). Jane's sense of wrong renders her, for Lady Eastlake, unlikeable—and Jane's spirited protests make her dangerously subversive.

Jane Eyre is throughout the personification of an unregenerate and undisciplined spirit, the more dangerous to exhibit from that prestige of principle and self-control which is liable to dazzle the eye too much for it to observe the inefficient and unsound foundation on which it rests. It is true Jane does right, and exerts great moral strength, but it is the strength of a mere heathen mind which is a law unto itself. No Christian grace is perceptible upon her. She has inherited in fullest measure the worst sin of our fallen nature—the sin of pride. Jane Eyre is proud, and therefore she is ungrateful too. It pleased God to make her an orphan, friendless, and penniless— yet she thanks nobody, and least of all Him, for the food and raiment, the friends, companions, and instructors of her helpless youth—for the care and education vouchsafed to her till she was capable in mind as fitted in years to provide for herself. On the contrary, she looks upon all that has been done for her not only as her undoubted right, but as falling far short of it. The doctrine of humility is not more foreign to her mind than it is repudiated by her heart. It is by her own talents, virtues, and courage that she is made to attain the summit of human happiness, and, as far as Jane Eyre's own statement is concerned, no one would think that she owed anything either to God above or to man below. . . .

Altogether the auto-biography of Jane Eyre is pre-eminently an anti-Christian composition. There is throughout it a murmuring against the comforts of the rich and against the privations of the poor, which, as far as each individual is concerned, is a murmuring against God's appointment—there is a proud and perpetual assertion of the rights of man, for which we find no authority either in God's word or in God's providence—there is that pervading tone of ungodly discontent which is at once the most prominent and the most subtle evil which the law and the pulpit, which all civilized society in fact has at the present day to contend with. We do not hesitate to say that the tone of mind and thought which has overthrown authority and violated every code human and divine abroad, and fostered Chartism and rebellion at home, is the same which has also written Jane Eyre.

Still we say again this is a very remarkable book. We are painfully alive to the moral, religious, and literary deficiencies of the picture, and such passages of beauty and power as we have quoted cannot redeem it, but it is impossible not to be spell-bound with the freedom of the touch. It would be mere hackneyed courtesy to call it 'fine writing.' It bears no impress of being written at all, but is poured out rather in the heat and hurry of an instinct, which flows ungovernably on to its object, indifferent by what means it reaches it, and unconscious too. As regards the author's chief object, however, it is a failure—that, namely, of making a plain, odd woman, destitute of all the conventional features of feminine attraction, interesting in our sight. We deny that he has succeeded in this. Jane Eyre, in spite of some grand things about her, is a being totally uncongenial to our feelings from beginning to end. We acknowledge her firmness—we respect her determination—we feel for her struggles; but, for all that, and setting aside higher considerations, the impression she leaves on our mind is that of a decidedly vulgar-minded woman—one whom we should not care for as an acquaintance, whom we should not seek as a friend, whom we should not desire for a relation, and whom we should scrupulously avoid for a governess.[49]

For Lady Eastlake, as for Kingsley reviewing *Princess Ida*, the self-conscious heroine is an un-Christian and vulgar woman, a threat not only to the womanly ideal but to the values of Victorian society. Both reviewers implicitly accept the mission laid out for women by such writers as Sarah Lewis, to exemplify Christian selflessness and resignation in a selfish male world. Margaret Oliphant confirmed Lady Eastlake's fears seven years later when she wrote that *Jane Eyre* had initiated "the most alarming revolution of modern times"—at least for the heroines of literature.[50] Brontë's plain-featured woman was, for Victorian readers, the first powerful heroine who was emphatically "not an angel," who combined the temperament of the strong-minded female with superior moral strength and yet wanted, and obtained, marriage and a home.

By the time Elizabeth Barrett Browning published *Aurora Leigh* (1856), and George Eliot wrote *Middlemarch* (1872), reviewers found the strong heroine a familiar character. Like Princess Ida, Aurora begins by rejecting marriage for intellectual and personal independence (see Illustration 5), and ends by acknowledging the importance of love and family. Some reviewers insist on reading Aurora's story, like Ida's, as an either/or dilemma: the independent mind *or* the angelic role. And because they identify Browning so closely with her heroine, critics disagree about which alternative the poet is advocating. Some critics base their remarks on Aurora's character in the early part of the poem; others on her final "reformation" and its parallels in Browning's life. Periodicals as politically diverse as the conservative *Blackwood's* and the radical *Westminster Review* blame the author for her strong heroine despite the poem's conclusion. *Blackwood's* finds Aurora "not a genuine woman" because she lacks "instinctiveness, which is the greatest charm of women." Aurora's "extreme independence detracts from the feminine charm, and mars the interest which we otherwise might have felt in so intellectual a heroine."[51] The *Westminster Review* agrees that "she thinks too much of herself. . . . Aurora's self-consciousness repels."[52] *Dublin University Magazine* points to Aurora's un-

5. The Tryst. Aurora Refusing Romney
Arthur Hughes, 1860 (The Tate Gallery, London)

Forth from a curtained window,
  The glad light comes and goes;
In the richly furnished chamber,
  The fitful firelight glows;
But the woe of the stricken master—
    Who knows?

Standing without on the pavement,
  Where the bitter north wind blows,
A woman leans, anguished and smitten,
  Wrapped up as it were in her woes;
But the hope of that weary spirit—
    Who knows?

For often a grief falls the harder
  On one who has felt but few blows,
When life still seems worth the living,
  When a scent is still left in the rose;
But the hope of the earthly-stranded,
    Who knows?

                    G.W.

6. Lights and Shadows
Cassell's Family Magazine, 1878

pleasant competitiveness: "a jealous and morbid sense of the misappreciation of woman by man, a 'struggling for woman's empery,' and even for something beyond it."[53] Others praise or blame the poem's conclusion. When Aurora finally accepts Romney, the *Athenaeum* feels that

> [it] amounts to an admission of failure. . . . Thus, as in all the works of its kind, which women have so freely poured out from their full hearts during late years, we see the agony more clearly than the remedy. We are shown, at first, restlessness disdaining quiet; till, fevered and forlorn, as time and grief do their work, the restless heart ends in courting the very repose it so scorned when first tendered.[54]

Other critics see the conclusion as the triumph of womanly instinct—like the *Christian Examiner*, which calls Browning "the great woman-poet of our time."

> In the final triumph of the woman over the artist, Mrs. Browning enforces another great truth; namely, that noble and glorious as Art is, the pursuit of it will never satisfy the heart, nor insure a perfect development of character, if "the artist's instincts" are to be exalted "at the cost of putting down the woman's." If she recognizes fully, not only woman's right to labor, but its Christian necessity, she is no advocate of any regulations that are to supersede religious and natural ties. Her own sweet instincts were too powerful, and she knows too well in what consists the happiness and true welfare of woman, to desire either to unsex her or unsphere her.[55]

The most significant aspect of the contemporary reception of *Aurora Leigh*, however, is the number of critics who do not find the spectacle of an independent-minded heroine fulfilling the angelic role to be either unnatural or impossible. Twentieth-century readers, like the Victorians quoted above, tend to interpret *Aurora Leigh's* conclusion as capitulation, but two laudatory American articles of 1857 single out Aurora's—and Elizabeth Barrett Browning's—move from intellectual independence to marriage as a triumph for the strong woman. *North American Review* writes:

> Besides the relation in which the "Aurora Leigh" stands to the great question of life in general, it has a particular application to the questions which have been started in regard to the nature and

position of woman. It is often thought that a large mental culture tends to unfit her for the more tender and domestic relations of life. Here is illustrated the reverse of this. Aurora and Romney could not meet in the highest union of love until they had each attained to the highest development of which they were separately capable. When this was accomplished, they became united in a love as much more noble than that of common lovers, as their individual development was more perfect than that of ordinary individuals. This view is entitled to great consideration, as coming from one who has herself passed through both stages, that of the lonely struggle and of the reward.[56]

Putnam's, in a long and self-congratulatory article, finds Aurora's success as both writer and woman a sign of the age's greatest achievement: the recognition that strength of mind is entirely compatible with the traditional womanly ideal, proved in real life by Charlotte Brontë and Elizabeth Barrett Browning.

The victim, in her childhood, like "Jane Eyre," of a decent tyranny, and, in her womanhood, like Tennyson's "Princess," the proud dreamer of a prouder dream, Aurora Leigh, fortunate in her genius, neither loses heart under the tyranny, nor goes mad in the dream.

. . . never, until now, never until this nineteenth century, has it been possible to say that men were approaching a general recognition of the absolute value of the female character, and of female genius; a general, and, therefore, tacit, easy, and unconstrained admission of woman's claim to be held for a power in the world. While people are quarreling in conventions about "Woman's Sphere," and pamphleteers are doing battle for and against her right to vote, and to hold property, to command steamers, and to preach in churches, and to work mills, and to cure diseases, and to break horses, the growing good sense and advancing appreciation of the civilized world are gradually, but surely, coming to the righteous conclusion of the whole matter. . . .

The blue-stocking of the last century, terror of gods and men, is happily extinct, having gone out with the dodo about thirty years since; the Laura Matilda is rarely to be found, excepting in the more remote villages of the interior; and the "strong-minded" woman of the present day excites, in both sexes, such intense emotions of dislike and disgust as human nature keeps in reserve for monsters alone, woman being no longer expected to be weak or odious. . . . a woman may now enjoy the reputation of being clever without ceasing to be regarded as a woman, so far that the noblest truths and the loftiest principles are not necessarily brought to scorn when they are spoken by a woman's lips, or written by a woman's pen.

This is a glory of our age which should never be forgotten by those who mean to paint its portrait, or to analyze its character—a present glory and the herald of brighter glories yet to be. For the world can no more spare the intellect of woman than it can dispense with the affections of man; and infinite good will result to us and to our children, we may be sure, from the growing recognition of this truth, and the consequent acceptance, into our literature and our life, of a new and noble spirit. When the follies of the fanatical friends of "Woman's Rights" shall have been utterly forgotten . . . and that golden year arrives, of which the poet prophesies, the year of the

> "World's great bridals, chaste and calm,
> Whence springs the crowning race of human kind;"

when mannish women and womanish men shall have become alike impossible, and each respecting each, and each by the other respected, man and woman find peace at last and harmony in the ordered freedom of dual but equal lives, then at least, if not before, the names of the women who have illustrated the literature of the present age will become as stars in the minds of men for the "sweet influences" they shall forever rain upon the race. . . . The lioness is now become at least as common and familiar a creature as the lion, and it is simple truth, which nobody fears to utter, that one meets with women who have not ceased to be women in becoming authors, quite as often as with men who, in becoming authors, have continued to be men. . . .

That the intellect of woman could fill its sphere and wield its authority in the wider circle of the world, without drawing away into itself the precious life of her affections and her graces, men used to doubt. But they can doubt no longer. It was idle to appeal, against this skepticism, to the examples of exceptional women in the past; but, beneath the constellated heaven of the present, skepticism has become ridiculous.

Though not all of one genius, most of the female writers, whose names are likely to survive the present age, have been of one spirit with Charlotte Brontë, and, like her, have done honor to their sex in doing service to their art. What author of our times has held more loyally to the great aims of authorship than Elizabeth Browning, and yet where shall we look for a more womanly woman than she?[57]

Putnam's celebrated the triumph of the strong-minded but womanly woman somewhat prematurely. In the decade that followed *Aurora Leigh*, popular fiction displayed a new female type who combined angelic and strong-minded qualities in a very different manner. But the sensation heroine (see Chapter 4)—hiding her will, passion, and criminal history beneath an angelic exterior—was a passing phenomenon. The equally popular but unsensational heroines of sentimental literature in the 1860s chose not to prove their strength in a man's world, like Jane Eyre or Aurora Leigh, but to draw their heroes into a female sphere and teach them womanly virtues.[58] The heroine of George Eliot's *Middlemarch* provided readers in the early 1870s with one of the greatest and last examples of the strong but womanly woman caught between the two spheres.

Dorothea Brooke possesses many of the qualities readers had come to expect in the strong heroine—passion, intelligence, spirit—but apparently none of the subversive desires. She uses all her attractive strengths in passionate self-submission as the helpmate wife. In her two marriages, however, Dorothea is not allowed to become either the martyred angel of an unworthy man or the inspiring angel of a great one. Critics were disappointed and perplexed by the ordinary fate which George Eliot had assigned to so promising a heroine. What had kept Dorothea from greatness? In the novel's epilogue Eliot suggested that society was to blame, but for most readers the novel itself did not support that conclusion. (Eliot herself later removed the disputed passage.) The novel seems to test the adequacy of the angelic ideal for the extraordinary woman: what is her potential for greatness in that role, as literary heroine and as human being? George Eliot's conclusion is not clear.

Many critics, however, made up their own minds. Though they admired Dorothea for her lofty aspirations, her nobleness, her enthusiastic and high-minded pursuit of the womanly ideal, they blamed her as much as society for her failure to achieve sainthood. In her marriage to the pedantic Casaubon, particularly, critics disputed George Eliot's suggestion of social pressures, and blamed Dorothea's willful insistence on her own judgment. For these critics Dorothea's behavior confirmed the dangers of a strong mind—even in an aspiring angel. As the *British Quarterly Review* points out in 1873,

> We hardly see how Dorothea could have been better protected against her first mistake than the picture of social life in Middlemarch represents her as having actually been protected. We note

this point only because we find in this passage a trace that George Eliot is, on reviewing her own work, a little dissatisfied with her own picture of the 'prosaic conditions' to which she ascribes Dorothea's misadventures; and that she tries to persuade herself that they were actually more oppressive and paralyzing than they really were. It is obvious, we think, that Dorothea's character was one of much more impetuous self-assertion, of much more adventurous and self-willed idealism than this passage would suggest. She is painted from the first as groping her way with an imperious *disregard* of the prevailing conventional ideas,—ideas quite too mean and barren for the guidance of such a nature,—and as falling, in consequence of that imperious disregard, into her mistake—the mistake being due about equally to her hasty contempt for the existing social standards of conduct, and to her craving for nobler standards not supplied. It was rather the ambitious idealism and somewhat wilful independence of Dorothea's nature than any want of a sound general opinion about the matter, which is represented as leading her into the mistake of her marriage with the pedantic bookworm, Mr. Casaubon; and George Eliot is hardly fair to the society she has herself so wonderfully portrayed, when she throws the responsibility of Dorothea's first great mistake upon it.[59]

Another critic was convinced that Dorothea's unheroic life, unsatisfying as it might be, was not a condition that Eliot really proposed to change. Leslie Stephen, in a *Cornhill* retrospective review (1881) of Eliot's work, points out that she does not push beyond her melancholy conviction that the age of heroism, especially for women, is over. Eliot's modern heroines are indeed strong, Stephen notes, but they never achieve a wider sphere for heroic action. Their struggles and their triumphs remain private, silent, and unseen.

Without going into the question fully, one thing may be said: the modern Theresa, whether she is called Dorothea, or Maggie, or Dinah, or Janet, is the central figure in the world of George Eliot's imagination. We are to be brought to sympathise with the noble aspirations of a loving and unselfish spirit, conscious that it cannot receive any full satisfaction within the commonplace conditions of this prosaic world. How women are to find a worthier sphere of action than the mere suckling of babes and chronicling of small beer is a question for the Social Science Associations. Some people answer it by proposing to give women votes or degrees, and others would tell us that such problems can only be answered by reverting to Saint Theresa's method. The solution in terms of actual conduct lies beyond the proper province of the novelist. She

THE WOMAN QUESTION—LITERARY ISSUES

has done all that she can do if she has revealed the intrinsic beauty of such a character, and its proper function in life. She should make us fall in love with Romola and Maggie, and convert us to the belief that they are the true salt of the earth.

Up to a certain point her success is complete, and it is won by high moral feeling and quick sympathy with true nobility of character. We pay willing homage to these pure and lofty feminine types, and we may get some measure of the success by comparing them with other dissatisfied heroines whose aspirations are by no means so lofty or so compatible with delicate moral sentiment. But the triumph has its limits. In the sweet old-world country life a Janet or a Dinah can find some sort of satisfaction from an evangelical preacher, or within the limits of the Methodist church. If the thoughts and ways of her circle are narrow, it is in harmony with itself, and we may feel its beauty without asking awkward questions. But as soon as Maggie has left her quiet fields and reached even such a centre of civilisation as St. Ogg's, there is a jar and a discord. *Romola* is in presence of a great spiritual disturbance where the highest aspirations are doomed to the saddest failure; and when we get to *Middlemarch* we feel that the charm has somehow vanished. Even in the early period, Mrs. Poyser's bright common-sense has some advantages over Dinah Morris's high-wrought sentiment. And in *Middlemarch* we feel more decidedly that high aspirations are doubtful qualifications; that the ambitious young devotee of science has to compound with the quarrelling world, and the brilliant young Dorothea to submit to a decided clipping of her wings. Is it worth while to have a lofty nature in such surroundings? The very bitterness with which the triumph of the lower characters is set forth seems to betray a kind of misgiving. And it is the presence of this feeling, as well as the absence of the old picturesque scenery, that gives a tone of melancholy to the later books. Some readers are disposed to sneer, and to look upon the heroes and heroines as male and female prigs, who are ridiculous if they persist and contemptible when they fail. Others are disposed to infer that the philosophy which they represent is radically unsatisfactory. And some may say that, after all, the picture is true, however sad, and that, in all ages, people who try to lift their heads above the crowd must lay their account with martyrdom and be content to be uncomfortable. The moral, accepted by George Eliot herself, is indicated at the end of *Middlemarch*. A new Theresa, she tells us, will not have the old opportunity any more than a new Antigone would "spend heroic piety in daring all for the sake of a brother's funeral; the medium in which these ardent deeds took shape is for ever gone." There will be many Dorotheas, and some of them doomed to worse sacrifices than the Dorothea of *Middlemarch*, and we must be content to think that her influence spent itself through many invisible channels, but was not the less potent because unseen.

Perhaps that is not a very satisfactory conclusion. I cannot here ask why it should not have been more satisfactory. We must admit that there is something rather depressing in the thought of these anonymous Dorotheas feeling about vaguely for some worthy outlet of their energies, taking up with a man of science and discovering him to be an effete pedant, wishing ardently to reform the world, but quite unable to specify the steps to be taken, and condescending to put up with a very commonplace life in a vague hope that somehow or other they will do some good. Undoubtedly we must admit that, wherever the fault lies, our Theresas have some difficulty in fully manifesting their excellence. But with all their faults, we feel that they embody the imperfect influence of a nature so lofty in its sentiment, so wide in its sympathies, and so keen in its perceptions, that we may wait long before it will be adequately replaced.[60]

Two contemporary reviewers challenge Dorothea's fate. Florence Nightingale protests that Eliot was wrong: there are plenty of opportunities for a modern Saint Theresa in the new areas of reform work for women.[61] Henry James, writing for *Galaxy* in 1873, criticizes the novel's technical failure to focus on its promising heroine and implies that that failure is also a mistaken moral choice. George Eliot, he feels, wastes Dorothea Brooke's potential as a literary figure by casting her as a mere wife and woman, and displacing her from the center of the book. Dorothea's struggle with herself and her culture is reduced from tragic to trivial.

[George Eliot's] heroines have always been of an exquisite quality, and Dorothea is only that perfect flower of conception of which her predecessors were the less unfolded blossoms. An indefinable moral elevation is the sign of these admirable creatures; and of the representation of this quality in its superior degrees the author seems to have in English fiction a monopoly. To render the expression of a soul requires a cunning hand; but we seem to look straight into the unfathomable eyes of the beautiful spirit of Dorothea Brooke. She exhales a sort of aroma of spiritual sweetness, and we believe in her as in a woman we might providentially meet some fine day when we should find ourselves doubting of the immortality of the soul. By what unerring mechanism this effect is produced—whether by fine strokes or broad ones, by description or by narration, we can hardly say; it is certainly the great achievement of the book. Dorothea's career is, however, but an episode, and though doubtless in intention, not distinctly enough in fact, the central one.

. . . The reader indeed is sometimes tempted to complain of a tendency . . . which we are at loss exactly to express—a tendency to make light of the serious elements of the story and to sacrifice them to the more trivial ones. Is it an unconscious instinct or is it a deliberate plan? With its abundant and massive ingredients "Middlemarch" ought somehow to have depicted a weightier drama. Dorothea was altogether too superb a heroine to be wasted; yet she plays a narrower part than the imagination of the reader demands. She is of more consequence than the action of which she is the nominal centre. She marries enthusiastically a man who she fancies a great thinker, and who turns out to be but an arid pedant. Here, indeed, is a disappointment with much of the dignity of tragedy; but the situation seems to us never to expand to its full capacity.[62]

Twenty-five years after *Jane Eyre* and *The Princess*, many Victorian critics had come to expect in their angels qualities once considered unnatural and unwomanly. But the synthesis of angel and strong-minded woman, worked out primarily by such high Victorian women writers as Elizabeth Gaskell, Charlotte Brontë, and Elizabeth Barrett Browning and revised by George Eliot, did not last. Brontë and Browning make controversial claims for the strong woman's happiness in both male and female spheres. Eliot's story deals with tensions and contradictions which seem to make the earlier vision unrealistic, perhaps even undesirable. James's demand for a larger role for Dorothea anticipates yet another change in the strong heroine: "new woman" fiction like his own 1881 novel, *The Portrait of a Lady*. Had George Eliot made Dorothea the center of *Middlemarch*, James concludes, she might have written "the first of English novels. . . .[*Middlemarch*] remains a very splendid performance . . . it sets a limit, we think, to the development of the old-fashioned English novel."[63] Dorothea's wasted potential, in James's view, is for tragedy. In the modern novel to which James looks forward, the strong-minded heroine declares her independence from the angelic ideal and takes her place as a representative, but also a sorely disappointed, human figure. Olive Schreiner's Lyndall in *The Story of an African Farm* (1883), George Gissing's Rhoda Nunn in *The Odd Women* (1893), Thomas Hardy's Tess and Sue Bridehead in *Tess of the D'Urbervilles* (1891) and *Jude the Obscure* (1895), James's Isabel Archer and Maggie Verver in *The Portrait of a Lady* (1881) and *The Golden Bowl* (1904), Dreiser's *Sister Carrie* (1900), Virginia Woolf's Mrs. Ramsey in *To the Lighthouse* (1927): these "new women" in fiction at the end of the century and after emerge as sympathetic characters who will not or cannot find happiness, despite their possession of both strong minds and womanly virtues.

4

Passionate Heroines
Fallen, Sensation, and Fleshly

Literature's commitment to the sexual purity of women prevails throughout the Victorian period and continues into the
twentieth century. (Hardy's *Tess of the D'Urbervilles* is bowdlerized
by *Graphic* in 1891, Dreiser's *Sister Carrie* is suppressed from 1900
to 1912.) A significant liberalization does occur, however, in the
second half of the nineteenth century—particularly in the
twenty years between two of the most controversial fallen-
woman novels, *Ruth* by Elizabeth Gaskell (1853) and *The New
Magdalen* by Wilkie Collins (1873). The 1850s and 1860s show an
increased concern with woman's passions. Prostitution, for example, is debated by Victorians with diverse interests in the
Woman Question (Volume II, Chapter 3). W.R. Greg's *Westminster*
article on prostitution praises Gaskell's *Mary Barton* and influenced, in turn, her next novel, *Ruth*; the public health writings of
Dr. Acton (Volume II, Chapter 2) and others lead to legislation
which prompts countercrusades by Josephine Butler in England
and by Susan B. Anthony and Frances Willard in America. Middle-
class men *and* women are forced to face more honestly their responsibilities for the sexual ills of society and to view more
humanely the passions which woman shares with man.

Making the culture face sexual facts of life is also the mission of many novelists and poets in the 1850s and 1860s. Fallen-woman novels proliferate. Still more numerous and shocking in the sixties are the new "sensational" and "fleshly" heroines. These passionate types resemble their strong-minded and their fallen sisters, but differ from them significantly. Like the strong-minded woman, the passionate heroine is willful; unlike the strong-minded, she is anything but angelic in the criminal and erotic acts to which her passions drive her. Such dangerous passions may seem to link the passionate and fallen women (and indeed the Victorians often equated them), but in fact the two differ substantially. In a sensation novel like Mary Elizabeth Braddon's *Lady Audley's Secret* (1862), the passive victim becomes the active victimizer. This difference is important. The sensation heroine of fiction and her fleshly sister in poetry and painting challenge social roles and moral laws as fallen women did not. The controversy here is not over the virtue of one woman but over the fate of society. In the very decade when doctors and scientists are intensely concerned about the sexual and psychological health of woman, sensational and fleshly writers are presenting heroines subversive enough to call into question the culture's moral health and the nature of womanhood.

By 1873, Anglo-American Victorians are thus both calmer and tenser, both more willing to deal publicly with the issue of female passions and more anxious before the magnitude of the problem. These changes determine our presentation of fallen, sensational, and fleshly heroines. The nature of these female types and the changing public attitudes toward female sexuality are mirrored in four great controversies. The first, over fallen women, centers on Gaskell's *Ruth* in 1853; still fiercer battles are fought in the sixties over both sensational and fleshly literature; finally, reactions to Collins' fallen woman of 1873 indicate what has and has not changed in the twenty years since *Ruth*. All four literary controversies raise a question basic to our understanding of Victorian attitudes toward female passion: To what extent do outraged reviewers speak for Victorian readers? Or, put another way, how can we reconcile numerous attacks by critics and substantial sales for authors? This tension between prescription and practice touches literature as it does every area of Victorian life. Like doctors (William Acton's heyday occurs largely between *Ruth* and *New Magdalen*), clerics, educators, legislators, editors, and private citizens, Victorian writers and reviewers were trying to account for those rapid social changes of which literature was both cause and effect.

I

Fallen women in early Victorian fiction—Dickens' lower-class Nancy and Emily in *Oliver Twist* (1837–38) and *David Copperfield* (1849–50) and his aristocratic Lady Dedlock in *Bleak House* (1852–53)—tend to conform to the traditional type. They are denied the role of protagonist and are subjected to the death mandatory for women with extra-marital relationships. What is potentially subversive about presenting such women in fiction appears in 1850, when a "Magdalen" at last becomes a heroine and laudatory reviewers of *The Scarlet Letter* respond in dangerously contradictory ways.

> We never, in our pity for the sufferer, lose our abhorrence of the sin.

> We almost forget the crime in the courage, and lose sight of the sinner in the heroine.[1]

Compassion for the fallen woman can shade readily into sympathy for unhallowed moral attitudes. Despite the mandatory death which Elizabeth Gaskell inflicts upon *her* fallen heroine three years later, *Ruth* shows enough sympathy with unorthodox attitudes to spark immediate and extensive controversy. The novel may seem tame today (an orphan, seduced by a handsome aristocrat, manages before her early death to win the community's respect), but its stands on important issues are radical in 1853. Gaskell shows and apparently approves of a wife disobeying her husband; she reveals tensions in the supposedly benign relations of fathers and daughters. More importantly, Gaskell challenges basic assumptions about the fallen woman— that the baby is the mother's badge of shame, that any expedient marriage should be agreed to, that fornication taints the woman irrevocably but leaves the man respectable.

Challenges so basic cannot go unheeded in 1853. "'An unfit subject for fiction' is *the* thing to say about it," Gaskell noted.[2] Two years later, *Blackwood's* can still say:

> the mistake lies in choosing such a heroine at all. Every pure feminine mind, we suppose, holds the faith of Desdemona—"I do not believe there is any such woman;" and the strong revulsion of dismay and horror with which they find themselves compelled to admit, in some individual case, that their rule is not infallible, produces at once the intense resentment with which every other woman regards the one who has stained her name and fame.[3]

Gaskell makes clear how intense and close to home the criticism was. "Now *should* you [her friend, Eliza Fox] have burnt the 1st vol. of Ruth as so *very* bad? even if you had been a very anxious father of a family? Yet *two* men have; and a third has forbidden his wife to read it; they sit next to us in Chapel and you can't think how 'improper' I feel under their eyes."[4]

Lest the Gaskell and *Blackwood's* remarks seem to oversimplify the *Ruth* controversy, two complicating facts should be noted. Gaskell herself admits that "of course it is a prohibited book in *this*, as in many other households; not a book for young people, unless read with someone older."[5] By sharing with other Victorian parents a recognition of *Ruth's* potentially subversive influence, Elizabeth Gaskell establishes that the Victorian fear of sexual laxity was not restricted to a few extremists. Moreover, when Gaskell says "the only comparison I can find for myself is to St Sebastian tied to a tree to be shot at with arrows,"[6] she is being thin-skinned. Responses to *Ruth* are less simple-minded than Gaskell suggests. Private and public praise is generous, and adverse comments are often astute.

Praise conveyed privately to Gaskell by eminent Victorians— Charlotte Brontë, Elizabeth Barrett Browning, Josephine Butler, Richard Cobden, Dickens, Guizot, Kingsley, Maurice, Nightingale, Catherine Winkworth[7]—is echoed in numerous laudatory reviews of *Ruth*. Besides applauding the moderate tone which Gaskell achieved with so volatile a theme, major periodicals espouse various of her unconventional stands on moral issues. *Westminster Review* and the *North British Review* agree, for example, that the child need not be the mother's badge of shame— *Westminster* arguing in terms of "nature," *North British* in terms more expressly Christian.

Admirable is the stroke of nature by which Ruth cannot be made to feel "sorry" that she is to have a baby! . . . It is new life, new strength, new hope! . . .

The author has treated this phase of the history of a fallen woman with immense truth and delicacy. She has separated the consequences of an action from the action itself. The natural and pure relationship between a mother and her child ought not to be considered as poisoned and vitiated, because the antecedents of that relationship are to be regretted; it is an opportunity afforded to her of rehabilitating her life, by nobly and courageously accepting the responsibility she has incurred, and qualifying herself to discharge the trust committed to her. If women who have placed themselves in Ruth's position only could find the moral courage to accept the duties entailed upon them by their own conduct, it would much lessen the misery and social evil that now follows in the train of illicit connexions.[8]

Again, in the unfolding of Ruth's character another truth shines out, clear and bright as day; the old truth which David expressed in a noble psalm—the truth which the Church of England has boldly embodied in her service of the churching of women, every word of which is as applicable to a harlot who had become a mother as to the Queen of England on her throne—the truth that "children and the fruit of the womb are an heritage and gift which cometh of the Lord." [Ps. 127:3] A very strange truth, indeed, now-a-days—a truth denied by every advertisement asking or offering the services of married men or women, "without incumbrances,"—a truth denied by the fearfully increasing number of cases of child-poisoning, child-murder, abandonment of children, and perhaps still more so by the perpetual verdicts of "concealment of birth." But the authoress of Ruth is a mother, and the duties of hallowed motherhood have taught her own pure soul what its blessings may be to the fallen. Ruth the seduced girl is made a noble Christian woman by the very consequences of her sin. Satan sent the sin—God sends the child. . . . Is there a harlot mother in whom the germs of these feelings cannot be found, if we only look deep enough for them? But no. It is so much easier to point the lesson of the sin through its consequence, to insist on the shame, on the trouble, on the expense of the unlawful motherhood! Another time, perhaps, a tiny corse will be found in the cess-pool.—Why should you wonder? Is it not one "incumbrance" the less in this world, both to the mother and to the country at large, over-population being taken into account?[9]

The general moral attitude fostered by *Ruth* is also celebrated by important periodicals. *Westminster Review* concludes eloquently:

"If women are to have their lives rehabilitated, it must be through the means of women, who, noble and pure in their own lives, can speak with authority, and tell them that in this world no action is final; and that, to set the seal of despair and reprobation upon any individual during any one point of his career, is to blot out the inner life by which we live."[10]

What makes *Ruth* particularly powerful is that its "moral" transcends the question of the fallen woman. Like William Thompson and George Drysdale who saw woman's wrongs in the context of human rights, Elizabeth Gaskell examines society's response to all suffering, to all outcasts. Arguing with incontrovertible orthodoxy that the essence of Christianity is love, Gaskell subversively reveals the gap between society's pretension to Christian principles and society's practice of righteous vindictiveness. *Ruth* threatened so many Victorians because it attacks the citadel from within.

Although no one periodical defines fully the subversive nature of Gaskell's novel, reviewers do recognize that *Ruth* involves more than one group of outcasts. For the *North British Review* the novel affirms the familial nature of society and the familial obligations of us all: *Bentley's Miscellany*, relating the moral to the form of *Ruth*, shows that the novel's dual plots reflect Gaskell's dual concern with female *and* male outcasts.

But the tracing out of the influence of Ruth's motherhood upon herself is but a part, we take it, of the larger and more general purpose of the book—of that lesson which it inculcates, along with every penitentiary, ill or well regulated, in the world, for those who choose to read the lesson—that, as the sin of unchastity in the woman is, above all, a breaking up or a loosening of the family bond—a treason against the family order of God's world—so the restoration of the sinner consists mainly in the renewal of that bond, in the realization of that order, both by and through and around herself. We are beginning to learn that whipping unchaste women, or putting them in prison, are not, as our forefathers thought, sufficient safeguards against vice; Now, if the authoress of Ruth had been a mere professed philanthropist, a setter up of systems, she would have placed her scene of action in some model penitentiary, and shewn us her notions of the regular machinery to be set at work for manufacturing virtuous women. . . . [But she knows] that all these same appliances of philanthropy, however praiseworthy, useful, pious, are but palliatives—remedies applied to urgent symptoms, whilst we cannot or dare not strike at the disease itself. . . . And so she goes at once to the root of the matter, and places poor erring Ruth in a family, between a brother and sister, and their old servant, with her wronged innocent child before her for a monument of past sin and life-long duty. And thus the erring girl, as we said, grows up into a noble Christian woman, and outlives the discovery of her shame to receive thanks from clergymen and medical men for her devotion to the sick in time of fever, and to die from attending on the man who ruined her. We are quite sure that, by a course like this, the authoress will have done far more real service to the cause (as the cant phrase is) of penitentiaries, and nurses' institutions, and sisterhoods, and deaconesses' institutes, and the rest, than if she had "taken up" any one of those subjects; simply because she has, as it were, lifted the veil from off their working, to shew us the principle by which alone they can stand or fall. (155–57)

Read in a right spirit and with a due appreciation of the writer's meaning, no nobler exhortation to charity can be conceived. It teaches that the difference between those who commit and those who do not commit certain offences against God and man, is to be found rather in circumstances than in themselves, and that we should never take account of the sin without also measuring the temptation. It beautifully indicates the difference between a sin, however great, and habitual sin, and suggests that it is want of charity among men that converts the former into the latter, and peoples the world with outcasts.

. . . Resolute that there shall be no mistake about it she introduces a second exemplification of the great truth in the person of the son of that rich dissenter, who dismisses the poor girl in disgrace from his immaculate household. Yes, his son, Mr. Bradshaw's son Richard, the pride of his heart, who had all the benefit of his severe teaching and his rigid example, actually commits a forgery and defrauds the poor dissenting preacher. The father [Mr. Bradshaw], in his austere Roman virtue, declares that he has not one rule for a stranger and another for a son, exhorts the minister to prosecute the young man, and shuts both his heart and his door resolutely against the offender. But Mr. Benson refuses to prosecute. He believes that such a course would only confirm the youth in his selfishness; and Mr. Bradshaw's partner, a man of a kindly nature, concurs in opinion with him. The result is, that young Bradshaw is saved . . . and the triumph of charity is complete.

. . . This additional enforcement is given to the lesson of charity, as though the authoress of "Ruth" would show that she is not pleading only for her own sex.[11]

Important periodicals are also astute in their adverse comments on *Ruth*. Anything but so hysterical as the bookburners whom Gaskell contemns, the best reviewers criticize two of the novel's aspects which trouble readers today. One is the presentation of Ruth's sexuality. The orphan grows up among sewing girls [Volume II, Chapter 3] and yet knows nothing of men or seduction; she then lives intimately with her lover, and yet shows no passion. Reviewers' responses to Ruth's nonsexuality form a spectrum of critical opinion. *North British Review* defends Gaskell unreservedly; *Gentleman's Magazine* criticizes her presentation but sympathizes with her predicament; *Literary Gazette* attacks Gaskell fiercely.

> The most marking characteristic of the book, we should say, is its perfect simplicity, truthfulness, its following out, step by step, of nature in all its parts, together with its exquisite purity of feeling in dealing with a subject which so many would shrink from. For instance, the latter part of the first volume shews us Ruth living with her seducer at a Welsh inn—a grand opportunity for commonplace moralists to picture to us terrible struggles of conscience in one or both of them—the debasement of the one, the corrupting influence of the other. The wife and mother who wrote "Ruth" does no such thing. Ruth is still the simple girl, country-bred, delighted with the new sight of mountain-scenery, with all her sympathies not deadened, but heightened, by the new power which has been developed in her, the entire devotion of a most humble, most trustful love. (151)

> We think that it would have been more true to paint Ruth as both more alive and less simple. She ought not to have gone astray from stupidity or from fear, but with all her poetic love of beauty should have been less passive, more enkindled—more of the woman in short; ensnared from within as well as from without, though still possessed of a young heart's delicacy. At the same time we are far from insensible to Mrs. Gaskell's difficulty. Had Ruth erred from passion rather than from ignorance, scenes must have been constructed in accordance with that view, and then we should have had the usual objectionable draggings through dangerous mazes of sentiment and suffering, which a pure writer would of course much prefer shunning altogether.[12]

> The story is radically faulty in its heroine. The most extravagant demands are made upon the reader's credulity in regard to

her character throughout the first portion of the work, and throughout the rest she is elevated into a pure and saintly pattern of sweetness and excellence, which it is hard to reconcile with her former imbecility. A lapse in chastity, committed in ignorance of the nature of the sin, and expiated by a life of suffering and martyrlike piety, is the theme upon which the story turns; but the authoress, while continually dwelling upon this plea of ignorance, has in fact cut the ground from under the heroine's feet, by elaborately introducing incidents, and placing her in circumstances where she must very early have been taught the truth, and learned the penalties which society attaches to delinquency like hers.

The novel opens after her parents' death, and shows her to us at the age of sixteen, in a large establishment of sewing girls, in a considerable country town. She must there, if not before, have learned something about sweethearts and irregular attachments . . . yet when, having yielded to her seducer's solicitation to accompany him, she next appears upon the scene at a Welsh inn, where she is living with him as his mistress, we are asked to suppose that she is in total ignorance of having committed any breach of the laws either of God or of society![13]

A second major problem with *Ruth* is that the heroine of this innovative novel succumbs finally to a conventional fate. Gaskell maintains privately that there can be no other way. But many Victorians, like most readers today, disagree. Elizabeth Barrett Browning asks, "was it quite impossible but that your Ruth should *die*?"[14] Charlotte Brontë, after praising the novel's practical and theoretical usefulness, says

> Yet—hear my protest!
> Why should she die? Why are we to shut up the book weeping?
> My heart fails me already at the thought of the pang it will have to undergo. And yet you must follow the impulse of your own inspiration. If *that* commands the slaying of the victim, no bystander has a right to put out his hand to stay the sacrificial knife; but I hold you a stern priestess in these matters.[15]

Probably the most telling criticism comes from a reviewer who clearly sympathizes with and respects Gaskell's attempt to portray the fallen woman humanely. W.R. Greg did not, like some reviewers, simply espouse Ruth's right to live. "The False Morality of Lady Novelists" *National Review* (1859) makes a more general (and to Gaskell, no doubt, a more painful) criticism. Greg accuses her of that very righteousness which she sought to extirpate; and, worse still, he indicts such righteousness in the name of what Gaskell held most sacred—Christian love.

Novelists err grievously and habitually in their estimates of the relative culpability of certain sins, failings, and backslidings. It must be admitted that the church and the world too generally err as grievously, and in the same direction.

Provided a man is strictly honest, decorous in demeanor, and what we call "moral"—that is, not impure—in conduct, he is accepted unrebuked before the altar;—though he be a tyrannical husband and a brutal father. . . .

But provided a woman, however young, however ignorant in the world's ways, however desolate and sorely tried, has unloosed for one moment the girdle of her maiden innocence,—though the lapse may have been instantaneous, delirious, instantly repented and resolutely retrieved,—though in her essential nature she may still be all that is noble, affectionate, devoted, womanly, and unstained,—she is punished without discrimination as the most sunk of all sinners; and, what is more especially to our present purpose, all writers of fiction represent her as acquiescing in the justice of the sentence.

Now we say unhesitatingly that these are not righteous, as most assuredly they are not Christian, judgments. Far be it from us to say one word calculated to render less strong, less lofty, less thorny, or less insurmountable, the barrier which protects female chastity in our land, or to palliate untruly that frailty which is always a deplorable weakness and often a heinous sin.

Yielding to temptation must be always sinful; but yielding to wishes not in themselves nor at all times wrong, cannot justly be condemned so sternly as yielding to passions inherently and invariably violent and criminal. In this direction, at least, lay the judgment and the sympathies of Jesus, as the whole tenor of his words and deeds proclaim; for while he denounced the hard and cruel rulers of the land, the grasping lawyer and the supercilious Pharisee, with an indignation that is refreshingly human, he comforted and pardoned the frail wife and the weeping Magdalen with a grave tenderness that is unmistakeably divine.

These remarks have been suggested to us by the re-perusal of a most beautiful and touching tale, wherein the erroneous moral estimate we are signalising appears in a very mild form; and which, indeed, would appear to have been written with the design of modifying and correcting it, though the author's ideas were not quite clear or positive enough to enable her to carry out boldly or develop fully the conception she had formed. This man [Bradshaw], reeking with the sins Christ most abhorred, turns upon the unhappy Ruth (who, after six years of exemplary life, has become a governess in his house), as soon as he accidentally learns her history, with a brutal savage violence and a coarse unfeeling cruelty which we need not scruple to affirm constituted a far greater sin than poor Ruth had committed, or would have committed had her lapse from chastity been willful and persistent instead of unconscious, transient, and bitterly and nobly atoned for. Something of this very conviction was evidently in Mrs. Gaskell's mind. . . . But what we object to in her book is this: that the tone and language habitually adopted throughout, both by Ruth herself and by her friends when alluding to her fault, is at war with this impression and with the true tenor of the facts recorded. Mrs. Gaskell scarcely seems at one with herself in this matter. Anxious above all things to arouse a kinder feeling in the uncharitable and bitter world towards offenders of Ruth's sort, to show how thoughtless and almost unconscious such offenses sometimes are, and how slightly, after all, they may affect real purity of nature and piety of spirit, and how truly they may be redeemed when treated with wisdom and with gentleness,—she has first imagined a character as pure, pious, and unselfish as poet ever fancied, and described a lapse from chastity as faultless as such a fault can be; and then, with damaging and unfaithful inconsistency, has given in to the world's estimate in such matters, by assuming that the sin committed was of so deep a dye that only a life of atoning and enduring penitence could wipe it out. If she designed to awaken the world's compassion for the ordinary class of betrayed and deserted Magdalenes, the circumstances of Ruth's error should not have been made so innocent, nor should Ruth herself have been painted as so perfect. If she intended to describe a saint (as she has done), she should not have held conventional and mysterious language about her as a grievous sinner.[16]

After *Ruth*, numerous British and American works feature fallen women. Elizabeth Barrett Browning's *Aurora Leigh* (1856), George Eliot's *Adam Bede* (1859), Mrs. Henry Wood's *East Lynne* (1861), Rebecca Harding Davis' *Margaret Howth* (1862), Caroline Norton's *Lost and Saved* (1863), Bayard Taylor's *John Godfrey's Fortunes* (1864), Meredith's *Rhoda Fleming* (1865), Elizabeth Stuart Phelps's *Hedged In* and Anthony Trollope's *The Vicar of Bullhampton* (1870). Critical indignation at these fallen women is less severe and widespread than we might assume today. Some criticism on moral grounds does occur, of course, but in most cases the author's attitude toward the fallen woman precludes major cultural concern. George Eliot, for example, is obviously intent upon presenting Hetty Sorel's shallowness in *Adam Bede*; the novel received by and large excellent reviews, and a substantial part of the negative comments is either retracted later or patently special pleading.[17] Mrs. Wood *is* sympathetic enough with her fallen Isabel to prompt some reviewers to lump *East Lynne* with sensational disgraces, but Wood visits the mandatory suffering and death upon Isabel so rigorously that Harriet Martineau and the *Times* applaud the novel, and even the severe *Saturday Review* admitted that it "touched every woman's heart."[18] The most problematic author of fallen-woman fiction is probably Caroline Norton. Reviewers hit her so hard because *Lost and Saved* hits society so hard.[19] Norton allows her heroine to escape the mandatory death and to enjoy a happy future; in turn, Norton questions the morals and the intentions of society's privileged classes. *Lost and Saved* was called "sensational" in 1863 and, of all *Ruth's* progeny, it points most clearly to the real center of controversy in the sensational 1860s. Fallen-woman novels generally were not seen by the Victorians as a movement, like the sensation and fleshly schools, and did not in the 1860s generate controversies as these schools did. The most wayward heroines are not fallen at all. Whether sensational or fleshly, they are not passive victims. They attack.

II

The new fiction which shocks the 1860s is called "sensational," though the Victorians cannot decide who coined the term or what it means precisely.[20] "Fast novels," "bigamy novels," "crime novels," "adultery novels" (*Punch* even suggested "arsenical novels") are sometimes equated with and sometimes distinguished from "sensation novels." For certain, sensation fiction features—in varying proportions—crime, mystery, passion, social commentary, and questions of identity, in a contemporary setting. *The Woman in White* (1860) and *Lady Audley's Secret* (1862) lead the way, generating for Wilkie Collins and Mary Elizabeth Braddon enormous sales, controversy, and imitation.[21] More titles and authors followed rapidly. Collins writes *No Name* (1862) and *Armadale* (1866); Braddon produces more than one novel a year, her best being probably *Aurora Floyd* (1863). Such established, controversial writers as Charles Reade and G.A. Lawrence contribute *Griffith Gaunt* and *Sans Merci* (1866),[22] and the spread of sensationalism does not stop here. It also touches such basically unsensational writers as Trollope and Eliot; it evokes from Gaskell and Eliza Lynn Linton such sensational titles as *A Dark Night's Work* (1863), *Sylvia's Lovers* (1864), and *Sowing the Wind* (1867); and it even tempts such neophytes as lawyer-anthropologist J. MacGregor Allan [Volume II, Chapter 2] to try his inept hand with *Nobly False* (1863). What is particularly important for the Woman Question is that many of the new novels come from women. In England, Ouida, Rhoda Broughton, and Mrs. Wood joined Braddon among the decade's best-sellers. American sensationalism is harder to define (America's most shocking fiction may in fact be women's *religious* novels), but certainly the spectacular sales of *East Lynne* and *Lady Audley's Secret* prompt Louisa May Alcott, Bella Spencer, and others to write lurid tales for the sensation presses, as Jo does in *Little Women*.[23]

Viewing the sensation controversy in light of the Woman Question is rewarding because so much of the controversy involves woman's changing role. The sensation novels written by women were primarily about women and are largely for women. Also, the most sustained evaluation of sensation fiction came from the foremost female reviewer of the period, Margaret Oliphant. Defining fully woman's involvement in sensationalism requires a three-stage analysis. The cultural aspects of and the critical response to the sensation controversy must each be established; then, with this context for Margaret Oliphant, we can see how much her complex response to woman as the writer-reader-subject of sensation fiction reveals about a representative voice and a major controversy of the Victorian period.

Sensation fiction appears in a decade which the Victorians themselves recognize as "sensational." Besides the well-documented throngs that watched Blondin balancing on the high wire, Leotard flying from the trapeze, Ohman walking on the ceiling, and the Colleen Bawn high-diving in Boucicault's play, Britain and America both stand rapt before the supreme spectacle—the Civil War.

TEN years ago the world in general had come to a singular crisis in its existence. The age was lost in self-admiration. . . . It is a changed world in which we are now standing. If no distant sound of guns echoes across seas and continents upon our ears as we wander under the South Kensington domes, the lack of the familiar sound will be rather disappointing than satisfactory. That distant roar has come to form a thrilling accompaniment to the safe life we lead at home. On the other side of the Atlantic, a race *blasée* and lost in univeral *ennui* has bethought itself of the grandest expedient for procuring a new sensation; and albeit we follow at a humble distance, we too begin to feel the need of a supply of new shocks and wonders. Those fell Merrimacs and Monitors, stealing forth with a certain devilish invulnerability and composure upon the human ships and men to be made fire and carnage of, are excitement too high pitched for comfort; but it is only natural that art and literature should, in an age which has turned to be one of events, attempt a kindred depth of effect and shock of incident.[24]

Sensationalism is particularly upsetting to many Victorians because it spreads beyond battlefields and popular amusements. Reviewers note that "Professor Kingsley sensationalizes History" and that "theology itself has not wholly escaped its influence."[25] Even the sacred realm of womanhood is implicated. What are Victorians to think, for example, when they read in *Westminster Review*:

When Richardson, the showman, went about with his menagerie he had a big black baboon, whose habits were so filthy, and whose behavior was so disgusting, that respectable people constantly remonstrated with him for exhibiting such an animal. Richardson's answer invariably was, 'Bless you, if it wasn't for that big black baboon I should be ruined; it attracts all the young girls in the country.' Now bigamy has been Miss Braddon's big black baboon, with which she has attracted all the young girls in the country.[26]

Women are also shockingly evident at the great murder trials which thrill the period. Frequently the defendant is female; worse still, female interest in and sympathy for the defendant are so substantial that the bench and the press cry out repeatedly.

Fancy women with pretensions to purity, education, and refinement scrambling and struggling to hear the public revelations concerning an admitted adulteress and an alleged murderess! What filth they must have in their hearts! What greed of lustful curiosity!

What smug hypocrisy in their offenseless faces! What a dunghill of dirt seething and stinking behind their modest eyes and placid brows! For the women there is no excuse![27]

Similar outcries are visited upon sensation novels because women's behavior here is also decidedly antisocial. The passive victim has become the active victimizer. The heroines of Braddon and Ouida are second to no man in their potential for evil and their ability to act. More ephemeral titles—*Hidden Fire, Treason at Home, Which Should It Be, The Woman of Spirit*—reflect authors' common determination to present female sexuality with unprecedented frankness. The new heroine's appearance indicates, for Eliza Lynn Linton, a cultural turn-about in novels.

> Our later novelists, however, have altered the whole setting of the palette. Instead of five foot ten of black and brown, they have gone in for four foot nothing of pink and yellow. Instead of tumbled masses of raven hair, they have shining coils of purest gold. . . . their worst sinners are in all respects fashioned as much after the outward semblance of the ideal saint as they have skill to design.[28]

Orthodoxy is justifiably worried. Dethroning the angel means discontent in the house. How satisfactory can traditional roles be if adultery, bigamy, and spouse-killing captivate millions of readers? *Westminster Review* in 1865 reflects the general sense of dislocation when it plays upon traditional maxims about women.

> The New Woman, as we read of her in recent novels, possesses not only the velvet, but the claws of the tiger. She is no longer the Angel, but the Devil in the House. . . . Man proposes, woman disposes, is the new proverb. The Fathers, after all, were right when they said Adam was more tempted by Eve than by the Devil.[29]

What must also be acknowledged, however, is that shocking novels boasted morally impeccable endings. Sympathy for the forward woman varies with each novel, but she is finally chastized in almost every case. (Alcott's "Behind a Mask" is an exception.) Adapt to orthodox notions of womanhood or die, is the general rule. Lady Audley and Cigarette go too far to return.

Now that recent scholarship has recognized the subversive element in sensation fiction, there is a danger of swinging to the other extreme and dismissing the orthodoxy of these novels.

Biographical and cultural data suggest not neat polarities but uneasy mixes. In their private lives, Wood, Broughton, and even the temporarily compromised Braddon cherish traditional values, particularly the sacredness of the family; in their careers, all three authors moved on to less flamboyant novels of social comment and character study. These women reflect, not simply discontent with old ways, but a tension between discontent and a disinclination to adopt radically new ways. The same is true of their readers. Analyzing what impelled Madeleine Smith to seek premarital sex with the lower-class French lover whom she murdered imperiling her arranged marriage, Mary S. Hartman suggests, "that she intended nothing more than a secret fling."[30] To indulge subversive feelings within a context of still-secure values is a need recognized by Victorian reviewers of sensation fiction. "They read, especially women, of Margaret Dacre [in Yates's *Land at Last*] as boys read of Captain Kidd, forgetting the criminality of the deed in the excitement of the danger."[31] Victorian women can experience emotional needs more serious than the Captain Kidd analogy suggests—and still need the orthodox values which prevail at the end of sensation novels. These readers can find pleasure both in sympathetic Lady Audley's wild rebellion and in misogynistic Robert Audley's orthodox marriage. Granted that such poetic justice does not, as several Victorian reviewers noted, deal satisfactorily with the problems raised in sensation fiction: this does not make the poetic justice merely a sop thrown to Mrs. Grundy and Mr. Mudie. The unsatisfying tension between plot and denouement in sensation novels reflects the ambivalence of sensation readers who feel subversive emotions but still espouse woman's sphere.

This tension between the subversive and the orthodox means that sensation literature inevitably evokes wildly contradictory responses—everything from outrage to laughter, with various defenses in between. The major positions along this spectrum are valuable both as expressions of Victorian attitudes and as critical context for Margaret Oliphant. So, before focusing on her, here is the spectrum: from W. Fraser Ray and *Christian Remembrancer*, to Justin MacCarthy, to *Saturday Review* and the *Times*, to Bret Harte.

Outraged critics from the Archbishop of York to Mrs. E.B. Duffey attack sensation literature. Most, like *Victoria*, judge expressly "from a social [rather] than an art-critical point of view";[32] but some, like W. Fraser Ray, espouse critical analysis. "We shall purposely avoid applying a moral test to these productions. . . . A novel which deserves censure from a literary point of view cannot merit high eulogy solely on account of its morality." What Ray's supposedly "impartial" analysis indicates, however, is how endemic moral stereotyping is to Victorian criticism.

> In drawing her [Lady Lucy Audley], the authoress may have intended to portray a female Mephistopheles; but, if so, she should have known that a woman cannot fill such a part. The nerves with which Lady Audley could meet unmoved the friend of the man she had murdered, are the nerves of a Lady Macbeth who is half unsexed, and not those of the timid, gentle, innocent creature Lady Audley is represented as being.[33]

The first sentence states a moral assumption about life: a woman cannot be a Mephistopheles. The second sentence makes an aesthetic judgment about literature: expectations generated by the presentation of Lucy-as-Angel are falsified by the subsequent revelation of Lucy-as-Demon. This aesthetic judgment is hardly impartial. Ray is limiting Braddon to the confines of that very Angelic Womanhood which *Lady Audley's Secret* subverts. Ray does the same thing when Aurora Floyd whips her servant for hurting an injured dog. "We are certain that, except in this novel, no lady possessing the education and occupying the position of Aurora Floyd could have acted as she is represented to have done" (98). A woman could not be a lady—have education and standing—and still thrash her servant. For Ray, an ideal of conduct coincides with the act of individuals. This coincidence of precept and practice allows Ray finally to admit what has been obvious all along—that literary and moral criteria are one.

> From a lady novelist we naturally expect to have portraits of women which shall not be wholly untrue to nature. . . .
> Tested, then, by a purely literary standard, these works must be designated as the least valuable among works of fiction. They glitter on the surface, but the substance is base metal. Hence it is that the impartial critic is compelled, as it were, to unite with the moralist in regarding them as mischievous in their tendency, and as one of the abominations of the age. Into uncontaminated minds they will instil false views of human conduct. (97, 104)

Ray is symptomatic of what confronts sensation writers. Outraged critics—expressly or covertly—stress "moral" criteria because sensationalism seems to threaten social life itself. The two-pronged nature of this threat is clearly defined in a *Christian Remembrancer* review which accuses sensation writers of both exalting passion and disparaging ordinary life.

Sensation writing is an appeal to the nerves rather than to the heart; but all exciting fiction works upon the nerves, and Shakespeare can make "every particular hair to stand on end" with anybody. We suppose that the true sensation novel feels the popular pulse with this view alone—considers any close fidelity to nature a slavish subservience injurious to effect, and willingly and designedly draws a picture of life which shall make reality insipid and the routine of ordinary existence intolerable to the imagination. There is nothing more violently opposed to our moral sense, in all the contradictions to custom which they present to us, than the utter unrestraint in which the heroines of this order are allowed to expatiate and develop their impulsive, stormy, passionate characters. We believe, it is one chief among their many dangers to youthful readers that they open out a picture of life free from all the perhaps irksome checks that confine their own existence, and treat all such checks as real hindrances, solid impediments, to the development of power, feeling, and the whole array of fascinating and attractive qualities. . . . the victim of feeling or passion sinks at once into the inspired or possessed animal, and is always supposed to be past articulate speech; and we have the *cry,* the *smothered cry of rage,* the *wail,* the *low wailing cry,* the *wail of despair,* with which, if our readers are not familiar, *ad nauseam,* we can only say we *are.* The curious thing is, that probably no writer ever heard a woman utter this accepted token of extreme emotion, which would indeed be a very intolerable habit in domestic life; but it is evidently accepted by a very large circle as *the* exponent of true, thoroughgoing passion. . . . [Moreover, the reward for such passion is all too often orthodox. In *Lost and Saved,* sensational Beatrice] is taken up and restored to society by kind friends, marries an Italian count . . . and the curtain closes on the young mother hanging over the cradle of her baby. For calm, serene, domestic felicity, the very last thing these heroines of many stormy adventures are fit for, is always the haven assigned to them. It is easier, in fact, to turn nun, hospital nurse, or sister of mercy, to take up and carry through the professed vocation of a saint, than to work out the English ideal of wife, mother, and presiding spirit of the house, after any wide departure from custom and decorum; and it is one of the most mischievous points of a bad moral that leads the young and inexperienced reader to suppose otherwise.[34]

Partisans of the sensation novel defend it in several ways. New York's *Round Table* expresses substantial Anglo-American sentiment when it blames the rise of shocking fiction on the inadequacy of didactic moralizing. "The Satanic School comprises a bad lot, to be sure, but even it is better than the soporific school."[35] Going further, Justin MacCarthy in *Westminster Review* turned the tables on hostile critics by maintaining the moral *superiority* of sensationalism. MacCarthy's "Novels with a Purpose" (1864) makes one of the great Victorian arguments for literary rebellion.

> That sense of propriety which is satisfied by simply pretending that we do not see and hear things which no human precaution can shut out from our eyes and ears, is worthy of nothing but contempt. The innocence which is ignorance becomes impossible after a certain age, and if it were not impossible it would be merely despicable. When Mrs. Norton published her "Lost and Saved" she was criticized rather sharply because of the peculiar nature of her subject. She was reminded by one reviewer that such reading was not good for the young. Her defence of herself was, we think, unassailable. . . . The book was not intended to be read by the young. Its peculiar nature was to be sought for in the fact that it was not meant to be reading for the young.
> . . . We would not teach women that they are mere puppets of man's passion, soulless creatures for whom, as for children, an absence of all individual responsibility may be claimed. . . . The author of a recent novel entitled "Recommended to Mercy" has had the courage to strike out something of a new path. . . . The Helen of this novel frankly despises marriage, and is, like Dryden's Antony, all for love. She braves society, lives with the man she loves, is abandoned by him, and redeems her error of principle or judgment by a life devoted to active and unwearying benevolence. . . . The story degenerates into an ordinary tale of complicated mystery and extravagant sensation. Its general purport, however, seems to be a healthful insistance that . . . here at least is one woman for whose fall beneath society's surface of smooth propriety none of the conventional excuses of romance is pityingly urged. The heroine sees and understands her risk, accepts it, suffers for her venture, and pays the penalty with a brave heart.

The error was committed by herself, and her fate is redeemed by herself. We own to a much greater sympathy with this description of heroine, than with the forlorn creatures of the ordinary British novel, who are always crying "I didn't mean to do it" when the evil is done, and for whose individual errors the pitying author makes society a whipping-boy. If any real good can come of treating such social questions through the medium of fiction, the good, it seems to us, must be attained rather by endeavouring to increase than to lessen the sense of individual responsibility. . . .

Each of the four books [Meredith's *The Ordeal of Richard Feverel* and *Emilia in England,* Norton's *Lost and Saved,* anon. *Recommended to Mercy*] we have noticed is a practical protest, more or less direct and bold, against the tacit arrangement by which fiction in our day is expected to ignore all the perplexities, dangers, and sufferings springing from the relations between man and woman. We think the protest was needed. We can see no reason whatever why the novelist should be expected to shrink from taking into account one of the greatest sources of human trial, difficulty, and fall. We sympathize with the author who feels impelled to infuse more reality into his work than is necessary to make a pretty prose idyll or humorous caricature. . . . The world of most of our British novelists of the present day is really no more like the real world which we all see around us, than the pastoral life of the opera is like the actual condition of the Swiss mountain peasantry. . . . The great source of human temptation, and discord, and unhappiness affects the romance people not in the least. The hero has but one desire in his life—to marry the heroine; and as he never felt any movement of passion before his eyes fell upon her, so having married her, all human weakness, all anger, envy, jealousy, selfishness, impatience, are purged thoroughly out of him, and he and his wife are rapt away in a roseate cloud from the ken of common-place mortality. The women of course have no passions at all. . . .

There is no good end attained by trying to persuade ourselves that women are all incorporeal, angelic, colourless, passionless, helpless creatures, who are never to suspect anything, never to doubt anyone, who regard the whole end and passion of human life as ethereal, Platonic love, and orderly, parent-sanctioned wedlock. Women have especial need, as the world goes, to be shrewd, self-reliant, and strong; and we do all we can in our literature to render them helpless, imbecile, and idiotic. When Charlotte Brontë endeavoured to do otherwise, we can all recollect that a prudish scream was raised against her, and genteel virtue affected to be horrified with the authoress who drew women and girls endowed with human passion.

. . . We are so thoroughly impressed with the conviction that art and morals alike suffer by the prudish conventionalities of our present English style, that we are inclined to welcome rebellion against it merely because it is rebellion. . . . While it is coldly, stiffly, prudishly agreed to paint for us as a rule only such life as might be lectured on in a young ladies' boarding-school, we feel thankful to the novelist who has the courage to approach some of the great problems of existence, and to show us human creatures as we know them around us, tried by the old passions and quivering with the old pains.[36]

While MacCarthy shares with his opponents the belief that sensationalism has immense moral consequences, his fellow partisans farther along the critical spectrum are not so sure. The usually severe *Saturday Review* calls *Aurora Floyd* "harmless. . . . The literary market just now demands excitement without transgression of morality; and here the literary market gets its supply. All the crime is done under proper reprobation, and yet the writer and readers have all the benefit of the crime."[37] This benefit could—according to partisans still farther along the spectrum—be enjoyed without raising the moral question at all. In a review which *Christian Remembrancer* lamented as an "imprimatur" of respectability, the *Times* of London proclaims the sheer enjoyment of reading *Lady Audley's Secret*.

It is a good galloping novel, like a good gallop, to be enjoyed rather than criticized. It is full of rapid incident, well put together. When we begin to read we cannot choose but go on. . . . the present writer has laid her hands upon some well-known materials, but she has turned them to such good account that in the general interest we forget the imperfections of detail, and in the rush of events take little note of what is new or what is hackneyed.
. . . This is the age of lady novelists, and lady novelists naturally give the first place to the heroine. But, if the heroines have the first place, it will scarcely do to represent them as passive and quite angelic, or insipid—which heroines usually are. They have to be pictured as high-strung women, full of passion, purpose, and movement—very liable to error. Now, the most interesting side of a woman's character is her relation to the other sex, and the errors of women that are most interesting spring out of this relation. Hence unwonted prominence has of late been given to a theme which novelists used formerly to shrink from; and we are honored with descriptions of the most hidden feelings of the fair sex which would have made our fathers and grandfathers stare. . . .

Lady Audley's character is well conceived, and develops itself naturally. In the first few chapters, she appears as a perfect angel. The beauty of the country, the delight of her husband, the beloved and admired of all who come within the reach of her spells. Gradually we discover a mask. She is a heartless creature who plays a heartless game. . . . It is not easy to represent a woman in such a position, or with a character capable of such acts; to combine so much beauty with so much deformity; to depict the lovely woman with the fishy extremities. Miss Braddon would be entitled to rank as the first of lady novelists if she had perfectly succeeded in reconciling these contradictions; nevertheless her portraiture is by no means feeble, and gives promise of great success hereafter.[38]

On beyond the *Times*, at the opposite end of the critical spectrum from *Christian Remembrancer*, are readers who respond to sensation fiction by laughing. They satirize both the silliness of shocking excesses and the overseriousness of certain critics. Even the dour *Blackwood's* musters a (not too funny) jingle, "HOW TO MAKE A NOVEL, a sensation song." Besides a poem of its own, *Punch* contributes a five-part serial, "Mokeanna; or, The White Witness," plus a parodic "Prospectus of a New Journal" to be called "The Sensation Times," a "Sensation Census" listing supposed injuries to actors in "exciting Sensational Productions," and an *Almanac* cartoon, "The Sensation Novel". Rev. Francis Paget writes a novel, *Lucretia; or, the Heroine of the Nineteenth Century*; Lewis Carroll, a poem "Poeta Fit, Non Nascitur"; and W.S. Gilbert composes both a Bab ballad, "Sensation Captain," (1868) and a play, *Sensation Novel* (1871).[39] Although the conception and certain sections of the play are probably the most brilliant of the sensation parodies, Gilbert does not excerpt so well as another contemporary, Bret Harte. Harte's *Condensed Novels* (1867) satirizes Collins, Dickens, Charlotte Brontë, Reade, G.A. Lawrence, and other writers of the day. Harte's "Selina Sedilia By Miss M.E. B—dd-n and Mrs. H-n-y W—d" parodies one particular kind of sensation fiction, the ghostly tale, but manages to capture what is common to all sensation fiction—the multiple crimes and manifold identities, the instability of sexual relationships, the extravagance of diction and incident.

"Edgardo! You here?" [said Selina Sedilia]
"Yes, dearest."

"And—you—you—have—seen nothing?" said the lady in an agitated voice and nervous manner, turning her face aside to conceal her emotion.

"Nothing—that is, nothing of any account," said Edgardo. "I passed the ghost of your aunt in the park, noticed the spectre of your uncle in the ruined keep, and observed the familiar features of the spirit of your great-grandfather at his usual post. But nothing beyond these trifles, my Selina. Nothing more, love, absolutely nothing."

The young man turned his dark, liquid orbs fondly upon the ingenuous face of his betrothed.

"My own Edgardo!—and you still love me? You still would marry me in spite of this dark mystery which surrounds me? In spite of the fatal history of my race? In spite of the ominous predictions of my aged nurse?"

"I would, Selina;" and the young man passed his arm around her yielding waist. The two lovers gazed at each other's faces in unspeakable bliss. Suddenly Selina started.

"Leave me, Edgardo! leave me! A mysterious something—a fatal misgiving—a dark ambiguity—an equivocal mistrust oppresses me. I would be alone!"

The young man arose, and cast a loving glance on the lady. "Then we will be married on the seventeenth."

"The seventeenth," repeated Selina, with a mysterious shudder.

They embraced and parted. . . .

"The seventeenth," she repeated slowly, with the same fateful shudder. "Ah!—what if he should know that I have another husband living? Dare I reveal to him that I have two legitimate and three natural children? Dare I repeat to him the history of my youth? Dare I confess that at the age of seven I poisoned my sister, by putting verdigris in her cream-tarts,—that I threw my cousin from a swing at the age of twelve? That the lady's-maid who incurred the displeasure of my girlhood now lies at the bottom of the horse-pond? No! no! he is too pure,—too good,—too innocent, —to hear such improper conversation!" and her whole body writhed as she rocked to and fro in a paroxysm of grief. . . .

. . . a hand was laid upon her arm, and with a shriek the Lady Selina fell on her knees before the spectre of Sir Guy.

CHAPTER II.

"Forbear, Selina," said the phantom in a hollow voice.

"Why should I forbear?" responded Selina haughtily, as she recovered her courage. "You know the secret of our race?"

Passionate Heroines: Fallen, Sensation, and Fleshly   133

"I do. Understand me,—I do not object to the eccentricities of your youth. I know the fearful destiny which, pursuing you, led you to poison your sister and drown your lady's-maid. I know the awful doom which I have brought upon this house! But if you make away with these children"—

"Well," said the Lady Selina hastily.

"They will haunt you!"

"Well, I fear them not," said Selina, drawing her superb figure to its full height.

"Yes, but, my dear child, what place are they to haunt? The ruin is sacred to your uncle's spirit. Your aunt monopolises the park, and, I must be allowed to state, not unfrequently trespasses upon the grounds of others. The horse-pond is frequented by the spirit of your maid, and your murdered sister walks these corridors. To be plain, there is no room at Sloperton Grange for another ghost. I cannot have them in my room,—for you know I don't like children. Think of this, rash girl, and forbear! Would you, Selina," said the phantom mournfully,—"would you force your great-grandfather's spirit to take lodgings elsewhere?"

Lady Selina's hand trembled; the lighted candle fell from her nerveless fingers.

"No," she cried passionately; "never!" and fell fainting to the floor.

CHAPTER III.

EDGARDO galloped rapidly towards Sloperton. When the outline of the Grange had faded away in the darkness, he reined his magnificent steed beside the ruins of Guy's Keep. . . . "Come what may, she is mine," he continued, as his thoughts reverted fondly to the fair lady he had quitted. "Yet if she knew all. If she knew that I were a disgraced and ruined man,—a felon and an outcast. If she knew that at the age of fourteen I murdered my Latin tutor and forged my uncle's will. If she knew that I had three wives already, and that the fourth victim of misplaced confidence and my unfortunate peculiarity is expected to be at Sloperton by to-night's train with her baby. But no; she must not know it. Constance must not arrive; Burke the Slogger must attend to that.

"Ha! here he is! . . . Hark ye, serve my purpose . . . The 5.30 train from Clapham will be due at Sloperton at 9.25. *It must not arrive!*"

The villain's eyes sparkled as he nodded at Edgardo.

. . . [Having toppled the bridge into the chasm] Burke the Slogger,—for it was he,—with a fiendish chuckle seated himself on [the Sloperton side of] the divided railway track and awaited the coming of the train.

A shriek from the woods announced its approach. For an instant Burke the Slogger saw the glaring of a red lamp. The ground trembled. The train was going with fearful rapidity. Another second and it had reached the bank. Burke the Slogger uttered a fiendish laugh. But the next moment the train leaped across the chasm, striking the rails exactly even, and dashing out the life of Burke the Slogger, sped away to Sloperton.

The first object that greeted Edgardo, as he rode up to the station on the arrival of the train, was the body of Burke the Slogger hanging on the cow-catcher; the second was the face of his deserted wife looking from the window of a second-class carriage.[40]

Margaret Oliphant, like Eliza Lynn Linton, succeeds in the hectic world of Victorian publishing.[41] Supporting three children and a nephew (beyond their majority, in some cases), she writes novels, tales, and reviews for fifty years, ultimately producing an oeuvre larger than Dickens'. Oliphant's reviews are excellent specimens of Victorian criticism. At best, she shows how bright the reviewers could be; at worst, how righteous they often were. Oliphant is particularly adept at doing what Arnold admired so much in Burke—turning suddenly around and recognizing an opposing truth. She provides both sides of a debate by defining, often more eloquently than partisans, the excellences of a work which she ultimately condemns. This heterodoxy helps make Margaret Oliphant so representative a Victorian voice. She is as complex as the sensation novel and the period's response to it.

Oliphant's complexity appears immediately when we try to locate her on the critical spectrum of sensation reviews. She has affinities with both Justin MacCarthy and *Christian Remembrancer*. Like MacCarthy she recognizes that shocking novelists are responding to a very real cultural need which society has failed to satisfy; like the *Remembrancer* she finds this need subversive. This need also reveals another aspect of Oliphant's complexity. Like her sister conservatives, Eliza Lynn Linton and Geraldine Jewsbury,[42] Oliphant writes novels which reviewers related to the contemporary malaise. "Mrs. Oliphant is a writer of a very different stamp from those [sensation novelists] already described, but she seems equally incapable of appreciating the motives and principles of spiritual life. . . . [Even her *Chronicles of Carlingford*] have their sensational portions."[43]

Finally, and most important for this work, is Oliphant's complex response to women in fiction. As early as 1855 she laments in *Blackwood's* not only the aggressive "unsexed" quality of the heroines of women's fiction, but also the tepid fatuity of the heroines of men's fiction. She says of Dickens and Thackeray:

> . . . heroines are a sadly featureless class of well-intentioned young women in these days. . . . In the ordinary type of heroines —in the Agnes Wickfield, the Ada, the Kate Nickleby [*David Copperfield, Bleak House. Nicholas Nickleby*]—Mr Dickens is very generally successful. These young ladies are pretty enough, amiable enough, generous enough, to fill their necessary places with great credit and propriety, but to produce an individual woman is another and quite a different matter.
>
> . . . If we do not bid Mr Thackeray create a woman of the highest order, or if we are doubtful of his capacity for this delicate formation, we may still beg him to add a little common-sense to his feminine goodness. When these tender pretty fools are rational creatures, the world of Mr Thackeray's imagination will have a better atmosphere; for besides marrying, and contriving opportunities to give in marriage, besides the nursery and its necessities, there are certain uses for womankind in this world of ours, and we are not so rich in good influences as to forfeit any of them.[44]

Even Bulwer-Lytton, whom Oliphant considered the greatest Victorian novelist, could not escape her criticism.

> He would yield to no one in chivalrous devotion to woman's merits. . . . But the tone strikes us as a little out of keeping with the times. . . . In fact his conception of female excellence tastes a little of the old school. . . . Not that our author denies intellect to women, but he regards it as a misfortune. . . . Even the virtue of constancy . . . suffers in its dignity by this view of feminine nature: it is a sort of unreasoning fidelity.[45]

On the other hand, the male novelist whose women shocked many reviewers—Charles Reade—receives praise from Oliphant for his ability to excel at both types of heroines, the old and the new. Of traditional Lucy in *Love Me Little, Love Me Long* (1859), Oliphant says, "the great charm about her is that she is a perfect lady—courtesy is almost her passion"; of Reade's aggressive "new" women like Peg in *Peg Woffington* and Christie in *Christie Johnstone* (1853), Oliphant declaims:

> it is the very ideal of womankind . . . a being full of power and brilliancy, and daring, and intuitive perception—full, indeed, of what we can describe only as genius, in distinction from the more manageable and practical talents of ordinary life. . . . That Mr. Dickens never dreamed of such a being, nor even the broader intelligence of Mr. Thackeray, nor the more courtly and more diversified genius of Lord Lytton, it is unnecessary to say.[46]

Oliphant's various types of complexity come together in her response to sensation fiction. Here she is both representative and distinctive. She represents the many reviewers who recognized woman's intimate tie to sensationalism. *Saturday Review,* for example, links woman and sensationalism by refusing to distinguish between the major female literary efforts of the period—composing hymns and writing novels. "The stage of intellectual fever through which able men have passed when they were young is replaced, in the case of girls of talent, by a stage of moral morbidity. At first this finds vent in hymns, and it turns in the end to novels."[47] In America, *Round Table* echoes the laments of *London Quarterly* and *Athenaeum* in its highly rhetorical question about readers of illustrated sensation magazines: "What manner of wives and mothers are young girls to make, half whose lives are being passed in taking in such delectable mental nourishment?"[48]

Sharing such concern, Margaret Oliphant recognizes that if sensation novels victimize women, then the victimizers of women are women. Why do such novels exist, and why are they so popular with women? Either readers imagine that real life is as licentious as shocking fiction claims, and they enjoy reading about licentiousness; or readers recognize the unreality of the fiction, and still enjoy reading about licentiousness. In either case, the basic issue is the moral health of that enormous consumer of fiction, that supposed moral center of society—woman. This focus upon woman as reader distinguishes Oliphant from the male orientation of Geraldine Jewsbury, *Victoria,* and *Christian Remembrancer.* Jewsbury in a reader's report for Bentley's writes, "if I were a *man* reading this MS [*Dolly*] I shd enquire 'are the young women of England trying to qualify themselves for Courtezans?'—the breaking down of all sense of

shame & modesty, opens the way to that bottomless pit."[49]
Victoria expresses publicly this same worry about what *male* readers would think of women. "What, we may ask, will ultimately be the estimate of the other sex, if men put faith in such portraitures?" The answer? "It must rapidly sink to the lowest depths a Sensational author can crawl to, and principle, fidelity, and honour in a woman, will come to be regarded as unattainable as the philosopher's stone."[50] *Christian Remembrancer* is even more male oriented. Fearing "the triumph of mere feminine fascination, before which man falls, prostrate and helpless,"[51] the reviewer was envisioning castration. What will happen to society if oversexed women unsexed the all-providing male? This question is not primary for Oliphant.Her distinctive concern is the nature and destiny of woman.

Oliphant's four essays on sensation fiction appeared in *Blackwood's* in 1855, 1862, 1863, and 1867.[52] The 1855 essay is doubly prescient. Oliphant not only recognizes the phenomenon of sensationalism fully half a decade before *The Woman in White* officially inaugurates the shocking sixties; she was already concerned with woman's responsibility for sensational behavior in literature and life. "The grossness of the book [*Jane Eyre*] was such grossness as only could be perpetrated by a woman. . . . this furious love-making was but a wild declaration of the 'Rights of Woman' in a new aspect. . . . Here is your true revolution. France is but one of the Western Powers; woman is the half of the world."[53] Oliphant's ability to go on and celebrate the power of Charlotte Brontë—"*Jane Eyre* remains one of the most remarkable works of modern times" (558)—attests to her complexity, and allows her to accomplish a still more remarkable feat. In a postscript which tempered none of her reservations and insists again upon the "peculiar" quality of Brontë's power, Oliphant makes one of her wonderful reversals, generously and intelligently paying the tribute of a minor novelist to a major one.

> Since writing the above, we have heard of an event which will give to some of its comments an air of harsh and untimely criticism. The author of *Jane Eyre*, the most distinguished female writer of her time, has ended her labours, and exchanged these fretting shows of things for the realities which last for ever. To associate bodily weakness or waning life with the name of this remarkable woman, did not occur to us; nor can we think of cancelling now

what we have said; but we repeat again over her grave, the great admiration with which we have always regarded her wonderful powers. No one in her time has grasped with such extraordinary force the scenes and circumstances through which her story moved; no one has thrown as strong an individual life into place and locality. Her passionate and fearless nature, her wild, warm heart, are transfused into the magic world she has created—a world which no one can enter without yielding to the irresistible fascination of her personal influence. Perhaps no other writer of her time has impressed her mark so clearly on contemporary literature, or drawn so many followers into her own peculiar path; and she leaves no one behind worthy to take the pre-eminent and leading place of the author of *Jane Eyre*. (568)

In 1862 Margaret Oliphant writes another mixed review of sensationalism. Besides praising the ability of shocking writers (particularly Collins in *The Woman in White*) to build compelling plots, she acknowledges, as she did with Brontë, the power that morally ambiguous characters like Collins' Count Fosco exercises over her and the reading public. Oliphant warns, however, that works of such genius were dangerous models and that Collins' imitators, like Brontë's, would reproduce the moral limitations of his characters without achieving the attractive complications. By 1867 Oliphant has evolved considerably. Her final essay on sensationalism is less mixed than its predecessors because her worst fears seem confirmed. Charlotte Brontë has had no worthy successors; the passionate heroines and Fosco-figures who now dominate fiction lack Brontë's force and Collins' finesse. Even as she laments the impact and size of Braddon's school, however, Oliphant remains complex enough to give the devil her due. The three "honours" which partisan reviewers usually bestowed upon Braddon—historical importance, literary craft, moral orthodoxy—Oliphant acknowledges. "These are the real results which Miss Braddon has achieved, and we do not grudge her the glory of them."[54] Oliphant cannot, however, take sensational moralizing too seriously because she believes that the moral laxness which has "infected" the present generation of writers and readers is spreading to the next generation. Rhoda Broughton prompts so lengthy a discussion from Oliphant because the first novel of this talented young woman reveals strongly the influence of Braddon (when *Cometh Up as a Flower* appeared anonymously in 1867, Broughton's father forbade her to read it!). Oliphant's concern is again woman's nature and destiny. When Broughton's Nell scorns female society, Oliphant, despite her attempt to explain away this scorn, clearly fears that the strong passions which alienate woman from her "womanhood" will also alienate her from womankind. In her uniquely complex blend of the representative and the distinctive, Oliphant is more than a spokesperson for those many Victorians who fear sensationalism and increasingly doubt the quality of Anglo-American life and letters. Margaret Oliphant is also one of half the human race—attempting to deal with cultural changes which are redefining who she and her millions of sisters are and should be.

Writers who have no genius and little talent, make up for it by displaying their acquaintance with the accessories and surroundings of vice, with the means of seduction, and with what they set forth as the secret tendencies of the heart—tendencies which, according to this interpretation, all point one way. . . .

What is held up to us as the story of the feminine soul as it really exists underneath its conventional coverings, is a very fleshly and unlovely record. Women driven wild with love for the man who leads them on to desperation before he accords that word of encouragement which carries them into the seventh heaven. . . .

. . . The peculiarity of it in England is, that it is oftenest made from the woman's side—that it is women who describe those sensuous raptures—that this intense appreciation of flesh and blood, this eagerness of physical sensation, is represented as the natural sentiment of English girls, and is offered to them not only as the portrait of their own state of mind, but as their amusement and mental food. Such a wonderful phenomenon might exist, and yet society might be innocent of it. It might be the fault of one, or of a limited school, and the mere fact that such ravings are found in print might be no great argument against the purity of the age. But when it is added that the class thus represented does not disown the picture—that, on the contrary, it hangs it up in boudoir and drawing-room—that the books which contain it circulate everywhere, and are read everywhere, and are not contradicted— then the case becomes much more serious. . . . the perplexing fact is that the subjects of this slander make no objections to it.

Miss Braddon is the leader of her school, and to her the first honours ought naturally to be given, but her disciples are many. One of the latest of these disciples is the authoress of 'Cometh up as a Flower,' a novel which has recently won that amount of public approval which is conveyed by praise in the leading papers and a second edition. This book is not a stupid book. . . . The wonderful thing in it is the portrait of the modern young woman as presented from her own point of view. The last wave but one of female novelists was very feminine. Their stories were all family stories, their troubles domestic, their women womanly to the last degree, and their men not much less so. The present influx of young life has changed all that. It has reinstated the injured creature Man in something like his natural character, but unfortunately it has gone to extremes, and moulded its women on the model of men, just as the former school moulded its men on the model of women. The heroine of 'Cometh up as a Flower' is a good case in point. She is not by any means so disagreeable, so vulgar, or so mannish, as at the first beginning she makes herself out to be. Her flippancy, to start with, revolts the reader, and inclines him to pitch the volume to as great a distance from him as is practicable; but if he has patience a little, the girl is not so bad. She is a motherless girl. . . . Ill-brought-up motherless girls, left to grow anyhow, out of all feminine guardianship, have become the ideal of the novelist. There is this advantage in them, that benevolent female readers have the resource of saying "Remember she had no mother," when the heroine falls into any unusual lapse from feminine traditions; but it is odd, to say the least of it, that this phase of youthful life should commend itself so universally to the female novelist. . . .

"How did you get on with all those fine ladies?" inquired my father, kindly.

"Middling" said I; "I did not care much about them. I liked the men better. If I went into society, I should like to go to parties where there are no women, only men." . . .

"That is a sentiment that I think I should keep for home use, my dear, if I were you."

"Should you? Well, perhaps so; but women are so prying and censorious. All the time you are talking to them you feel sure that they are criticising the sit of your tucker, and calculating how much a-yard your dress cost. Now, if you're only pretty and pleasant—indeed, even if you're not either (I mentally classed myself under this latter head)—men are good-natured, and take you as they find you, and make the best of you."

My father did not dispute my position.

These are sentiments which everybody is aware a great many vulgar clever women think it clever and striking to enunciate. The misery of such unhappy ones as throw themselves out of the society of their own sex, their pitiful strivings after the recognition of any stray strong-minded woman who will look over their imperfections, should be sufficient answer to it in any serious point of view. . . . This [feeling of superiority toward women] is one of the popular bits of falsehood by which lively-minded young women are often taken in and led to misrepresent themselves.

And it is another curious feature in second-rate women's books. As a general rule, all the women in these productions, except the one charming heroine, are mean and envious creatures, pulling the exceptional beauty to pieces. Shall we say that the women who write ought to know? But the fact is, that a great many of the women who write live very contentedly in the society of other women, see little else, find their audience and highest appreciation among them, and are surrounded and backed up and applauded by their own sex in a way which men would be very slow to emulate. The pretence [of scorn for female society] seems to imply a certain elevation above her neighbours of the speaker; although the very same woman, if brought to the test, would shrink and recoil and be confounded if her silly and false aspirations could be realised. Of course the patent meaning of it on the lips of a girl like the heroine of the book before us is, that the society she prefers is that of the man with whom she is falling in love, and who has fallen in love with her, and that for the moment the presence of other people is rather a bore than otherwise.

This story, as we have already said, is interesting, not because of its particular plot or incidents, but as a sample of the kind of expression given by modern fiction to modern sentiments from the woman's point of view. Nelly Lestrange has no particular objections to meet her soldier out of doors whenever he pleases to propose it. He takes her in his arms after he has seen her about three times, and she has still no objection. The girl is innocent enough according to all appearance, but she has certainly an odd way of expressing herself for a girl. She wonders if her lover and she, when they meet in heaven, will be "sexless passionless essences," and says, God forbid! She speaks, when a loveless marriage dawns upon her, of giving her shrinking body to the disagreeable bridegroom. There may be nothing wrong in all this, but it is curious language, as we have said, for a girl. And here let us pause to make a necessary discrimination. A *grande passion* is a thing which has to be recognised as possible wherever it is met with in this world. . . . This [*grande passion*] is wrong, sinful, ruinous, but it is not disgusting; whereas those speeches about shrinking bodies and sexless essences are disgusting in the fullest sense of the word. Would that the new novelist, the young beginner in the realm of fiction, could but understand this! . . .

After our free-spoken heroine has come to the climax of her fate, she becomes consumptive and reflective after that loftily pious kind which generally associates itself with this species of immorality; for sensual literature and the carnal mind have a kind of piety quite to themselves, when disappointment and incapacity come upon them. . . . The intense goodness follows the intense sensuousness as by a natural law;—the same natural law, we presume, which makes the wicked witch of romance—the woman who has broken everybody's heart, and spent everybody's money, and desolated everybody's home—sink at last into the most devoted of sisters of charity. The good women who follow the rule of St Vincent de Paul would be little flattered by the suggestion. . . . It would be a task beyond our powers to enter into all the varieties of immorality which the novelists of the day have ingeniously woven into their stories. In these matters the man who writes is at once more and less bold than the woman; he may venture on positive criminality to give piquancy to his details, but it is the female novelist who speaks the most plainly, and whose best characters revel in a kind of innocent indecency, as does the heroine of 'Cometh up as a Flower.' Not that the indecency is always innocent; but there are cases in which it would seem the mere utterance of a certain foolish daring—an ignorance which longs to look knowing—a kind of immodest and indelicate innocence which likes to play with impurity. This is the most dismal feature among all these disagreeable phenomena. Nasty thoughts, ugly suggestions, an imagination which prefers the unclean, is almost more appalling than the facts of actual depravity, because it has no excuse of sudden passion or temptation, and no visible boundary. It is a shame to women so to write; and it is a shame to the women who read and accept as a true representation of themselves and their ways the equivocal talk and fleshly inclinations herein attributed to them. Their patronage of such books is in reality an adoption and acceptance of them. It may be done in carelessness, it may be done in that mere desire for something startling which the monotony of ordinary life is apt to produce; but it is debasing to everybody concerned. Women's rights and women's duties have had enough discussion, perhaps even from the ridiculous point of view. We have most of us made merry over Mr Mill's crotchet on the subject, and over the Dr Marys and Dr Elizabeths; but yet a woman has one duty of invaluable importance to her country and her race which cannot be over-estimated—and that is the duty of being pure. There is perhaps nothing of such vital consequence to a nation. Our female critics are fond of making demonstrations of indignation over the different punishment given by the world to the sin of man and that of woman in this respect. But all philosophy notwithstanding, and leaving the religious question untouched, there can be no possible doubt that the wickedness of man is less ruinous, less disastrous to the world in general, than the wickedness of woman. That is the climax of all misfortunes to the race. . . .

We are no preacher to call English ladies to account, and we have no tragical message to deliver even had we the necessary pulpit to do it in; but it certainly would be well if they would put a stop to nasty novels. It would be well for literature, well for the tone of society, and well for the young people who are growing up used to this kind of reading. Considering how low the tone of literary excellence is, and how little power of exciting interest exists after all in these equivocal productions, the sacrifice would not seem a great one. (258–60, 267–69, 274–75)

Two subsequent phases of the debate indicate in a brief, final way the complexity of the sensation controversy and of Margaret Oliphant. Braddon is befriended in the 1860s by two eminent Victorian novelists—the very two, in fact, whom Margaret Oliphant reveres most, Charles Reade and Bulwer-Lytton. After reading Oliphant's 1867 review, Braddon writes to Bulwer a letter which is a good antidote against seeing Braddon and other female sensationalists as too single-mindedly subversive. In her cry of outrage, Braddon interestingly assumes that the *Blackwood's* reviewer is male.

After a general condemnation of the sensual tone predominant in second rate novels the reviewer goes on to say "The girls of our acquaintance in general are very nice girls; they do not, so far as we are aware—notwithstanding a natural proclivity towards the society, when it is to be had, of their natural companions in existence—pant for indiscriminate kisses, or go mad for indiscriminate men. And yet here stands the problem which otherwise is not to be solved. *It is thus that Miss Braddon* & Miss Thomas & a host of other writers explain their feelings. These ladies might not know, it is quite possible, any better. *They might not be aware how young women of good blood & good training feel."*

Now can anything exceed the covert insolence of this? Who is this writer who dares to tell me that I do not know how a virtuous or well-bred woman feels. Does he judge by the evidence of my books. I say boldly—No.

It is quite true that I have in Aurora Floyd endeavoured to tell the story of a foolish girl who eloped with her father's groom. But I declare that Aurora Floyd is not *"a woman who marries her groom in a fit of sensual passion"*—as the writer in Blackwood broadly states. Is this gentleman one of the "nice men," who are always nasty men, I wonder, by the bye. It is also true that in "The Doctor's Wife" I described the sentimental fancy of a young married woman for a man who seems to her the ideal of all her girlish dreams. And this study of a silly girl's romantic passion is not a story which I would care to place in the hands of "the young person," but I defy any critic—however nice, or however nasty—to point to one page or one paragraph in that book—or in any other book of mine—which contains the lurking poison of sensuality.

Why then should I be placed at the head of the list of those who have offended in this particular. Of all horrors sensuality is that from which I shrink with the most utter abhorrence—and to you, Lord Lytton, as a phrenologist, I may venture to say—without fear of provoking ridicule—that all those who have examined my head phrenologically know that this sin is one utterly foreign to my organization, that indeed, the great weakness of my brain is the want of that animal power—which, as I am told, gives force & activity to the higher organs.

Forgive me for boring you with this long letter. I daresay I write foolishly—illogically—but I am stung to the very quick by this most false cruel imputation.[55]

In turn, Margaret Oliphant gets in the last word. Looking back in *The Victorian Age of English Literature* (1892), she evaluates Braddon as she did Brontë in the 1855 postscript—in terms not of the moral decline which Oliphant had feared, but of the literary craft which she, as a professional, can ultimately acknowledge as primary.

Miss Braddon, now Mrs. Maxwell, is perhaps the most complete story-teller of the whole, [sensation school] and has not confined herself to that or any other type of character, but has ranged widely over all English scenes and subjects, always with a power of interesting and occupying the public, which is one of the first qualities of the novelist. If it has ever happened to the reader to find himself, while travelling, out of the reach of books and left to the drift of cheap editions for the entertainment of his stray hours, he will then appreciate what it is, among the levity and insignificance of many of the younger writers, to find the name of Miss Braddon on a title-page, and know that he is likely to find some sense of life as a whole, and some reflection of the honest sentiments of humanity, amid the froth of flirtation and folly which has lately invaded, like a destroying flood, the realms of fiction.[56]

III

The Victorian critics who were disturbed by sensation fiction in the 1860s were equally troubled by a parallel phenomenon in poetry: the exploration, primarily by men, of *their* heterodox perceptions of women in love. George Meredith's *Modern Love* (1862), A.C. Swinburne's *Poems and Ballads, First Series* (1866), and D.G. Rossetti's *Poems* (1870) provoke heated protests against what Robert Buchanan calls the "fleshliness" of their creations. Reviewers note the connection between sensation fiction and "fleshly" poetry.[57] One writer calls Swinburne "the poet of what is known as the sensation school of literature," a school he defines as "appealing not to the intellect and the moral reason, not to the imagination and the affections, but to the senses and the appetites."[58] To alarmed critics serious poetry as well as popular fiction seems suddenly bent on probing "a deep and painful subject": "the miseries of married love as it exists in our modern society" and the still more perplexing miseries of unmarried love—"the rotten places in our social system."[59] The poets respond with a defense as extreme as these attacks. Swinburne insists that his art deals with purely aesthetic problems. Twentieth-century readers have usually followed his lead. But Victorian readers point out that what the poets wish to escape are not current social questions but conventional answers about the behavior of men and women in love. Critics recognize a close connection between "aesthetic" or "fleshly" poetry and a topic of immediate public concern in the sensation sixties: sensuality, in men *and* women. Two articulate reviewers explicitly draw this connection: Alfred Austin attacks "The Poetry of the Period" as proof of the effeminization of English literature, and Walter Pater defends "Aesthetic Poetry" as an example of contemporary philosophical interest in moments of intense experience.

The women portrayed by "fleshly" poets share with the heroines of sensation fiction both a passionate nature and an unsettling beauty, a particular beauty often associated with Pre-Raphaelite painting. The young English painters who signed themselves "PRB" (Pre-Raphaelite Brotherhood) in the early 1850s adopted an austere style which first struck critics by the tense awkwardness of its figures, painted in painfully vivid color and relentlessly sharp detail. The effect, critics felt, was a disturbing sense of the unnatural. Among the most vivid images of the new painting were its women: John Everett Millais' *Ophelia* (1851-52) D.G. Rossetti's Mary (*Ecce Ancilla Domini!*) (1850), Holman Hunt's kept woman in *The Awakening Conscience* (1853). Unbound hair, parted lips, bright color, and luxuriant detail hint at a suppressed life at odds with unsensuous faces and figures in these apparently religious or poetic works. In the 1860s, Rossetti's lush paintings of massive, sensuous female figures hint more strongly at a dark, half-hidden power in the Pre-Raphaelite woman (see Illustration 7). Contemporary viewers and writers recognize her latent eroticism. When sensation novelist M.E. Braddon wants to tell readers of *Lady Audley's Secret* that the angelic Lucy Grahame is not what she seems, Braddon has her hero discover Lucy's portrait:

> Yes, the painter must have been a pre-Raphaelite. No one but a pre-Raphaelite would have painted, hair by hair, those feathery masses of ringlets, with every glimmer of gold, and every shadow of pale brown. No one but a pre-Raphaelite would have so exaggerated every attribute of that delicate face as to give a lurid brightness to the blonde complexion, and a strange, sinister light to the deep blue eyes. No one but a pre-Raphaelite would have given to that pretty pouting mouth the hard and almost wicked look it had in the portrait.
>
> It was so like, and yet so unlike. It was as if you had burned strange-colored fires before my lady's face, and by their influence brought out new lines and new expressions never seen in it before. The perfection of feature, the brilliance of coloring, were there; but . . . my lady, in his portrait of her, had something of the aspect of a beautiful fiend.[60]

When in the same year George Meredith publishes his sonnet sequence *Modern Love,* the reviewer who suggests that a better title would be *Modern Lust* accuses Meredith of "poetic pre-Raphaelitism."[61]

In fact the "fleshly" or Pre-Raphaelite woman differs from the sensation heroine in several important respects. In the first place, fleshly women, though not angels, fallen or otherwise, are never unmasked as devils or villains and put aside by their lovers for more conventional partners. Fleshly poems and paintings lack the reassuring orthodox moral framework of sensation novels. In the second place, despite suggestions of physical power, the fleshly woman remains a largely silent, inactive, and mysterious figure, usually presented in painting or poem as she might be viewed from a distance by her troubled, uncomprehending lover or creator. Meredith's *Modern Love* opens with a striking image of the sensual but psychologically alienated relation between men and women explored by these painters and poets.

7. Lady Lilith
Dante Gabriel Rossetti, 1867 (The Metropolitan Museum of Art,
Rogers Fund, 1908)

8. The Adams Memorial (Clover Hooper Adams)
Augustus Saint-Gaudens (Rock Creek Cemetery, Washington, D.C.)

> By this he knew she wept with waking eyes:
> That, at his hand's light quiver by her head,
> The strange low sobs that shook their common bed,
> Were called into her with a sharp surprise,
> And strangled mute . . .
> . . . .
> Like sculptured effigies they might be seen
> Upon their marriage-tomb, the sword between;
> Each wishing for the sword that severs all.

The scene is laid in the shocking intimacy of the marriage bed, but husband and wife could not be more radically divided.

The male protagonist in *Modern Love* and other "fleshly" poems glimpses but cannot completely overcome the perceptual barriers erected by conventional notions of masculine and feminine behavior in love. In Rossetti's "The Blessed Damozel" these barriers are represented by the separation of death. The dead woman of his poem is physically present but separated from her lover by a spiritual gulf; she stands, literally, on the floor of heaven, stooping and speaking across the clouds to him on earth "Until her bosom must have made/The bar she leaned on warm." Lover and damozel, however, are clearly not speaking the same language, and when at last the lover does manage to hear her, he can only make out their separation, and her despair:

> And then she cast her arm along
>   The golden barriers,
> And laid her face between her hands,
>   And wept. (I heard her tears.)

Rossetti's "Jenny" repeats the same theme—the passionate woman viewed from a distance—in a more modern setting, but criticizes the masculine attempt to comprehend the woman. The poem is a monologue by a man to a pretty young prostitute who has (innocently) fallen asleep and so cannot answer his questions.

> Why, Jenny, as I watch you there,—
> For all your wealth of loosened hair,
> Your silk ungirdled and unlac'd
> And warm sweets open to the waist,
> All golden in the lamplight's gleam,—

. . . .
I wonder what you're thinking of.
    If of myself you think at all,
What is the thought? . . .

Characteristically, the speaker has moments of insight in his
monologue, but his insights are constantly obscured by more
conventional responses—though sometimes he is perceptive
enough to realize when he has stopped being honest. He can
notice that Jenny is, after all, not so very different from "my
cousin Nell," can then forget the real woman for the "cipher of
man's changeless sum of lust," and finally can admit his own
failure to overcome conventional reactions to the prostitute:

And must I mock you to the last,
Ashamed of my own shame,—aghast
Because some thoughts not born amiss
Rose at a poor fair face like this?

The speaker hopes finally that his half-suppressed thoughts will
prove "a far gleam which I may near,/A dark path I can strive to
clear."

Swinburne's poems explore more exotic varieties of passion
and insist emphatically on the acuteness of physical desire. He,
too, often uses male speakers to address a silent, enigmatic,
passionate, and provocative woman. For Swinburne, as for Rossetti, there is something valuable in passionate desire, not to be
grasped by conventional notions of love. As he puts it in the
rather extravagant mock-litany, "Dolores":

Time turns the old days to derision
    Our loves into corpses or wives;
And marriage and death and division
    Make barren our lives.
. . . .
Thou [Dolores] wert fair in the fearless old fashion,
    And thy limbs are as melodies yet,
And move to the music of passion
    With lithe and lascivious regret.
What ailed us, O gods, to desert you
    For the creeds that refuse and restrain?
Come down and redeem us from virtue,
    Our Lady of Pain.

Swinburne is more successful than Rossetti or Meredith at dramatizing the passionate voice of the woman herself—his "Anactoria," a monologue by Sappho, was especially objectionable to critics. But among the fleshly poets Swinburne is an exception. Most fleshly poetry, though disturbingly sensual, could be said to be a troubled inversion of Victorian woman-worship. Woman is no longer the angel-wife but her fallen sister, an erotic icon whose worshipper is beset by doubts he can neither resolve nor overcome.

The Pre-Raphaelite woman provokes especially strong responses when she appears in poetry, partly because poetry claims attention as serious art. It is addressed, not to female readers or to those whose tastes have been whetted by sensational journalism, but to the highly respectable audience that Tennyson created. Attacks on Meredith's *Modern Love* express a common feeling that Meredith has violated literary as well as social decorum by putting a study of contemporary adultery into serious verse. The reaction to *"Modern Lust"* is mild, however, compared to the storm which follows the publication of Swinburne's *Poems and Ballads* in 1866. John Morley, writing for the *Saturday Review*, is aesthetically as well as morally offended by the violence of Swinburne's descriptions of women: "we may ask him whether there is really nothing in women worth singing about except 'quivering flanks' and 'splendid supple thighs,' 'hot sweet throats' and 'hotter hands than fire,' and their blood as 'hot wan wine of love'? Is purity to be expunged from the catalogue of desirable qualities? . . . Every picture is hot and garish with this excess of flaming violent colour."[62]

The poems in Rossetti's 1870 volume are less "hot and garish," but here too critics are troubled by the combination of a lush style with imagery of spiritual love drawn from the Bible and Dante. The *Quarterly Review* is repelled by the "revolting picturesqueness" of Rossetti's descriptions, objecting particularly because Rossetti "endeavours to attach a spiritual meaning to the animal passions. . . . Descriptions repulsively realistic are mixed up with imagery like that in Solomon's Song." The reviewer concludes that "Love, as he [Rossetti] represents it, appears not as romantic passion, or even as natural ardour, but as pious sensuality."[63] In all three poets, and in the PRB painters, critics were irritated by what seemed an inappropriate conjunction of sensuous style with elevated feeling, and of sensational subject with the forms of high art.

Robert Buchanan, the most persistent and outspoken critic of Pre-Raphaelitism, finds style as subervisive as subject matter in the presentation of the "fleshly" woman. According to Buchanan's famous diatribe in the *Contemporary Review* (1871), "The Fleshly School of Poetry: Mr. D.G. Rossetti," the over-wrought style of the Pre-Raphaelite poets simply mirrors the fundamental immorality of their attitudes toward love and women. They exalt flesh over spirit.

[Fleshliness] . . . may indeed be described as the distinct quality held in common by all the members of the last sub-Tennysonian school, and it is a quality which becomes unwholesome when there is no moral or intellectual quality to temper and control it. Fully conscious of this themselves, the fleshly gentlemen have bound themselves by solemn league and covenant to extol fleshliness as the distinct and supreme end of poetic and pictorial art; to aver that poetic expression is greater than poetic thought, and by inference that the body is greater than the soul, and sound superior to sense; and that the poet, properly to develop his poetic faculty, must be an intellectual hermaphrodite, to whom the very facts of day and night are lost in a whirl of aesthetic terminology. . . . It would be scarcely worth while, however, to inquire into the pretensions of the writers on merely literary grounds, because sooner or later all literature finds its own level, whatever criticism may say or do in the matter; but it unfortunately happens in the present case that the fleshly school of verse-writers are, so to speak, public offenders, because they are diligently spreading the seeds of disease broadcast wherever they are read and understood. Their complaint too is catching, and carries off many young persons. What the complaint is, and how it works, may be seen on a very slight examination of the works of Mr. Dante Gabriel Rossetti, to whom we shall confine our attention in the present article.

. . . [The same] qualities, which impress the casual spectator of the photographs from his pictures, are to be found abundantly among his verses. There is the same thinness and transparence of design, the same combination of the simple and the grotesque, the same morbid deviation from healthy forms of life, the same sense of weary, wasting, yet exquisite sensuality; nothing virile, nothing tender, nothing completely sane; a superfluity of extreme sensibility, of delight in beautiful forms, hues, and tints, and a deep-seated indifference to all agitating forces and agencies, all tumultuous griefs and sorrows, all the thunderous stress of life, and all the straining storm of speculation.

. . . Mr. Swinburne was wilder, more outrageous, more blasphemous, and his subjects were more atrocious in themselves; yet the hysterical tone slew the animalism, the furiousness of epithet lowered the sensation; and the first feeling of disgust at such themes as "Laus Veneris" and "Anactoria," faded away into comic amazement. It was only a little mad boy letting off squibs; not a great strong man, who might be really dangerous to society. "I *will* be naughty!" screamed the little boy; but, after all, what did it matter? It is quite different, however, when a grown man, with the self-control and easy audacity of actual experience, comes forward to chronicle his amorous sensations, and, first proclaiming in a loud voice his literary maturity, and consequent responsibility, shamelessly prints and publishes such a piece of writing as this sonnet on "Nuptial Sleep":—

> *At length their long kiss severed, with sweet smart:*
> *And as the last slow sudden drops are shed*
> *From sparkling eaves when all the storm has fled,*
> *So singly flagged the pulses of each heart.*
> *Their bosoms sundered, with the opening start*
> *Of married flowers to either side outspread*
> *From the knit stem; yet still their mouths, burnt red,*
> *Fawned on each other where they lay apart.*

> Sleep sank them lower than the tide of dreams,
>   And their dreams watched them sink, and slid away.
> Slowly their souls swam up again, through gleams
>   Of watered light and dull drowned waifs of day;
> Till from some wonder of new woods and streams
>   He woke, and wondered more: for there she lay.

This, then, is "the golden affluence of words, the firm outline, the justice and chastity of form." Here is a full-grown man, presumably intelligent and cultivated, putting on record for other full-grown men to read, the most secret mysteries of sexual connection, and that with so sickening a desire to reproduce the sensual mood, so careful a choice of epithet to convey mere animal sensations, that we merely shudder at the shameless nakedness. We are no purists in such matters. We hold the sensual part of our nature to be as holy as the spiritual or intellectual part, and we believe that such things must find their equivalent in all; but it is neither poetic, nor manly, nor even human, to obtrude such things as the themes of whole poems. It is simply nasty. Nasty as it is, we are very mistaken if many readers do not think it nice.

. . . We cannot forbear expressing our wonder, by the way, at the kind of women whom it seems the unhappy lot of these gentlemen to encounter. We have lived as long in the world as they have, but never yet came across persons of the other sex who conduct themselves in the manner described. Females who bite, scratch, scream, bubble, munch, sweat, writhe, twist, wriggle, foam, and in a general way slaver over their lovers, must surely possess some extraordinary qualities to counteract their otherwise most offensive mode of conducting themselves. It appears, however, on examination, that their poet-lovers conduct themselves in a similar manner. They, too, bite, scratch, scream, bubble, munch, sweat, writhe, twist, wriggle, foam, and slaver, in a style frightful to hear of. Let us hope that it is only their fun, and that they don't mean half they say. At times, in reading such books as this, one cannot help wishing that things had remained for ever in the asexual state described in Mr. Darwin's great chapter on Palingenesis. We get very weary of this protracted hankering after a person of the other sex; it seems meat, drink, thought, sinew, religion for the fleshly school. There is no limit to the fleshliness. . . . Whether he is writing of the holy Damozel, or of the Virgin herself, or of Lilith, or Helen, or of Dante, or of Jenny the streetwalker, he is fleshly all over, from the roots of his hair to the tip of his toes; never a true lover merging his identity into that of the beloved one; never spiritual, never tender; always self-conscious and aesthetic.

. . . A poem is a poem, first as to the soul, next as to the form. The fleshly persons who wish to create form for its own sake are merely pronouncing their own doom. But *such* form![64]

The very vividness and vociferousness of such attacks provoke objections from some more moderate critics. *Fraser's* is indignant at the moral hypocrisy of both the critics and the society they claim to protect from Swinburne's indecencies.[65] The *Nation* reviewer, though he finds Swinburne's passionate women and men rather low than lofty, confesses himself "not wholly sorry" to get "a knowledge of characters and passions that we should hardly be able to conceive were they not presented with such extraordinary power by so great a genius."[66] Richard Grant White in the *Galaxy* challenges the notion that purity means sexual innocence.

. . . the woman who cannot read any of these herself without harm, is already long past mental contamination. The question is plainly this, Is sexual love in itself impure? or is it in itself entirely without moral character, and under certain circumstances as rightful as it is joyful, and under others criminal and in the end full of bitterness? Will men who have wives and mothers, and women who hope to be wives and mothers decide for the former? And if it is not impure, filling, as it does, so large a place and having so important a function in man's life, shall it be excluded from the domain of art, of high art? . . . Let every man who can see in this passage only blasphemy and impurity, let every man who measures a woman's innocence by her physiological ignorance and her bodily torpidity, exclude this book from his house and the houses of all those in whom he takes an interest, as he would keep poison from his table; for it swells to bursting with such venom. There will be others who, perceiving at once the dramatic spirit through the lyric form of these poems, will find in them neither blasphemy nor the intention of blasphemy, and who, breathing the same moral atmosphere as the poet, will find in his song impurity neither of word nor thought. To all such readers they will not only be harmless, but full of deep and strong delight. Their beauty, and the joy they give, is heroic, and will consume small souls. It is like the beauty of the poet's "Dolores," to whom he says:

> Thou wert fair in the fearless old fashion,
> And thy limbs are as melodies yet.

His whole book is an expression of beauty and of passion in this fearless old fashion: naked, free and strong. Naked not for the sake of nakedness, but for the sake of freedom, strength and beauty.[67]

Swinburne himself took the offensive shortly after his *Poems and Ballads* were published. In *Notes on Poems and Reviews* (1866) he attacks his critics for invoking the pure woman reader in order to make moral judgments on aesthetic questions. Though his poetry seemed to most readers to flout accepted moral standards, Swinburne the critic argues that great literature should be moral. But he protests that "feminine" purity must not define "masculine" morality for art.

The question at issue is wider than any between a single writer and his critics, or it might well be allowed to drop. It is this: whether or not the first and last requisite of art is to give no offence; whether or not all that cannot be lisped in the nursery or fingered in the schoolroom is therefore to be cast out of the library; whether or not the domestic circle is to be for all men and writers the outer limit and extreme horizon of their world of work. For to this we have come; and all students of art must face the matter as it stands. Who has not heard it asked, in a final and triumphant tone, whether this book or that can be read aloud by her mother to a young girl? whether such and such a picture can properly be exposed to the eyes of young persons? If you reply that this is nothing to the point, you fall at once into the ranks of the immoral. Never till now, and nowhere but in England, could so monstrous an absurdity rear for one moment its deformed and eyeless head. In no past century were artists ever bidden to work on these terms; nor are they now, except among us. The disease, of course, afflicts the meanest members of the body with most virulence. Nowhere is cant at once so foul-mouthed and so tight-laced as in the penny,twopenny, threepenny, or sixpenny press. Nothing is so favourable to the undergrowth of real indecency as this overshadowing foliage of fictions, this artificial network of propierties. *L'Arioste rit au soleil, l'Arétin ricane à l'ombre.* The whiter the sepulchre without, the ranker the rottenness within. Every touch of plaster is a sign of advancing decay. The virtue of our critical journals is a dowager of somewhat dubious antecedents: every day that thins and shrivels her cheek thickens and hardens the paint on it; she consumes more chalk and ceruse than would serve a whole courtful of crones. 'It is to be presumed,' certainly, that in her case 'all is not sweet, all is not sound.' The taint on her fly-blown reputation is hard to overcome by patches and per-fumery. Literature, to be worthy of men, must be large, liberal, sincere; and cannot be chaste if it be prudish. Purity and prudery cannot keep house together. Where free speech and fair play are interdicted, foul hints and evil suggestions are hatched into fetid life. And if literature indeed is not to deal with the full life of man and the whole nature of things, let it be cast aside with the rods and rattles of childhood. . . .

When England has again such a school of poetry, so headed and so followed, as she has had at least twice before, or as France has now; when all higher forms of the various art are included within the larger limits of a stronger race; then, if such a day should ever rise or return upon us, it will be once more remembered that the office of adult art is neither puerile nor feminine, but virile; that its purity is not that of the cloister or the harem; that all things are good in its sight, out of which good work may be produced. . . . Then all accepted work will be noble and chaste in the wider masculine sense, not truncated and curtailed, but out-spoken and full-grown. . . .[68]

Insisting that his poetry was both pure and "virile," Swin-burne attempted to redefine the meaning of "masculine" and "feminine." Most readers found his definition hard to accept. The *Spectator* replied, "it is precisely the unmanliness of the book . . . that is so suffocating. . . . We hold that, in this volume at least, Mr. Swinburne is both unmasculine and un-feminine. He is unmanly or effeminate, which you please, and they mean morally the same thing."[69] Pre-Raphaelite men and women fit no simple, polarized norms of masculine and feminine behavior. The women were neither wholly married angels nor wholly abandoned prostitutes; the men who loved them con-fessed that they were unable to keep separate their feelings of chivalrous devotion and physical desire. From an orthodox view, "fleshly" poetry portrayed unacceptable feelings in both men and women.

A few critics viewed fleshly poetry, like sensation fiction, as the symptom of a major cultural change. Alfred Austin links not only Swinburne but even Tennyson and Trollope to Braddon and her passionate sensation heroines. Writing for *Temple Bar* in 1869, Austin takes up Swinburne's argument for a "masculine" literature and turns it against his poetry in an all-out attack on "feminine" art. For Austin the source of the trouble is clear. The literature of the period, like the Girl of the Period, has been infected by the Woman Question. Woman's influence is to blame.

If we were asked to sum up the characteristics of Mr. Tennyson's compositions in a single word, the word we should employ would be "feminine," and if we had to do the same for Mr. Browning's genius, the word inevitably selected would be "studious." The pen of the latter is essentially the pen of a student; the muse of the former is essentially—we must not say the muse of a woman, for we should be rendering ourselves liable to misconception, but—a feminine muse. And in these two salient qualities they are un-questionably representative men, and typify two of the prominent tendencies of the time. We have just had, from a much revered source, an essay on the Subjection of Women; but we think it would not be difficult to show that men, and especially in the domain of Art, are, and have for some time been, quite as subject to women, to say the least of it, as is desirable. In the region of morals, women may, in modern times, have had a beneficent influence; though, as we shall see when we come to treat of Mr. Swinburne's particular genius, recent phenomena have somwhat shaken our once favourable opinion on that score. But there can be no question that, in the region of Art, their influence has been unmitigatedly mischievous. They have ruined the stage; they have dwarfed painting till it has become little more than the representa-tive of pretty little sentiment—much of it terribly false—and mawkish commonplace domesticities; and they have helped poetry to become, in the hands of Mr. Tennyson at least, and of his disciples, the mere handmaid of their own limited interests, susceptibilities, and yearnings. We do not say that Mr. Tennyson is never by any chance and on occasion fairly manly, though we think no one can doubt who considers the matter, that he is not even fairly manly very often, and never conspicuously so; and the most unreasonable of his worshippers would not dare for one moment, in describing his supposed merits as a poet, to call him masculine. That feminine is the proper word to apply to his compositions, taken in their entirety, no impartial judge, we feel convinced, would dream of denying. . . .

Now, on the first blush, it would seem as though Mr. Swinburne's poetry were a genuine revolt against that of Mr. Tennyson, and as though he had struck a distinct and even antagonistic note. That Mr. Swinburne himself thinks so is evident from some observations dropped by him in his "Notes on Poems and Reviews": a defence of his muse "against the strictures of those who complained —in our opinion, with absurd extravagance—of its alleged indecency and profanity." . . .

The question therefore arises, Has Mr. Swinburne, acting up to his excellent theory, turned his back on the haunts of feminine muses, struck out a masculine strain, and wrung from strenuous chords nervous and extolling hymns worthy of men and gods? Alas! Who shall say it? True, he has given us no more idylls of the farm and the mill, of the dining-room and the deanery; nor will any one pretend that his lyrics and ballads are fit for the sole or even for part of the diet of girls. But what have men—to say nothing of gods—men brave, muscular, bold, upright, chivalrous —we will not say chaste, for that is scarcely a masculine quality ("I will find you twenty lascivious turtles ere one chaste man," says no less an authority than Shakespeare), but at any rate clean— men with "pride in their port, defiance in their eye," men daring, enduring, short of speech and terrible in action—what have these to do with Mr. Swinburne's Venuses and Chastelards, his Anactorias and Faustines, his Dolores, his Sapphos, or his Hermaphroditus? If these be his Olympus, we prefer the deanery and the dining-room, or even the drawing-room. We do not say that they are not fair, much less that they are illegitimate, subjects for the poet's pen; but are they masculine? That is the question. Mr. Swinburne need fear no prudish or bigoted criticism from us. Venus or virgin, it is all one to us, provided he can make fine poetry out of either; though, of course, we should always reserve to ourselves the right of deciding which was the nobler theme. . . . For to this clear charge and distinct conclusion must we come: that far from Mr. Swinburne being more masculine even than Mr. Tennyson, he is positively less so. Where has he given us, to use his own words, "Literature worthy of men, large, liberal, sincere?" Where the "literature that deals with the full life of man and the whole nature of things?" We readily grant that the "lilies and languors of virtue" do not constitute the full life of man and the whole nature of things; but we must protest that neither do "the roses and raptures of vice." . . .

But we must grapple still more closely with the relations existing between the muse of Mr. Tennyson and the muse of Mr. Swinburne, inasmuch as in giving a serious account of the "Poetry of the Period" almost everything turns upon it. We regard each muse alike as essentially feminine, and we will proceed at once to illustrate what we mean.

Let us for a moment step aside from the province of poetry proper, and direct our attention to one in which imagination, however, plays a leading part—the province of prose romance. . . . During the last twenty or thirty years, and more decidedly during the last ten than the last twenty, and during the last twenty than during the last thirty, the heroines of novels have been more important than the heroes; and when they were not actually intended to be such by their author or authoress, they have been determinedly invested with more interest by the general public. We have not space to go into detail; but let us take one single instance, fairly typical of the tones and tendencies to which we are alluding. Let us compare Sir Walter Scott and Mr. Anthony Trollope. There we have the whole matter in a nutshell—the representative novelists of their time brought face to face and contrasted. It were sheer waste of time to demonstrate the self-evident; that, though Scott can of course be relished by women, girls, and children too, he is pre-eminently a masculine novelist, writing for men in a manly spirit, and from a man's point of view; whilst Mr. Trollope, though he can be relished by men, scarcely by boys, and much less by children, is a feminine novelist, writing for women in a womanly spirit and from a woman's point of view. . . . In these [times], as far as the faculty of the imagination and the objects on which it is exerted are concerned, we have as novelists and poets only women or men with womanly vices, steeped in the feminine temper of the times, subdued to what they work in, and ringing such changes as can be rung on what—we mean no disrespect or depreciation of the sex, that is both fair, devout, dear, and indispensable—has well been called "everlasting woman." Open Mr. Tennyson's first volume, and read the table of contents straight off: "Claribel," "Lilian," "Isabel," "Mariana," "Madeline," "Adelmine," and so on. What are "The Lady of Shalott," "Oriana," "Fatima," "Eleanore," "Œnone," "The May Queen," "The Miller's Daughter," "The Gardener's Daughter," "Lady Clara Vere de Vere," "Love and Duty," "Locksley Hall," and the rest, all about?

All about woman. What is "Maud" about? Woman. What is "The Princess" about? Woman, woman. What are the four "Idylls of the King" about? Woman, woman, woman, woman. We wonder what the Flos Regum Arthurus and all the Table Round would have thought had they known that their names and deeds would have served this one small purpose in the nineteenth century. We think they would have somewhat grimly smiled as they clanked their spurs and rattled their spears. "He loves and he rides away" is the refrain of an old song about "a gay young knight," which we remember hearing in the nursery. That is just about what gay young knights used to do, for

"Love is in man's life a thing apart;"

or, at any rate, ought to be.

But what has Mr. Swinburne got to do with all this? Surely a great deal. . . . Surely, it will be said, Mr. Swinburne's muse is not a feminine muse in the same sense that Mr. Tennyson's is; and surely he does not sing of love, woman, and all that is concerned with and gathers about woman, in the same way Mr. Tennyson does? Certainly not. But there is such a thing as the "one step farther," and Mr. Swinburne has taken it. Again, we must have recourse to our writers of prose romance, to those who exert the faculty of imagination in novels. We have spoken of Mr. Anthony Trollope, and have called him a feminine novelist, at the same time pointing him out as the fair analogue, in prose novels, of Mr. Tennyson. Now Mr. Trollope is a very "proper" writer, as no doubt in manner and usually in matter Mr. Tennyson also is. But is Mr. Trollope the only feminine novelist of the time? And are all the feminine novelists of the time as "proper" as himself? More than that: are not the most "improper" of them—we are obliged to use the word in vogue, in order to be understood, though we wish to convey no ethical opinion of our own in doing so—are not the most "improper" of them not only feminine, but actually women? Mr. Trollope writes of love, still love; but it is the sentimental love of youths and maidens, of coy widows and clumsy middle-aged men, beginning in flirtation and ending in marriage. In a word, it is pretty, pious, half-comical, domestic love—love within the bounds of social law. But what is the love of which many of our men-novelists—men, at least, as far as nominal sex is concerned, though certainly not men as authors or in any literary sense—and nearly all our women-novelists, so freely discourse? It is the love—had we not better call it the lust?—which begins with seduction and ends in desertion, or whose agreeable variations are bigamy, adultery, and, in fact, illicit passion of every conceivable sort under every conceivable set of circumstances. Nor have we yet given to the matter its full proportions. In the novels to which we refer, and they may be counted by hundreds, it is not men so much as women who are represented as the leading tempters. The heroines are more animal and impassioned than the heroes. . . . It is the feminine element at work when it has ceased to be domestic; when it has quitted the modest precincts of home, and courted the garish light of an intense and warm publicity. It is the feminine element, no longer in the nursery, the drawing-room, or the conjugal chamber, but unrestrainedly rioting in any and every arena of life in which an indiscriminating imagination chooses to place it. It is the "one step farther" of which we have already spoken, but a step that was inevitable and sure to be taken, when the first wrong step—that of making women too conspicuous in life and literature—had once been fatally indulged in. Our "proper" feminine novelists have but led the way for our "improper" feminine novelists; and the, on the whole, "proper" feminine muse of Mr. Tennyson was only the precursor of the "improper" feminine muse of Mr. Swinburne. There is nothing masculine about the one any more than about the other; or what advantage there is on either side in that particular lies, as we have said, with the muse of the former. Both, however, are substantially feminine muses; only one is the feminine muse of the Hearth, whilst the other is the feminine muse of the Hetairae.[70]

Surely eccentric in his sweeping inclusion of Tennyson and Trollope, Austin may nonetheless have expressed in extreme form the uneasy suspicions to which thirty years of public debate had roused even the most scornful conservative on the Woman Question. In Austin's eyes, fleshly poetry and sensation fiction were but the most outrageous symptoms of what writers then and since have called the effeminization of England and America.

The most eloquent and famous defense of the new poetry as a symptom of cultural change is Walter Pater's. Pater's essay, first published in 1868, becomes a manifesto for advanced young men in the seventies and continues to influence the generation of the nineties. For these young men Pater is the apologist for what one writer calls the philosophy of sensationalism,[71] or, as Pater terms it, of aestheticism.

Pater sees analogues for the peculiarly tense emotional atmosphere of Pre-Raphaelite, fleshly, or "aesthetic" poetry in the "wild convulsed sensualism" of medieval Provençal poetry, the product of "a passion of which the outlets are sealed." In that poetry, Pater reminds his readers, "religion shades into sensuous love, and sensuous love into religion." The new poetry, he implies, is the fruit of another age of repressed passion. Its pervasive, melancholy sense of loss and separation, on the other hand, he compares to Greek literature, finding the Greek awareness of life's shortness and death's finality echoed in the conclusions of modern psychology and philosophy.

. . . let us see what modern philosophy, when it is sincere, really does say about human life and the truth we can attain in it, and the relation of this to the desire of beauty.

. . . The service of philosophy, and of religion and culture as well, to the human spirit, is to startle it into a sharp and eager observation. Every moment some form grows perfect in hand or face; some tone on the hills or sea is choicer than the rest; some mood of passion or insight or intellectual excitement is irresistibly real and attractive for us for that moment only. Not the fruit of experience but experience itself is the end. A counted number of pulses only is given to us of a variegated, dramatic life. How may we see in them all that is to be seen in them by the finest senses? How can we pass most swiftly from point to point, and be present always at the focus where the greatest number of vital forces unite in their purest energy?

To burn always with this hard gem-like flame, to maintain this ecstasy, is success in life. Failure is to form habits; for habit is relative to a stereotyped world; meantime it is only the roughness of the eye that makes any two things, persons, situations—seem alike. While all melts under our feet, we may well catch at any exquisite passion, or any contribution to knowledge that seems by a lifted horizon to set the spirit free for a moment, or any stirring of the senses, strange dyes, strange flowers and curious odours, or work of the artist's hands, or the face of one's friend. Not to discriminate every moment some passionate attitude in those about us and in the brilliance of their gifts some tragic dividing of forces on their ways, is on this short day of frost and sun to sleep before evening. With this sense of the splendour of our experience and of its awful brevity, gathering all we are into one desperate effort to see and touch, we shall hardly have time to make theories about the things we see and touch. . . . The theory or idea or system which requires of us the sacrifice of any part of this experience, in consideration of some interest into which we cannot enter, or some abstract morality we have not identified with ourselves, or what is only conventional, has no real claim upon us.

. . . Well, we are all *condamnés*, as Hugo somewhere says: we have an interval and then we cease to be. Some spend this interval in listlessness, some in high passions, the wisest in art and song. For our one chance is in expanding that interval, in getting as many pulsations as possible into the given time. High passions give one this quickened sense of life, ecstasy and sorrow of love, political or religious enthusiasm, or the "enthusiasm of humanity." Only, be sure it is passion, that it does yield you this fruit of a quickened, multiplied consciousness. Of this wisdom, the poetic passion, the desire of beauty, the love of art for art's sake, has most; for art comes to you professing frankly to give nothing but the highest quality to your moments as they pass, and simply for those moments' sake.[72]

For Pater both the critics' accusation that the poets sought passion for passion's sake, and the poets' defense that they wrote art for art's sake, are equally true. The new poetry is both fleshly and aesthetic. But Pater's explanation makes the woman who inspires passion or art indeed an icon, not the real passionate woman that Meredith, Swinburne, and Rossetti tried at moments to comprehend. Pater's own fleshly woman, his 1873 prose description of Leonardo's *Mona Lisa*, is removed by art and history from the miseries of modern love.

> The presence that rose thus so strangely beside the waters, is expressive of what in the ways of a thousand years men had come to desire. Hers is the head upon which all "the ends of the world are come", and the eyelids are a little weary. It is a beauty wrought out from within upon the flesh, the deposit, little cell by cell, of strange thoughts and fantastic reveries and exquisite passions. Set it for a moment beside one of those white Greek goddesses or beautiful women of antiquity, and how would they be troubled by this beauty, into which the soul with all its maladies has passed! All the thoughts and experience of the world had etched and moulded there, in that which they have of power to refine and make expressive the outward form, the animalism of Greece, the lust of Rome, the mysticism of the middle age with its spiritual ambition and imaginative loves, the return of the Pagan world, the sins of the Borgias. She is older than the rocks among which she sits; like the vampire, she has been dead many times, and learned the secrets of the grave; and has been a diver in deep seas, and keeps their fallen day about her; and trafficked for strange webs with Eastern merchants; and, as Leda, was the mother of Helen of Troy, and, as Saint Anne, the mother of Mary; and all this has been to her but as the sound of lyres and flutes, and lives only in the delicacy with which it has moulded the changing lineaments, and tinged the eyelids and the hands.[73]

The woman created and worshipped here may be passionate, mysterious, and sinister, but she is too remote to be shocking. She can even be, in one of her guises, the Virgin's mother. By 1873 the sensational sixties were over.

IV

In an 1874 retrospective essay on Gaskell, *Cornhill* declared:

> *Ruth*, a story which has generally been one of the chief favorites with readers, is remarkable for the manner in which it deals with a question that requires the utmost delicacy of treatment. We have seen the subject repeatedly treated in the most objectionable and unsatisfactory manner, notably by a popular writer just recently. In enlisting the sympathy of the public with the unfortunate heroine of his story, he purposely threw a false halo round her character. . . . we mention this instance particularly with a view of correcting what is too common an error.[74]

The "popular writer" who has "just recently" treated the fallen woman is Wilkie Collins, whose *The New Magdalen* appeared in play and novel versions the previous year. *Cornhill* can look back nostalgically to *Ruth* because Gaskell's evident compassion for her heroine did not stay the mandatory death. Collins' heroine, on the other hand, wins a halo not in the next life but in this one. What *Cornhill* (and many other reviews) find false about the halo is simply its presence. After a career in prostitution and an interlude impersonating an heiress, Mercy Merrick acknowledges her transgressions and achieves moral apotheosis. That readers today agree with Collins' Victorian critics about the book's artistic flaws should not obscure what is innovative about his effort. In 1873 Wilkie Collins constituted—in at least three ways—an emblem of the twenty-year controversy over female passion in literature. He embodies the subversive determination of writers to challenge orthodoxy; and his *New Magdalen* controversy is emblematic both of the mixed feelings with which the public read shocking fiction and of the limited extent to which writers finally liberalized Victorian attitudes.

First, Collins as emblem of the subversive spirit of the age. Wilkie Collins knows the shocking writers personally, Swinburne, Reade, and Meredith particularly; his private life—he lives out of wedlock with two women—is as unconventional as their own.[75] More importantly, Collins shares with shocking writers the determination to challenge the repressive power of orthodoxy. When, for example, the son of actor Alfred Wigan is dismissed from school in 1858 because of his father's profession, Collins writes for *Household Words* an article, "Highly Proper," which worries the magazine's editor, Charles Dickens. Dickens was Collins' close friend and was not averse to dramatizing social ills in his own fiction, but as editor Dickens must admonish his assistant-editor, W.H. Wills: "I particularly wish you to look well to Wilkie's article, and not to leave anything in it that may be sweeping, and unnecessarily offensive to the middle class. He has always a tendency to overdo that—and such a subject gives him a fresh temptation."[76] Collins is no less aggressive in his fiction. As early as 1852 he shocks the public with *Basil: A Story of Modern Life.* Here a fiancé listens at a wall as his fiancée is seduced in the next room by a rake! Collins reissues *Basil* in the sensational sixties and, still more aggressively, says of his *Armadale* in its 1866 preface: "estimated by the clap-trap morality of the present day, this may be a very daring book. Judged by the Christian morality which is of all time, it is only a book that is daring enough to speak the truth."[77] In *The New Magdalen* Collins goes beyond allowing the fallen woman a chance for repentence and allows her a real future. Instead of serving well and dying young, Mercy weds the Rev. Gray and presumably prospers. This wedding of repentance and Christian love is, Collins insists, the only hope in a complexly "gray" world which mocks the black-white simplicities of moral absolutes. In allowing Mercy to wed her cleric as Ruth could never wed Rev. Benson, Collins shows how much the sensational interlude of the sixties had prompted writers to boldness.

Collins is also an emblematic figure because the controversy over Mercy Merrick reflects the mixed minds of readers after twenty years of shocking literature. *The New Magdalen* evokes a critical spectrum substantially different from *Ruth*'s in 1853. Since repentance had become a standard feature of fallen woman stories by 1873, critical attention to moral issues is no longer inevitable. Instead of a spectrum ranging from moral outrage to moral ecstasy, critics now range from those who concentrate upon "the moral," to those who discuss both moral and artistic matters, to those who focus exclusively upon artistry. The *New York Times*, for example, calls *The New Magdalen* "a grand, an unquestionable, but not an unqualified success."[78] The review goes on to define the qualification—which is not that a good play is flawed by a bad moral, but that a good play is flawed by bad acting. Clearly, the *New York Times* and its readers take Collins' shocking moral sufficiently in stride that they can concentrate upon the artistic aspects of the play.

Toward the center of the critical spectrum is the *Times* of London. Its reviewer acknowledges the problem of the play's moral, but sees it as a fact of social history and not as a threat to be met polemically.

> In these days we are used to rehabilitation, but we are certain that in the time of our fathers, when the clemency of the Stranger, in the play of that name, was severely censured by moral judges, the conclusion of the New Magdalen's history would not have been tolerated. . . . The piece is evidently written in that didactic spirit which distinguishes the works of Mr. Wilkie Collins, who in this case would extol to the highest possible degree the virtue of contrition. Most writers whose ethics take the same direction end their story with the death of the penitent. . . . Mercy [Merrick] has sunk lower in the scale of degradation than Mrs. Haller, and therefore . . . Collins has shown himself a bolder man than Kotzebue, teaching, as he does, that penitence sufficiently over-balances any amount of guilt, and merits a reward in this world as well as in the next.
>
> Considered simply as a work of dramatic art, the *New Magdalen* is entitled to high commendation.[79]

Polemic does, however, erupt on both sides of the Atlantic. Some reviewers attack Collins as they had Gaskell—for daring to raise the issue of fallen women at all. In New York, the *Daily Tribune* says, "its subject is one that ladies and gentlemen cannot discuss, and that seems to us a sufficient reason why it should not be obtruded from the stage."[80] More interesting is the anonymous reviewer for New York's *Daily Graphic*, "Matador," who recognizes that plays are not moral tracts, and yet still attacks Collins on moral grounds. "Matador"'s complexity is suggested by his use of Charles Reade's famous phrase "prurient prude." Reade had coined the phrase in his attack upon moral-izing critics which appeared the same year as Collins' "clap-trap morality" attack upon the same critics. "Matador" quotes Reade with approval, and then castigates Collins!

The "New Magdalen" has been produced at the Broadway Theater, and the shrinking modesty of the morning press has consequently undergone a violent shock.

There is a certain type of critic who demands that the theatre should be conducted so as to conceal from any hypothetical daughter he may at any time hereafter possess the knowledge that the world is not a perpetual Sunday-school class thirsting after moral truths, and oblivious of the existence of bad people who prefer peanuts in the churchyard to precepts in the class-room.

Naturally in the interest of the hypothetical daughter—these critics resent the "New Magdalen" as eminently calculated to bring a blush to the cheek of a young person. It is a grossly immoral play—so they tell us. It actually introduces a "Magdalen" on stage.

Yes! But does it not also introduce a clergyman?—such as he is. And if the "Magdalen" makes it immoral, does not the clergyman make it moral?

And then, if a play is indecent because it contains among its characters a modern "Magdalen", what are we to say of the Scriptures, which introduced to us the original person of that name?

. . . There are scores of people who affect to believe that adultery . . . is unfit for the purposes of dramatic art, for the reason that it is intrinsically "nasty." . . .

Now, the "New Magdalen" is the most vicious play that has ever been produced in this city, but it is not "nasty" in any sense, and I protest against the theory that the subject which it handles is unfit for the stage, or that it has necessarily any bearing upon the moral character of the play. . . . Whatever is not unfit for discussion by the press or the pulpit is not unfit to be treated by the dramatist. . . . "Show me the man," says Charles Reade, "who calls adultery 'nasty,' and I will show you a prurient prude." . . .

The fault of the play is not that it mentions the existence of vice, but that it holds the vicious woman up for our admiration, and impresses upon us the essential meanness and repulsiveness of virtue. . . .

Throughout the play Mercy Merrick is steadfastly represented as worthy of our warmest admiration. She is a noble creature, forced by circumstances to commit the indiscretion of prostitution and the trifling error of personating another woman and robbing her of her rights. The latter [Grace] is with equal steadiness held up to scorn as a mean-spirited, vindictive, virtuous woman, whose moral nature, never having been chastened by prostitution and sweetened by false impersonation and robbery, is, of course, in the highest degree repulsive to all generous and noble men.

The direct teaching of the "New Magdalen" is that impurity, when repented of, demands our admiration, and that the worst crime a woman can commit is atoned for by her confession.

. . . Every young man who goes to the Broadway Theatre tonight will learn that virtuous women, as typified by Grace Roseberry, are malignant and mean, and that only among prostitutes can be found women worthy to be loved and capable of loving in return. . . .

That an honest, upright gentleman like Wilkie Collins—a man whose sympathies are all on the side of healthy morality—could have been so blinded to the real nature of his work as he must have been when he wrote the "New Magdalen", is a marvel not to be explained.

A "nasty play"? If it had been as nasty as the sewers of New York, that would have been a small offense in comparison with the direct and powerful preaching of vice and the sure and steady depreciation of virtue which characterizes the "New Magdalen" throughout.[81]

These negative reviews are difficult to interpret. What percentage of the population do they speak for? Or, granted that the reviews reflect one part of a divided Victorian consciousness, what role did that part play in the daily life of the individual? The prescription-practice dilemma recurs: are "conservative" voices speaking for an accepted ideal, or are they advocating an ideal which the majority violated regularly? Indicating how heterogeneous the Victorian period is, the *Daily Graphic* reviews Collins' play *twice*. "Matador's" piece on November 17 follows an opening-night review on November 11. "A Lady Critic Gives Her Views About Wilkie Collins' Great Play" raises also the issue of Collins' moral. "Everybody has read the novel, and though the opinion pretty generally prevails that the moral is not what it should be, yet it must be conceded that it is not unlike what often is."[82] Enough said, the rest of the opening-night review focuses exclusively upon artistic aspects of *The New Magdalen*. Which of the *Graphic*'s two critics is more representative of 1873? Any answer must take into account the contemporary reception of the play.

American expectations on opening night are indicated by the fact that "the house was packed, there was not a seat vacant, though the night was unpleasantly cold."[83] Does *The New Magdalen* satisfy such expectations? "At the end of the fourth act Wilkie Collins, being summoned by loud applause, stood up in a stage box and bowed to the upper multitude. Again summoned, he came upon the stage, leading Miss Leclercq (the heroine)—to whom, with graceful gesture, he referred as the proper recipient of public homage. Still called, he emerged for the third time."[84] The opening-night audience in London also calls Collins onto the stage during the performance. This initial success is followed by a nineteen-week run in London, an extended provincial tour, and two revivals of the play later in the century. "*The New Magdalen* had the longest life of any Collins drama, serving as a vehicle for many famous actresses of the era and holding the stage throughout the nineteenth century and into the twentieth. Translations were made for performances in France, Italy and Austria."[85]

Putting adverse reviews into perspective, such success clearly indicates that a large number of respectable citizens on both sides of the Atlantic responded positively to the subject and treatment of *The New Magdalen*. Audience sympathy for Mercy Merrick suggests widespread interest in female sexuality and widespread approval of Collins' attack upon social righteousness. On the other hand, the fate of the novel version of *The New Magdalen* prevents us from defining the playgoers' response as *the* public response. Collins has great hopes for the novel.

> "I have done all I can to secure a double success. We are well in advance of the day this time (as to the story) and you [George Bentley] will be able to subscribe the book as soon as you see fit."
>
> "Subscribing a first edition" was largely a trade euphemism for getting an order from Mr. Mudie. He, for his part, scented something blasphemous about the name *The New Magdalen* and told Bentley, who was publishing on terms of ten per cent commission to himself, to change it. When he heard this, Wilkie was furious. "Nothing will induce me to modify the title," he told Bentley. . . .
>
> "The serious side of this affair is that this ignorant fanatic holds my circulation in his pious hands. Suppose he determines to check my circulation. What remedy have we?" . . .
>
> Wilkie decided to advertise the novel on the playbill and to gamble that Mr. Mudie would be forced by his subscribers to take a satisfactory number of the expensive two-volume first edition.[86]

The gamble fails. Mudie refuses to be pressured, and the novel version of *The New Magdalen* sells disastrously in England. Although Collins earns handsome profits from the play and from American sales of the novel, Mudie proves once again how much the English reading public is controlled by the spirit of Mrs. Grundy. But what, really, does "controlled" mean? Does Mrs. Grundy prevail because Mr. Mudie can personally deny books to millions of eager readers, or does he continue to articulate the moral attitudes of most Victorians? The power of Mudie's Circulating Library will last another twenty years; in America in the 1870s and 1880s, William A. Comstock wages a succesful war to repress books with sexual subjects [Volume 2, Chapter 2]. Comstock, Mudie, and the reviewers hostile to *The New Magdalen* can neither be dismissed as vestigial nor accepted as "the" Victorian spokesmen.

In England, then, a widely attended play and a little-read novel; in America, laudatory and antagonistic reviews in the same newspaper: these are fitting emblems of Victorian heterodoxy. Collins himself is finally an equally fitting emblem of the, at best, mixed success of shocking writers. Success there unquestionably was. Like many of the sensational school, Collins won fame and wealth. In 1883 he was voted the greatest living writer. This very accolade rings hollow, however, in a symptomatic way. By 1883, Thackeray, Dickens, Eliot, and Trollope are all dead. Collins' best writing is long since behind him, and the bloody controversies have taken their toll on other shocking writers too. Rossetti, physically broken and pathologically sensitive to criticism, has died in 1882; Swinburne is a recluse in a suburban London villa. Wilkie Collins is thus emblematic of the partial defeat of shocking literature: his career indicates that the substantial forces set against his school are in fact gaining the ascendancy, and his own fiction shows the extent to which Collins himself is as divided as his age.

The forces set against him are not only the Grundys and Mudies and Comstocks. In the 1880s the best of the shocking women novelists, Braddon, Wood, and Broughton, turn away from outré themes and write novels of manners and social criticism. Josephine Butler and the Purity Crusade in England and America [Volume 2, Chapter 2] agree with Collins that sexual realities have to be faced directly, but dissent from any ideal which includes passion and sexual equality. Their ideal is the angel out of the house who becomes actively engaged in the world so that the world may be raised to her level of purity. Likewise, apocalyptic feminism sees woman matching male activism, not so that she can gain the double standard, but so that men can be denied it.

In his own fiction, Collins, for all of his radicalism, reflects this same mixed attitude toward woman. His heroines are often aggressive, but they never seek the feminist goals of a professional career or a parliamentary seat. The goal of his aggressive women is in fact the goal of true woman—marriage with a decent man. As Mercy marries her cleric, the appropriately named heroine of *No Name* (1862), Madelaine, marries the appropriately named Captain Kirk of the good ship *Deliverance*. Collins indicates, then, how far attitudes have come from 1853 to 1873, and how far they have yet to go. An anecdote shows both how strong Mrs. Grundy remains and how time is siding with a new generation determined to open itself to the truths revealed by Collins, Braddon, Gaskell, and others. Not surprisingly, the new generation is represented in the anecdote by women.

The best bit of British criticism was one he encountered later in a railway car. He was traveling alone, musing somberly on the past and on Dickens, his former companion during so many a similar journey. A portly, prosperous clergyman with two daughters shared his compartment and attracted his attention.

"Before long," he noticed, "Papa fell asleep. After a sly look at him, one of the young ladies opened her bag and took out a book. She dropped it and I picked it up for her. It was . . . *The New Magdalen*. She reddened as she thanked me. I observed with interest the soft, round object sacred to British claptrap—the cheek of the young person—and I thought of a dear old friend, praised after his death by innumerable humbugs, who discovered the greatness of his art in its incapability of disturbing the complexion of 'young Miss.'

"She was really absorbed in her reading. 'It's perfectly dreadful,' she told her sister. Papa showed signs of returning to consciousness. *The New Magdalen* instantly disappeared, and the young person caught me looking at her cheek. It reddened a little again. Alas for my art, it was stuff which raised the famous blush, stuff registered in the Expurgatory Index of the national cant. Who will praise *The New Magdalen* when I am dead and gone? Not one humbug—thank God!"[87]

5

The American Girl
of the Period

One of the New World's products which has consistently received international attention is that free spirit, the American Girl.[1] How free were American young women, how free did they wish to be, how did marriage affect their freedom? These questions were asked consistently and answered variously by European visitors from the 1780s through the 1830s. Their answers form, in turn, the context for both the impressions of America's most dedicated student of the American Girl, Henry James, and the controversy stirred up by his most notorious young woman, Daisy Miller.

I

Before 1800, two French visitors—the Marquis de Chastellux and Moreau de St. Méry—agreed about the freedom of the American Girl and about the restraints on the American Wife.

When they [French soldiers] encamped at Alexandria, on the ground formerly occupied by Braddock, the most elegant and handsome young ladies of the neighborhood danced with the officers on the turf, in the middle of the camp, to the sound of military music; and (a circumstance which will appear singular to European ideas) the circle was in a great measure composed of soldiers, who, from the heat of the weather, had disengaged themselves from their clothes, retaining not an article of dress except their shirts, which in general were neither extremely long, nor in the best condition; nor did this occasion the least embarrassment to the ladies, many of whom were of highly polished manners, and the most exquisite delicacy. . . .

It is no crime for a girl to kiss a young man; it would indeed be one for a married woman even to show a desire of pleasing. Mrs. Carter, a young and pretty woman, whose husband is concerned in furnishing our army with provisions, and lives at present at Newport, once told me that, going down one morning into her husband's office, not much dressed up, but in a rather elegant informal French dress, a farmer from Massachusetts, who was there on business, seemed surprised at seeing her, and asked who this young lady might be. He was told that it was Mrs. Carter. "Well!" he replied, loud enough for her to hear him, "If she's a wife and a mother, she shouldn't be so well dressed."[2]

Although in general one is conscious of widespread modesty in Philadelphia, the customs are not particularly pure, and the disregard on the part of some parents for the manner in which their daughters form relationships to which they, the parents, have not given their approval is an encouragement of indiscretions which, however, are not the result of love, since American women are not affectionate.

But they are very ridiculous in their aversion to hearing certain words pronounced; and this scruple is frequently a confession of too much knowledge, rather than of ignorance. . . .

I have spoken of the unrestrained life of the young girls. . . . When a young woman marries, she enters a wholly different existence. She is no longer a giddy young person, a butterfly who denies herself nothing and whose only laws are her whims and her suitor's wish. She now lives only for her husband, and to devote herself without surcease to the care of her household and her home. In short, she is no more than a housekeeper. To put it more correctly, she is often the one and only servant.[3]

In the 1820s and 1830s, three British women visit America and comment upon the American Girl. Frances Wright finds more to praise than Frances Trollope or Harriet Martineau do, but Wright too laments those restrictions on the American Girl's education which limit the American Wife intellectually and politically. In *Views of Society and Manners in America* (1821), Wright says: "married without knowing anything of life but its amusements, and then quickly immersed in household affairs and the rearing of children, they command but few of those opportunities by which their husbands are daily improving in sound sense and varied information. . . . They enter very early into society; far too early, indeed, to be consistent with a becoming attention to the cultivation of their minds. I am, however, acquainted with striking exceptions to this general practice."[4]

The limitations noted by Wright are what Trollope and Martineau focus upon. Contrasting the "habitual insignificance" of American women and the considerable influence of their European counterparts, Trollope in *The Domestic Manners of the Americans* (1832) concludes that the American Girl, though pretty, lacks the inner substantiality essential for true attractiveness in a young woman and for real influence in an older one. In *Society in America* (1837), Harriet Martineau is less concerned with outward appearance. She blames the "slavery" of the American woman upon the nation's failure to help the American Girl escape social restraints and achieve full identity through education and experience. For Trollope and Martineau, as for Wright, the paramount issue is freedom.

> The women are certainly by far handsomer, speaking of them en masse, than those either of France or England. I have heard that women forgive every thing except being called ugly, and therefore I will venture after thus fully acknowledging their superiority in beauty, to express with equal freedom and sincerity my opinion on other points. . . . Generally speaking they want intelligence. What is far worse, they want grace. They want it in sitting, they want it in standing, they want it in expression, in accent, in tone. This is felt at every moment and scene, as it were, to neutralize every charm. Were they graceful, they would, from the age of fifteen to eighteen, be beautiful creatures indeed. They marry very early; once married, they seem to drop out of sight or of court, out of all competition with the blooming race that are following them.
>
> This, perhaps, is one reason why the drawing-room is so little attractive. From fifteen to eighteen the mind is not sufficiently developed to enable a woman to do her own honors well. Girls of that age make only a part, though a very lovely one, of the charm of society; but a flower garden possessing nothing but a bed of tulips would be no more imperfect than a salon with no other

ornaments than a knot or two of these bright blossoms. The piquant observation, the lively sally, the delicate coquetry, the playful yet acute remark, nay, even the abandon of enthusiasm or an elegant shadow of it, all, all meet in the varied and varying groups which form the centres round which all the stars of conversation revolve in the drawing-rooms of Europe. . . .

. . . I certainly believe the women of America to be the handsomest in the world, but as surely do I believe that they are the least attractive.[5]

While woman's intellect is confined, her morals crushed, her health ruined, her weaknesses encouraged, and her strength punished, she is told that her lot is cast in the paradise of women: and there is no country in the world where there is so much boasting of the "chivalrous" treatment she enjoys. That is to say,—she has the best place in stage-coaches . . . and, especially, her morals are guarded by the strictest observance of propriety in her presence. In short, indulgence is given her as a substitute for justice. Her case differs from that of the slave, as to the principle, just so far as this; that the indulgence is large and universal, instead of petty and capricious. In both cases, justice is denied on no better plea than the right of the strongest. . . .

The intellect of woman is confined by an unjustifiable restriction of both methods of education,—by express teaching, and by the discipline of circumstance. The former, though prior in the chronology of each individual, is a direct consequence of the latter, as regards the whole of the sex. As women have none of the objects in life for which an enlarged education is considered requisite, the education is not given. Female education in America is much what it is in England. There is a profession of some things being taught which are supposed necessary because everybody learns them. They serve to fill up time, to occupy attention harmlessly, to improve conversation, and to make women something like companions to their husbands, and able to teach their children somewhat. . . . There is rarely or never a careful ordering of influences for the promotion of clear intellectual activity. Such activity, when it exceeds that which is necessary to make the work of the teacher easy, is feared and repressed. This is natural enough, as long as women are excluded from the objects for which men are trained. . . . Accordingly, marriage is the only object left open to woman.[6]

In his celebrated *Democracy in America* (1835), Alexis de Tocqueville synthesizes the conflicting observations of his French and English predecessors, though in a unique and finally disturbing way. First, he, like previous Frenchmen, proclaims the unprecedented freedom of the American Girl.

> Long before an American girl arrives at the age of marriage, her emancipation from maternal control begins: she has scarcely ceased to be a child, when she already thinks for herself, speaks with freedom, and acts on her own impulse. . . . An American girl scarcely ever displays that virginal bloom in the midst of young desires, or that innocent and ingenuous grace which usually attend the European woman in the transition from girlhood to youth. It is rarely that an American woman at any age displays childish timidity or ignorance. Like the young women of Europe, she seeks to please, but she knows precisely the cost of pleasing. If she does not abandon herself to evil, at least she knows that it exists; and she is remarkable rather for purity of manners than for chastity of mind. . . . [Americans] have found out that in a democracy the independence of individuals cannot fail to be very great, youth premature, tastes ill-restrained, customs fleeting, public opinion often unsettled and powerless, paternal authority weak, and marital authority contested. Under these circumstances, believing that they had little chance of repressing in woman the most vehement passions of the human heart, they held that the surer way was to teach her the art of combating those passions for herself. . . . Far from hiding the corruptions of the world from her, they prefer that she should see them at once and train herself to shun them; and they hold it of more importance to protect her conduct, than to be over-scrupulous of her innocence.[7]

Tocqueville's portrait of the American Girl is not unqualified. If she is unprecedentedly free, she is clearly molded by immense social forces. That American adults are determined "to protect her conduct" indicates that *they* are deciding both the hierarchy of values and the means of preserving that hierarchy. Social restrictions upon freedom are most evident when Tocqueville takes up the marrying of the American Girl.

> In America the independence of woman is irrecoverably lost in the bonds of matrimony: if an unmarried woman is less constrained there than elsewhere, a wife is subjected to stricter obligations. The former makes her father's house an abode of freedom and of pleasure; the latter lives in the home of her husband as if it were a cloister. Yet these two different conditions of life are perhaps not so contrary as may be supposed, and it is natural that the American women should pass through the one to arrive at the other.

Religious peoples and trading nations entertain peculiarly serious notions of marriage: the former consider the regularity of woman's life as the best pledge and most certain sign of the purity of her morals; the latter regard it as the highest security for the order and prosperity of the household. The Americans are at the same time a puritanical people and a commercial nation: their religious opinions, as well as their trading habits, consequently lead them to require much abnegation on the part of women, and a constant sacrifice of her pleasures to her duties which is seldom demanded of her in Europe. Thus in the United States the inexorable opinion of the public carefully circumscribes woman within the narrow circle of domestic interests and duties, and forbids her to step beyond it.

Upon her entrance into the world a young American woman finds these notions firmly established; she sees the rules which are derived from them; she is not slow to perceive that she cannot depart for an instant from the established usages of her contemporaries, without putting in jeopardy her peace of mind, her honour, nay even her social existence; and she finds the energy required for such an act of submission in the firmness of her understanding and in the virile habits which her education has given her. It may be said that she has learned by the use of her independence, to surrender it without a struggle and without a murmur when the time comes for making the sacrifice. . . .

I by no means suppose, however, that the great change which takes place in all the habits of women in the United States, as soon as they are married, ought solely to be attributed to the constraint of public opinion; it is frequently imposed upon themselves by the sole effort of their own will. When the time for choosing a husband is arrived, that cold and stern reasoning power which has been educated and invigorated by the free observation of the world, teaches an American woman that a spirit of levity and independence in the bonds of marriage is a constant subject of annoyance, not of pleasure; it tells her that the amusements of the girl cannot become the recreations of the wife, and that the sources of a married woman's happiness are in the home of her husband. As she clearly discerns beforehand the only road which can lead to domestic happiness, she enters upon it at once, and follows it to the end without seeking to turn back.

A democracy committed to equality and freedom and given to eulogizing woman and her state proceeds to deny to women both equality and freedom. Tocqueville thus recognizes what Trollope and Martineau lament. He is less strident than they, agreeing with his travel-companion Beaumont that American homelife probably surpasses any in Europe, and denying that American women are in fact slaves ("the constraint of public opinion" is not solely responsible for "the great change" after marriage).⁸ But this great change, this virtually complete loss of freedom, is mentioned in Tocqueville's notes again and again. When he says that "she clearly discerns beforehand the only road which can lead to domestic happiness," Tocqueville clearly sees that only one road exists because society will view women one way. His overall presentation of and attitude toward American women is too complex to be explored fully in this chapter on the American Girl. But one thing is certain. Tocqueville's celebrated pronouncement—"if I were asked . . . to what the singular prosperity and growing strength of that people [Americans] ought mainly to be attributed, I should reply, To the superiority of their women"—must be seen in light of the price exacted from the American Woman. For what does the American Girl exchange her considerable freedom? At best? The genteel form of subjection is defined for Tocqueville by a young American wife. "I ventured the other day to ask one of these charming recluses just how, exactly, a wife could pass her time in America. She answered me, with great *sang-froid*: in admiring her husband."⁹ And at the worst? Tocqueville omitted from *Democracy in America* the following portrait of the American Girl who presents in extreme form various aspects of wifehood portrayed by other visitors.

Like the emigrant [her husband], this woman is in her prime; like him, she can recall the ease of her first years. Her clothes even yet proclaim a taste for adornment ill extinguished. But time has weighed heavily on her: in her prematurely pale face and her shrunken limbs it is easy to see that existence has been a heavy burden for her. In fact, this frail creature has already found herself exposed to unbelievable miseries. Scarce entered upon life, she had to tear herself away from the mother's tenderness and from those sweet fraternal ties that a young girl never abandons without shedding tears, even when going to share the rich dwelling of a new husband. The wife of the pioneer has torn herself in one instant and without hope of returning from that innocent cradle of her youth. It's against the solitude of the forests that she has exchanged the charms of society and the joys of the home. It's on the bare ground of the wilderness that her nuptial couch was placed. To devote herself to austere duties, submit herself to privations which were unknown to her, embrace an existence for which she was not made, such was the occupation of the finest years of her life, such have been for her the delights of marriage. Want, suffering, and loneliness have affected her constitution but not bowed her courage. 'Mid the profound sadness painted on her delicate features, you easily remark a religious resignation and profound peace and I know not what natural and tranquil firmness confronting all the miseries of life without fearing or scorning them.

Around this woman crowd half naked children, shining with health, careless of the morrow, veritable sons of the wilderness. From time to time their mother throws on them a look of melancholy and joy. To see their strength and her weakness one would say that she has exhausted herself giving them life and that she does not regret what they have cost her.[10]

II

Born soon after Tocqueville's book appeared in America, Henry James carries into the twentieth century the tradition of studying American women.[11] As late as 1907 he writes caustic essays on their speech and manners;[12] he recognizes that his "Julia Bride" of 1909 forms a "companion study" to his *Daisy Miller* of 1878. The continuity of these novellas reflects the larger continuity of a consciousness concerned—far more than readers realize who look only to James's novel on feminism, *The Bostonians* (1886)—with the fate of civilization and with the American Girl's role in that fate. Already in the 1860s James and Howells are dreaming of "a great American novel, in which the heroine might be infinitely realistic and yet neither a schoolmistress nor an outcast."[13] James is well equipped to write such a novel. He can view the American Girl not only from both native and British perspectives, but also with, as one contemporary noted, a uniquely sympathetic eye. "He seemed to look at women rather as women looked at them. Women look at women as persons; men look at them as women. The quality of sex in women, which is their first and chief attraction to most men, was not their chief attraction to James."[14]

In the decade before *Daisy Miller*, James raises in his fiction and his reviews many of the Woman Questions. One of his heroines says in 1867, "yes, they are cruel times . . . . They make one doubt all one has learnt from one's pastors and masters!"[15] Rejecting both the domestic angel and the sensation villainess, James denies that "the only escape from bread-and-butter and commonplace is into golden hair and promiscuous felony." In 1867 James mentions a possible alternative: "High-toned, free-thinking heroines." The key is free thinking. In the 1870s James's heroines sound repeatedly the theme of free thoughts and actions.

> "We women are so habitually condemned by fate to act simply in what is called the domestic sphere, that there is something intoxicating in the opportunity to exert a far-reaching influence outside of it."

> "Why should I suffer the restrictions of a society of which I enjoy none of the privileges?"

> "I had tried to get some insight into the position of woman in England. . . . she told me the position of a lady depended upon the rank of her father. . . . that proves to me that the position of woman in her country cannot be satisfactory."

James clearly agrees with one of his characters—and with foreign visitors from Chastellux to Tocqueville—that the "'prime oddity of ours . . . [is] the liberty allowed to young girls.'" The American Girl is too free to fit easily into conventional assigned roles. "'I have to pretend to be a *jeune fille* . . . an American girl is an intelligent, responsible creature,'" laments Aurora Church in "The Pension Beaurepas" (1879). Although the fact of liberty and the consequent freedom to transform and even invert traditional roles might seem to differentiate the American Girl sharply from her British and continental sisters, she is in fact a representative figure. *Atlantic Monthly* recognizes the representative status of James's first great heroine, Isabel Archer, as soon as *The Portrait of a Lady* (1881) appears.

> Our admiration is increased when reflection shows that, individual as Isabel is in the painting, one may fairly take her as representative of womanly life today. The fine purpose of her freedom, the resolution with which she seeks to be the maker of her destiny, the subtle weakness into which all this betrays her, the apparent helplessness of her ultimate position, and the conjectured escape only through patient forbearance,—what are all these, if not attributes of womanly life expended under current conditions?[16]

The 1860s and 1870s are, as we have seen, times when sensation fiction and social unrest are inverting traditional roles in literature and life. Compare Linton's remarks about sensation women belying their appearance [Chapter 4, p. 125] and a foreign visitor's comments in James's "The Pension Beaurepas":

> I have often noticed that contradiction in American ladies. You see a plump little woman, with a speaking eye and the contour and complexion of a ripe peach, and if you venture to conduct yourself in the smallest degree in accordance with these *indices*, you discover a species of Methodist—of what do you call it?—of Quakeress? On the other hand, you encounter a tall, lean, angular person, without color, without grace, all elbows and knees, and you find it's a nature of the topics! The women of duty look like coquettes, and the others look like alpenstocks![17]

James's heroines reflect the dislocations and uncertainties which characterized life on both sides of the Atlantic. By putting the New-World heroine into Old-World situations, James gives heightened expression to that ordeal of consciousness which was becoming increasingly important in fiction ("surely thoughts are free," cries the heroine of *East Lynne*) and which Anglo-American women were increasingly recognizing as a chief fact of their lives. How free does a young woman want to be, how free does society let her be, how free does marriage leave her? These are the questions not only of foreign visitors to America, but also of the Woman Question internationally. Henry James in 1878–79 raises all three questions in what he called *"pendent* or counterpoint"* novellas, *Daisy Miller* and *An International Episode*.[18]

Daisy Miller is notoriously the story of a free-spirited American girl who collides with orthodox society. Less well recognized is the fact that James's novella portrays *two* Miller women. Daisy's mother is virtually dysfunctional after years of marriage. Neither education nor experience has prepared Mrs. Miller to act in her husband's absence. Remaining largely in her room, she fails to supervise either her daughter's social conduct or her son's daily regimen. Randolph Miller eats sweets all day and stays up half the night. The role of mother devolves upon Daisy, who can no more manage her brother than she can save herself. By contrasting his heroine both with an American (if expatriate) society which restrains "free" behavior and with a wife-mother whom such restraints have maimed, James uses his new "international" format to dramatize the tensions and contradictions that foreign visitors have consistently seen in American women's lives. Public response to Daisy Miller will indicate much about our Girl of the Period.

Storm warnings appear even before publication. *Lippincott's Magazine* of Philadelphia, usually very receptive to James's work, returns his manuscript without even a letter of rejection. (Jingoistic outrage at an attack upon American girlhood?) Then the usually taciturn English editor Leslie Stephen accepts James's novella "enthusiastically" for *Cornhill*. (English delight at a satire on American institutions?) The storm which breaks in America after the novella's publication was chronicled by the *New York Times*. "There are many ladies in and around New York today who feel very indignant with Mr. James for his portrait of Daisy Miller, and declare it is shameful to give foreigners so untrue a portrait of an American girl."[19] Having defended James in the *Atlantic Monthly* against attacks which called him "brutally unpatriotic," William Dean Howells writes to James Russell Lowell that "Harry James waked up all the women with his *Daisy Miller*, the intention of which they misconceived, and there has been a vast discussion in which nobody felt very deeply, and everybody talked very loudly. The thing went so far that society almost divided itself into Daisy Millerites and anti–Daisy Millerites."[20] As with the Girl of the Period, the controversy over Daisy Miller spawns a vogue.

> The vogue set off by Daisy continued for a long time afterwards: she became a perennial figure—and "a Daisy Miller" was to be a much-used descriptive phrase whenever some particularly charming, forward young lady from America showed up in Continental surroundings. For a time there were "Daisy Miller" hats in the millinery shops, and presently another book appeared titled *An English Daisy Miller*, by a magazine writer named Virginia W. Johnson. . . . Henry's story was widely translated.[21]

James's contemporaries see Daisy Miller expressly in light of the Girl of the Period (G.O.P.). *Harper's* prophesies in 1879 that "Daisy Miller will become the accepted type and her name the sobriquet in European journalism of the American young woman of the period."[22] Comparing the Daisy Miller and G.O.P. controversies reveals one dramatic difference, however. Although no one today remembers the G.O.P. turmoil and many today associate Daisy Miller with a famous blowup, the fact is that *Daisy Miller* did *not* generate a controversy—if by controversy we mean what we meant with the G.O.P., a sustained public debate in the daily and periodical press.[23] Only one of James's many reviewers attacked his patriotism, and this review pulled its punches.

> If the anomalous mother and daughter who are the chief figures in Mr. James's *Daisy Miller* were seriously presented by him as typical representatives of our country-women—while admitting that such a mother and daughter are as much within the range of possibility as the Siamese Twins, and have as equitable a title to be set up as types—we should affirm that they have not enough of general or special resemblance to any really existent class to lend probability to caricature. It is obvious, however, that Mr. James had no such purpose in the brilliant and graceful trifle.[24]

The absence of acrimony in the press—especially considering the indubitable ire in private circles—raises at least as many cultural questions as a more conventional controversy would. Why, above all, do the reviews of *Daisy Miller* not reflect the private debate as G.O.P. reviews had? Could there be a sharp difference between male and female responses to the novella? Both the *New York Times* and the Howells letter focus upon woman as the irate party, whereas many of the most favorable reviewers are men—Richard Grant White for *North American Review*, Thomas Wentworth Higginson for *Literary World*, and Howells for *Atlantic Monthly*. Two important expressions of female opinion do exist, but both report *private* disagreements. Why do women not speak out more publicly? Since powerful female reviewers flourish on both sides of the Atlantic, it seems unlikely that women are denied access to public media. Are women indignant at what James has portrayed but chary of actually denying the truth of his portrait? Certainly women and men seem to differ in basic ways which suggest much about female roles and images in the later nineteenth century.

First, the public, male reaction. Today we are probably surprised at the maturity of America's public response to *Daisy Miller*, at the absence of national chauvinism. Not one reviewer seriously accuses James of "incivism." Above feeling the need to defend everything American, the reviewers are above the snobbery of asserting that no such thing could happen to us. These reviews manage at their best a blend of sympathy and tough-mindedness appropriate to James's complex story. Higginson says, "he [James] has achieved no greater triumph than when in . . . [*Daisy Miller*] he succeeds in holding our sympathy and even affection, after all, for the essential innocence and rectitude of the poor wayward girl whose follies he has so mercilessly portrayed."[25] In transcending one kind of snobbery, however, the reviewers often betray another. They avoid saying that Americans cannot be vulgar, but they say repeatedly that some Americans *are* vulgar. Cosmopolitan reviewers had no doubt known personal embarrassment at and for their countrymen abroad, especially under critical English eyes. But just as certainly the reviewers show a readiness, positively an eagerness, to get even—to lambaste Americans, and particularly American women, for lacking European polish. In however mild a fashion, the reviews reflect not only the anglophilia which characterized the genteel tradition, but also the sexual ambivalence which underlay that tradition's supposed benignity. Here is White:

> In Daisy Miller Mr. James has undertaken to give a characteristic portrait of a certain sort of American young woman, who is unfortunately too common. She has no breeding, little character, a headstrong will, in effect no mother, and with all this has personal attractions and a command of money which are very rare in Europe, even among people of rank. . . . It is perhaps well that he has made this study, which may have some corrective effect, and which should show European critics of American manners and customs the light in which the Daisy Millers are regarded by Americans themselves.[26]

The most insightful early analysis of *Daisy Miller* combines critically sympathetic and conventionally genteel attitudes. It is written by William Dean Howells.

> Daisy Miller was positively startling in its straightforward simplicity and what I can only call *authenticity*. It could not have been written—I am almost ready to say it cannot be appreciated—except by one who has lived so long abroad as to be able to look at his own people with the eyes of a foreigner. All poor Daisy's crimes are purely conventional. She is innocent and good at heart, susceptible of praise and blame; she does not wish even to surprise, much less outrage, the stiffest of her censors. In short, the things she does with such dire effect at Vevay and at Rome would never

for an instant be remarked or criticised in Schenectady. They would provoke no comment in Buffalo or Cleveland; they would be a matter of course in Richmond and Louisville. . . . Yet with such exquisite art is this study managed that the innocence and loveliness of Miss Miller are hardly admitted as extenuating circumstances in her reprehensible course of conduct. She is represented, by a chronicler who loves and admires her, as bringing ruin upon herself and a certain degree of discredit upon her countrywomen, through eccentricities of behavior for which she cannot justly be held responsible. Her conduct is without blemish, according to the rural American standard, and she knows no other. It is the merest ignorance or affectation, on the part of the anglicized Americans of Boston or New York, to deny this. A few dozens, perhaps a few hundreds, of families in America have accepted the European theory of the necessity of surveillance for young ladies, but it is idle to say it has ever been accepted by the country at large. In every city of the nation young girls of good family, good breeding, and perfect innocence of heart and mind, receive their male acquaintances *en tête-à-tête*, and go to parties and concerts with them, unchaperoned. Of course, I do not mean that Daisy Miller belongs to that category; her astonishing mother at once designates her as pertaining to one distinctly inferior. Who has not met them abroad? From the first word uttered by Miss Daisy to her rampant young brother in the garden at Vevay, "Well, I guess you'd better be quiet," you recognize her, and recall her under a dozen different names and forms. She went to dine with you one day at Sceaux, and climbed, with the fearless innocence of a bird, into the great chestnut tree. . . .

As to the usefulness of this little book, it seems to me as indubitable as its literary excellence. It is too long a question to discuss in this place, whether the freedom of American girls at home is beneficial or sinister in its results. But there is no question whatever as to the effect of their ignorance or defiance of conventionalities abroad. An innocent flirtation with a Frenchman or Italian tarnishes a reputation forever. All the waters of the Mediterranean cannot wash clean the name of a young lady who makes a rendezvous and takes a walk with a fascinating chance acquaintance. We need only refer to the darker miseries which often result from these reckless intimacies. A charming young girl, traveling with a simple-minded mother, a few years ago, in a European capital, married a branded convict who had introduced himself to them, calling himself, of course, a count. In short, an American girl, like Daisy Miller, accompanied by a woman like Daisy's mother, brought up in the simplicity of provincial life in the United States, has no more chance of going through Europe unscathed in her feelings and her character than an idiot millionaire has of amusing himself economically in Wall Street. This lesson is taught in Mr. James's story,—and never was necessary medicine administered in a form more delightful and unobtrusive.[27]

Female responses to *Daisy Miller* are of three types. The reaction of American women as reported in the *New York Times* and in the Howells letter requires some explanation. Daisy Millerism cannot have become a vogue if middle- and upper-class women are profoundly offended. Even Howells admits that no one felt too deeply. On the other hand, a substantial number of substantial women are undoubtedly offended by *Daisy Miller*. While male reviewers readily indict American vulgarity, the women whom they have primarily in mind cannot afford the luxury of such snobbery and must resort to the simpler snobbery of disavowing Daisy. Different as these counterclaims seem, they share a common donné—the ideal of the genteel angel. *Daisy Miller* threatens American women on a basic level. They can admit no deviation from the genteel ideal because most of them lack any viable alternative standard. For the individual and for the group, the basic choice remains perfection or perdition.

British women who are not amused at Daisy's vulgarity are as shocked as their American counterparts, but for a different reason. These British women debate not whether a creature like Daisy exists, but whether the creature perpetrates her outrages from innocence or viciousness. Firsthand documentation of how intensely this debate raged in private circles comes from Eliza Lynn Linton.

MY DEAR MR. JAMES,—As a very warm dispute about your intention in *Daisy Miller* was one among other causes why I have lost the most valuable intellectual friend I ever had, I do not think you will grudge me half a dozen words to tell me what you did really wish your readers to understand, so that I may set myself right or give my opponent reason. I will not tell you which side I took, as I want to be completely fair to him. Did you mean us to understand that Daisy went on in her mad way with Giovanelli just in defiance of public opinion, urged thereto by the opposition made and the talk she excited? or because she was simply too innocent, too heedless, and too little conscious of appearance to understand what people made such a fuss about; or indeed the whole bearing of the fuss altogether? Was she obstinate and defying, or superficial and careless?

In this difference of view lies the cause of a quarrel so serious, that, after dinner, an American, who sided with my opponent and against me, came to me in the drawing-room and said how sorry he was that any gentleman should have spoken to any lady with the "unbridled insolence" with which this gentleman had spoken to me. So I leave you to judge of the bitterness of the dispute, when an almost perfect stranger, who had taken a view opposite to my own, could say this to me![28]

MY DEAR MRS. LINTON,—I will answer you as concisely as possible—and with great pleasure—premising that I feel very guilty at having excited such ire in celestial minds, and painfully responsible at the present moment.

Poor little Daisy Miller was, as I understand her, above all things *innocent*. It was not to make a scandal, or because she took pleasure in a scandal, that she "went on" with Giovanelli. She never took the measure really of the scandal she produced, and had no means of doing so: she was too ignorant, too irreflective, too little versed in the proportions of things. . . . To my perception she never really tried to take her revenge upon public opinion —to outrage it and irritate it. In this sense I fear I must declare that she was not *defiant*, in the sense you mean. . . . The whole idea of the story is the little tragedy of a light, thin, natural, unsuspecting creature being sacrificed as it were to a social rumpus that went on quite over her head and to which she stood in no measurable relation. To deepen the effect, I have made it go over her mother's head as well. She never had a thought of scandalising anybody—the most she ever had was a regret for Winterbourne.[29]

The third response to *Daisy Miller* comes from Europeanized American women who know "the Daisy Miller type" first hand, and who exactly reverse the criticism made by their countrywomen at home. James has falsified the American Girl by making Daisy, not too crude, but too innocent and poetic. This debate James himself narrates years later.

It was in Italy again—in Venice and in the prized society of an interesting friend, now dead, with whom I happened to wait, on the Grand Canal, at the animated water-steps of one of the hotels. The considerable little terrace there was so disposed as to make a salient stage for certain demonstrations on the part of two young girls, children *they*, if ever, of nature and of freedom, whose use of those resources, in the general public eye, and under our own as we sat in the gondola, drew from the lips of a second companion, sociably afloat with us, the remark that there before us, with no sign absent, were a couple of attesting Daisy Millers. Then it was that . . . [my charming hostess protested] "How can you liken

THE WOMAN QUESTION—LITERARY ISSUES

those creatures to a figure of which the only fault is touchingly to have transmuted so sorry a type and to have, by a poetic artifice, not only led our judgement of it astray, but made *any* judgement quite impossible?" With which this gentle lady and admirable critic turned on the author himself. "You *know* you quite falsified, by the turn you gave it, the thing you had had, to satiety, the chance of 'observing': your pretty perversion of it, or your unprincipled mystification of our sense of it, does it really too much honour. . . . why *waste* your romance? There are cases, too many, in which you've done it again; in which, provoked by a spirit of observation at first no doubt sufficiently sincere, and with the measured and felt truth fairly twitching your sleeve, you have yielded to your incurable prejudice in favour of grace—to whatever it is in you that makes so inordinately for form and prettiness and pathos; not to say sometimes for misplaced drolling. Is it that you've after all too much imagination? Those awful young women capering at the hotel-door, *they* are the real little Daisy Millers that were; whereas yours in the tale is such a one, more's the pity, as—for pitch of the ingenuous, for quality of the artless—couldn't possibly have been at all." My answer . . . bristled of course with more professions than I can or need report here; the chief of them inevitably to the effect that my supposedly typical little figure was of course pure poetry, and had never been anything else; since this is what helpful imagination, in however slight a dose, ever directly makes for. As for the original grossness of readers, I dare say I added, that was another matter.[30]

The attack upon James here, and his reply, emphasize the aspect of the Daisy Miller furor which is most relevant for cultural history today. James frequently looked back upon early works—*The American* (1877) is the most famous example—and saw that what he had intended as realistic portraits were in fact imaginative transformations. Daisy Miller mirrors the workings of the artist and his society. James's portrait, colored by his imagination and interpreted by his audience, provokes a furor which is not in fact over Daisy or her real-life sisters. The furor concerns who the American Girl was and should be. Daisy's struggle in the novella is thus wonderfully reflected by responses to the novella. Women in the story react to Daisy Miller as women in their parlors react to *Daisy Miller*. In both cases the threat to social orthodoxy shuts female hearts against the female outcast. Male reactions to Daisy are—less precisely, but still substantially—reflected in the conduct of Frederick Winterbourne, whose sympathy with Daisy cannot finally outweigh his commitment to "proper" conduct. Both men and women react, not to Daisy Miller, but to an aberration from the genteel ideal.

Daisy Miller is ultimately about freedom. Daisy never escapes the preconceptions of her judges, her society and readers. If James shares with society the tendency to see the American Girl in light of his own imaginings, he is nonetheless allied with Daisy and against society. James may not have gotten so close to "life" as he initially imagined, but he got closer than many of his readers found comfortable. James paints the portrait of the American Girl, hangs it beside the icon of genteel womanhood, and records society's murderous preference for the latter. Dramatizing the Victorian debate over standards of female conduct, *Daisy Miller* asks what being a "lady" means. Two years later James will title his greatest early work, *The Portrait of a Lady*, in order to emphasize its examination of the heroine as lady. In *Daisy Miller*, James sympathizes strongly, as he says to Linton, with the "thin, natural, unsuspecting creature being sacrificed as it were to a social rumpus . . . to which she stood in no measurable relation." Since the "lady" issue was debated throughout the Victorian period, a writer interested in woman questions will dramatize the debate and readers attuned to their times will recognize the issue. The *New York Times* saw the American Girl furor as precisely a lady question.

Americans are often provoked at the ignorance which foreigners, more especially the English, display regarding them, but perhaps it seldom occurs to them how ignorant they themselves often are about themselves. It would, we believe, be almost impossible for an American to sit down and describe social life in his country in such a manner as would be generally recognized as true. . . . Many Americans bred in the fashionable life of great cities would certainly assure their English acquaintances that while *Daisy Miller* is a representative of an existing class, such a girl would *never* be received into "good society." This would puzzle the foreigner, who would want to know how it was, then, that she was received in good American society in Rome. Again, Mr. Howells, in his "The Lady of Aroostook" [1879], depicts a girl educated in a Massachusetts village, and brought up by a grandfather and aunt who would not seem to an educated Englishman to be above the level of his father's farm tenants, and whose language is tinctured with the broadest provincialisms. Yet this girl, although she perpetrates such solecisms as "I want to know," "Do tell," &c., is depicted as being in other respects entirely a lady. This again would puzzle the English man or woman. He would be perfectly ready to admit her moral and physical excellence and her innate charm, but they would not readily comprehend how she could be exactly "a lady," because in England "a lady" is associated with a certain recognized stamp of manner and language. For instance, if an elegantly-dressed young woman were to say, "Oh, it's elegant" or "She's very genteel," an English gentleman or lady would instantly jump to the conclusion that, however admirable, the fair speaker belonged to the lower grade of social life. Again, as to social customs, ask a young lady in highest grade of life in New York whether it is considered the correct thing to go to a theatre alone with a young man, and she will exclaim at such an idea; yet there are cities not many hours distant where her cousins, who occupy an equally good social position, do this with perfect propriety. It is an exceedingly difficult thing for foreigners to comprehend the great difference between persons of apparently the same social positions, in consequence of difference of place and circumstance. In England, the Earl has £10,000 a year, a castle, and a house in Grosvenor square, while his brother the parson lives in the depths of Devonshire on £800 a year; but the parson's sons and daughters speak just as good English as the Earl's, and their habits and manners are precisely the same.[31]

As a "counterpoint" to *Daisy Miller*, *An International Episode* turns the tables. Daisy was, as James told Linton, not really "defiant." Her defeat was so complete that she embodied only implicitly that critical tendency which her author directed against international society in *Daisy Miller*. Bessie Alden, the heroine who journeys to England and finally refuses a lord in *An International Episode*, is expressly critical. The American Girl represents, almost by definition, that free play of mind which passes judgment upon conventional roles and restraints. The best English review of *International Episode*, a long article in *Blackwood's*, recognizes this critical tendency in James's American travelers. Overall, however, the English reception is strident. James tells his family: "You may be interested to know that I hear my little 'International Episode' has given offense to various people of my acquaintance here. Don't you wonder at it? So long as one serves up Americans for their entertainment it is all right—but hands off the sacred natives! They are really, I think, thinner-skinned than we!"[32]

Bessie Alden represents that free play of mind which James as an artist exercises amid a genteel society he admires in many respects. Such intellectual mobility is a challenge to and an ideal for readers today because interpretative generalizations tend so often to oversimplify. To comment upon manners without necessarily indicting every member of a heterodox civilization is what James defines as his task in *An International Episode*, what female novelists from Charlotte Brontë to Elizabeth Stuart Phelps and Olive Schreiner attempt to accomplish, and what reviewers then and since have failed repeatedly to understand. For James, a mind is freest when it is evaluating both the strengths and the weaknesses of a culture, and is reserving judgment on many matters. Such intellectual freedom is ultimately the issue when an Englishwoman prompts from James a reply sharper than his letter to Eliza Lynn Linton. Reviewing for the *Daily News*, Mrs. Frank H. Hill expresses English irritation at that freedom which animates the American Girl and enables James to challenge generalizations about both his society and his art.

We feel bound to protest against the manners of Lord Lambeth and Mr. Percy Beaumont, in "An International Episode" being conceived as typical of the manners of English gentlemen. As individual characters, we take them on their merits and judge them accordingly, but true as types they certainly are not. There are undoubtedly, in England, and out of it, plenty of 'Arries, 'Arries in all grades of society, 'Arries even going abroad with the dread title of "lord." Had Mr. James chosen to draw for our amusement an 'Arry, he would have done it with all his wonted humour and truth, and greatly amused we should have been. But Lord Lambert and Percy Beaumont are not 'Arries. They are very worthy stupid honest gentlemen, and acquit themselves consistently as such in all they do. Why then should they be represented as habitually talking like arrant 'Arries? Men who have presumably been to a public school and college do not preface all their remarks with "Oh, I say!" This is not the slang of the stable or the club. That is the slang of the street. And Mr. James does not choose his English titles happily, nor are the manners of his English fine ladies pretty. Perhaps he does not consider that English manners are pretty.[33]

My dear Mrs. Hill—

I must thank you without delay for the little notice of *Daisy Miller* and the "Three Meetings," in this morning's Daily News, in which you say so many kind things so gracefully. You possess in great perfection that amiable art. But, shall I confess it? (you will perhaps guess it,) my eagerness to thank you for your civilities to two of my tales, is slighty increased by my impatience to deprecate your strictures with regard to the third. I am distressed by the evident disfavour with which you view the "International Episode;" and meditating on the matter as humbly as I can, I really think you have been unjust to it. No, my dear Mrs. Hill, *bien non*, my two Englishmen are not represented as "Arries"; it was perhaps the fond weakness of a creator, but I even took to myself some credit for the portrait of Lord Lambeth, who was intended to be the image of a loveable, sympathetic, excellent-natured young personage, full of good feelings and of all possible delicacies of conduct. That he says "I say" rather too many times is very probable (I thought so, quite, myself, in reading over the thing as a book): but that strikes me as a rather venial flaw. . . . A year ago I went for six months to the St. James's Club, where (to my small contentment personally) the golden youth of every description used largely to congregate, and during this period, being the rapacious and shameless observer that you know, I really made studies in London colloquialisms. I certainly heard more "I says" than I had ever done before; and I suppose that nineteen out of twenty of the young men in the place had been to a public school. However, this detail is not of much importance. . . . the Lord Lambeths of the English world are, I think, distinctly liable, in the turn of their phrases, just as they are in the gratification of their tastes—or of some of them—to strike quiet conservative people like your humble servant as vulgar. . . . I should go on to say that I don't think you have been liberal to the poor little women-folk of my narrative. (That liberal, by the way, is but a conciliatory substitute for some more rigid epithet—say *fair*, or *just*.) I want at any rate to remonstrate with you for your apparent assumption that in the two English ladies, I meant to make a resumé of my view of English manners. My dear Mrs. Hill—the idea is fantastic! The two ladies are a picture of a special case, and they are certainly not an over-charged one. They were very determined their manners should not be nicer; it would have quite defeated the point they wished to make, which was that it didn't at all suit them that a little unknown American girl should marry their coveted kinsman. Such a consummation certainly does not suit English duchesses and countesses in general—it would be quite legitimate to draw from the story an induction as to my conviction on that point. The story was among other things an attempt at a sketch of this state of mind. . . . A man in my position, and writing the sort of things I do, feels the need of protesting against this extension of his idea in which in many cases, many readers are certain to indulge. One may make figures and figures without intending generalizations— generalizations of which I have a horror. I make a couple of

English ladies doing a disagreeable thing—*cela c'est vu:* excuse me!— and forthwith I find myself responsible for a representation of English manners! Nothing is my *last word* about anything.[34]

The English are particularly upset by *An International Episode* because their century-long fear—that westward goes the course of empire, that the future belongs to America—seems confirmed by the apotheosis of the American Girl. New-World heiresses in increasing numbers are marrying into the European aristocracy (Winston Churchill's mother will be one) and British young women in increasing numbers are craving the freedom flaunted by their American sisters.

In their anxiety, however, the British overlook one central fact of *Daisy Miller.* Daisy, for all her freedom, dies. Henry James, for all his interest in free-spirited American women, chronicles the inevitable limitations of liberty. As visitors to the New World saw the American girl's freedom in light of the American wife's subjugation, so James dramatizes in *The Portrait of a Lady* how his free-spirited Isabel finds marriage an enslavement. Especially since the progress made by the Women's Movement in the 1860s and 1870s will slow depressingly in the 1880s and 1890s, James's emphasis in 1881 on the limitations of freedom is as prescient as his reflection of the girl-woman dichotomy is accurate. He learns in fact from experience. In 1875–76, the two heiresses to the Newberry fortune had, like Daisy Miller, gone to Rome and died. Closer to James personally are two other American girls, Minnie Temple, his cousin, and Clover Hooper, the future wife of Henry Adams [see illust. 8]. James contrasts the dowdiness of English women and the free-spiritedness of these American Girls. "I revolt from their [the British woman's] dreary deathly want of—what shall I call it?—Clover Hooper has it—intellectual grace—Minnie Temple has it—moral spontaneity."[35] By 1885, Minnie Temple is dead of tuberculosis and Clover Hooper Adams is dead by her own hand. Woman's physical and psychological health, so much debated internationally, is inescapably part of the American Girl's fate. The other side of freedom is inevitably limitation. And about that fact, if about nothing else in the Woman Question, there can be no debate.

Afterword

Despite the limitations to her freedom, the American Girl was not inevitably doomed to an early death. Nor were the aspirations for which she had come to stand. To be sure, by 1883 many of the famous voices in the Victorian debate were silent: Margaret Fuller, Charlotte Brontë, George Eliot, and John Stuart Mill were dead. With the publication of the initial volumes of their *History of Woman Suffrage* in 1881 and 1882, Stanton and Anthony closed the covers on the first phase of their long struggle. A few of the most fiercely debated issues of the preceding fifty years were resolved; the final resolution of many others had been, apparently, indefinitely postponed. In Britain the Married Woman's Property Act of 1882 was succeeded by suspension of the Contagious Diseases Acts in 1883, but suffrage was defeated in the following year. In America suffrage received a favorable committee report in Congress for the first time in 1883, but the Nineteenth Amendment was still more than a quarter century away. Nonetheless the question of woman was hardly dead as a subject for public discussion—nor can it be said that a restrictive atmosphere cut off the youthful ferment of Victorian debate. In the Social Purity movement of the next twenty years, or in the New Woman literature of the

1890s, women's claims were pressed, and resisted, quite as strongly as before, though the tone and many of the issues shifted. And in the private realm, the spectacular drop in the birthrate suggests increased use of birth control and thus the possibility that woman was gaining more control over that perennial battleground—her own body.

Daisy Miller, Minny Temple, and Clover Hooper Adams, or Margaret Fuller and George Eliot's Maggie Tulliver (drowned at nineteen in *The Mill on the Floss*) are less representative of the fate of woman in the nineteenth century than two of James's and Eliot's other heroines. Isabel Archer and Dorothea Brooke have provoked from readers and critics divergent, often contradictory, reactions which reflect the diverse alternatives which lay open to and threatened Victorian women. On the one hand, Dorothea and Isabel are defeated. Neither woman achieves that freedom of action in a larger sphere to which she aspired. Dorothea plays second fiddle to a husband who never achieves enough to provide her with any subsequent chance for action. Isabel at the end of *Portrait* returns to a marriage dead forever to passion. Why? Because she accedes to society's demands for wifely fidelity? Because she fears true sexuality when she finds it in Caspar Goodwood and in her own response to him? Because she can assume the Angel role with her stepdaughter while in fact refusing to be a bonafide angel in her now-moribund home? On the other hand, Isabel and Dorothea do have their triumphs, small but intensely valuable. Both women have freed themselves, at no little cost, from the errors in perception which had led to their confinements in bad marriages. And both refuse, in the end, to accept "freedom" from the hands of another. Dorothea resigns the independent income her first husband has given her, because it binds her to him; Isabel turns away from Caspar Goodwood's offer to free her from her marriage, because, she tells him, she must "get away from *you*!" If neither woman can fully choose her own future—James even questions whether full freedom of consciousness is possible—both do take up conventional domestic roles with an unconventionally active consciousness of the nature of these roles and of the alternatives to them. Disappointed, Dorothea and Isabel do not die. They, like the vast majority of their Victorian sisters, survive to trouble us with their mixed fates.

The representative Victorian women persisted—as did the Queen herself. When Albert died in 1861, Victoria was convinced her life was over, but she retained, evidently, the will to go on. Without the help of the husband who was father and mother as well as spouse, Victoria nonetheless lived out the century. She remained as tenacious a presence in the public discourse of Victorians as the subject she abhorred, the Woman Question.

Notes

For long quotations, references are given first to pages from which quotation has been made; inclusive page numbers for the entire article are given in square brackets.

Chapter 1

1 [W.B.O. Peabody], "Mrs. Sigourney and Miss Gould," *North American Review*, 41 (1835), 432.

2 "Women in the Domain of Letters," *Sharpe's*, 40 (1864), 252.

3 Bessie Rayner Parkes Belloc, *Essays on Women's Work* (London, 1865), p. 121.

4 "To William Ticknor," January, 1855, *Hawthorne and His Publisher*, ed. Caroline Ticknor (Boston: Houghton Mifflin, 1913), p. 141.

5 [G.H. Lewes], "A Gentle Hint to Writing Women," *Leader*, 1 (1850), 189. Lewes also satirizes the woman writer in his novel *Rose, Blanche, and Violet* (1848). Hester Mason, the stout-legged "Walton Sappho," writes bad poetry, runs off with an elderly gentleman, and becomes a prostitute. For Charlotte Brontë's criticism of the character, see "To W.S. Williams," May 1, 1848, *The Brontës: Life & Letters*, ed. Clement Shorter (London: Hodder and Stoughton, 1908), I, 412.

6 Isaac Disraeli, *The Literary Characteristics of Men of Genius* (1840; rpt. New York, 1880), pp. 272–73, 275.

7 Critics assumed that the male poet had a female muse. In "'Come Slowly—Eden': An Exploration of Women Poets and Their Muse," *Signs*, 3 (1978), 572–87, Joanne Feit Diehl reverses the model. Her theory that nineteenth-century women poets were forced to confront a composite male figure who is father, lover, and muse has been challenged by Lillian Faderman and Louise Bernikow in *Signs*, 4 (1978), 188–91 and 191–95, respectively.

[8]"The Female Character," *Fraser's*, 7 (1833), 601 [591–601].

[9][Edward Bulwer-Lytton], "On the Influence and Education of Women," *New Monthly Magazine*, 34 (1832), 230–31 [227–31].

[10]"Literary French Women," *All the Year Round*, 9 (1863), 489–92; "Literary Women," *London Review*, 8 (1864), 329.

[11]"To Mrs. Jameson," February 24, 1855, *The Letters of Elizabeth Barrett Browning*, ed. Frederic G. Kenyon (New York, 1897), II, 187–90.

[12]Harriet Taylor, "Enfranchisement of Women," *Westminster Review*, 56 (1851), 160; rpt. in *Essays on Sex Equality*, ed. Alice Rossi (Chicago: Univ. of Chicago Press), p. 119.

[13]J.S. Mill, *The Subjection of Women* (1869; rpt. in *Essays on Sex Equality*), pp. 209–11.

[14]For further study of the writers' attitude toward domesticity, see Ellen Moers, *Literary Women: The Great Writers* (Garden City, N.Y.: Doubleday, 1976), esp. Ch. 1; Tillie Olsen, *Silences* (New York: Delacorte Press, 1978), esp. pp. 203–12; and Elaine Showalter, *A Literature of Their Own: British Women Novelists from Brontë to Lessing* (Princeton: Princeton Univ. Press, 1977), esp. Ch. 2. Victorian women who address the issue but are not cited in the chapter include Charlotte Brontë, "To Robert Southey," March 16, 1837, *The Brontës: Life and Letters*, I, 129–30; Mrs. E.B. Duffey, "Women in Literature," *Victoria Magazine*, 28 (1877), 277–85; Charlotte Perkins Gilman in her unpublished diaries quoted by Mary Hill in *Charlotte Perkins Gilman: The Making of a Radical Feminist* (Philadelphia: Temple Univ. Press, 1980), esp. Ch. 6; and Harriet Beecher Stowe in *The Life of Harriet Beecher Stowe Compiled from Her Letters and Journals by Her Son* (Boston: Houghton Mifflin, 1889), pp. 93–98, 103–5, 133–40.

[15]"Female Authorship," *Fraser's*, 33 (1846), 460–61, 463, 465 [460–66].

[16]*Autobiography & Letters of Mrs. M.O.W. Oliphant*, ed. Mrs. Harry Cogshill (1899; rpt. Leicester: Leicester Univ. Press, 1974), pp. 23–24.

[17]Elizabeth Gaskell, *Life of Charlotte Brontë* (1857; rpt. London: J.W. Dent, 1970), pp. 237–38. Gaskell's influential biography made Charlotte Brontë a less passionate woman and a more respectable writer. Winifred Gerin analyzes Gaskell's motives and explains her numerous mistakes in *Elizabeth Gaskell: A Biography* (Oxford: Clarendon Press, 1976), pp. 159–78. Gerin also explores the relationship between motherhood and authorship in Gaskell's life.

[18]"To Eliza Fox," ca. February, 1850, *The Letters of Mrs. Gaskell*, ed. J.A.V. Chapple and Arthur Pollard (Manchester: Manchester Univ. Press, 1966), pp. 106–7.

[19]"Unknown," September 25 [? 1862], *Letters of Mrs. Gaskell*, pp. 694–95 [693–96].

[20]Fanny Fern, *Folly As It Flies* (New York, 1868), pp. 61–64. See Ann Douglas Wood, "'The Scribbling Women' and Fanny Fern: Why Women Wrote," *American Quarterly*, 23 (1971), 3–24, for a good analysis of attitudes toward women writers in nineteenth-century America.

[21]"Female Intellect," *Saturday Review*, 19 (1865), 366–67.

[22]M[ary] A[nn] Stodart, *Female Writers: Thoughts on Their Proper Sphere and on Their Powers of Usefulness* (London, 1842), p. 22.

[23]Disraeli, p. 270. In Chs. 1 and 2 of *The Madwoman in the Attic: The Woman Writer and the Nineteenth Century Imagination* (New Haven: Yale Univ. Press, 1979), Sandra Gilbert and Susan Gubar provide extensive analysis of the sexual metaphors used in the criticism of women writers.

[24][John Neal], "Men and Women," *Blackwood's*, 16 (1824), 289–94 [287–94].

Notes

Patricia Spacks gives helpful background on eighteenth-century ideas about sex and imagination in "'Every Woman Is at Heart a Rake,'" *Eighteenth Century Studies*, 8 (1974), 27–46.

25 Maria Grey and Emily Shirreff, *Thoughts on Self-Culture Addressed to Women* (Boston, 1851), pp. 399–400, 404–6. See also Edward W. Ellsworth, *Liberators of the Female Mind: The Shirreff Sisters, Educational Reform, and the Women's Movement* (London: Greenwood Press, 1979). A similar American text arguing for the cultivation of the female imagination is Ch. 5 of Lydia Maria Child's *The Mother's Book* (Boston, 1831).

26 Stodart, pp. 134–35. Inga-Stina Ewbank discusses Stodart in *Their Proper Sphere: A Study of the Brontë Sisters as Early-Victorian Female Novelists* (Cambridge, Mass.: Harvard Univ. Press, 1968).

27 "Literary Women," p. 329. On Sand's image as a woman writer, see Ch. 2, n. 43.

28 [G.H. Lewes], "The Lady Novelists," *Westminster Review*, 58 (1852), 133–34 [129–41].

29 See, for example, Thackeray's "Miss Bunion," in *Mrs. Perkins's Ball* (1847); rpt. in the Christmas Books of *The Oxford Thackeray*, ed. George Saintsbury (London: Oxford Univ. Press, 1911), pp. 32–33.

30 Ann Douglas Wood, "Mrs. Sigourney and the Sensibility of the Inner Space," *New England Quarterly*, 45 (1972), 166.

31 Olive Schreiner, *Woman and Labour*, 3rd ed. (New York: Frederick Stokes, 1911), pp. 162–64. Schreiner's efforts to free women from late Victorian assumptions about gender differentiation are discussed in Joyce Avrech Berkman, *Olive Schreiner: Feminism on the Frontier* (St. Alban's, Vt.: Eden Press, 1979) and Ruth First and Ann Scott, *Olive Schreiner* (New York: Schocken, 1980).

32 Anna Jameson, *Winter Studies and Summer Rambles* (London, 1838), I, 201–4. Jameson lived apart from her husband; it seems likely that the marriage was never consummated. For the details of her life, refer to Clara Thomas, *Love and Work Enough: The Life of Anna Jameson* (Toronto: Univ. of Toronto Press, 1967); for her ideas about art, see Adele M. Holcomb, "Anna Jameson (1794–1860): Sacred Art and Social Vision," in *Women as Interpreters of the Visual Arts, 1820–1979*, ed. Claire Richter Sherman and Adele M. Holcomb (Westport, Conn.: Greenwood Press, 1981), pp. 93–121. Her criticism of women's working conditions is analyzed in Vol. II, Ch. 3.

33 "To Jane Carlyle," October 6, 1851, *Selections from the Letters of Geraldine Endsor Jewsbury to Jane Welsh Carlyle*, ed. Mrs. Alexander Ireland (London, 1892), pp. 425–27 [424–28]. In their study of two aspiring nineteenth-century writers, William Taylor and Christopher Lasch suggest that women's commitment to the literary life often involved an ideal of pure friendship; see "'Two Kindred Spirits': Sorority and Family in New England, 1839–1846," *New England Quarterly*, 36 (1963), 23–41. Charlotte Yonge's friendship with Marianne Dyson led to the formation of a new "family": Dyson was mother, Yonge was father, and such famous characters as Guy and Ethel were their children; see Christabel Coleridge, *Charlotte Mary Yonge: Her Life and Letters* (London: Macmillan, 1903), pp. 166, 170–81, 188, 191. For recent studies of the ways women writers have acted as muses, mothers, and sisters to one another, see Louise Bernikow, *Among Women* (New York: Harper & Row, 1980); Cathy N. Davidson and E.M. Broner, eds., *The Lost Tradition: Mothers and Daughters in Literature* (New York: Ungar, 1980);

Lillian Faderman, "Emily Dickinson's Letters to Sue Gilbert," *Massachusetts Review*, 18 (1977), 197–225; Moers, *Literary Women*.

Chapter 2

[1] Maria Grey and Emily Shirreff, *Thoughts on Self-Culture Addressed to Women* (Boston, 1851), pp. 410–11.

[2] Nineteenth-century texts which reveal critical interest in the "poetess" as a new phenomenon include: "Mrs. Hemans's Poems," *North American Review*, 24 (1827), 443–63; [W.B.O. Peabody], "Mrs. Sigourney and Miss Gould," *North American Review*, 41 (1835), 430–454; [H.N. Coleridge], "Modern English Poetesses," *Quarterly Review*, 66 (1840), 374–418. During the twentieth century, American poetesses have received more attention than the English. Bradford A. Booth tabulates their contributions to the annuals in "Taste in the Annuals," *American Literature*, 14 (1942), 299–302. In *The Poetry of American Women from 1632 to 1945* (Austin: Univ. of Texas Press [1977]), Emily Stipes Watts documents the sudden appearance and widespread success of Sigourney and other poetesses. In *The Feminization of American Culture* (New York: Knopf, 1977), Ann Douglas studies the influence of poetesses and sentimental novelists on the development of popular culture; her argument that Sigourney and others used the pose of helpless passivity to engage in aggression and self-aggrandizement is also developed in "Mrs. Sigourney and the Sensibility of the Inner Space," *New England Quarterly*, 45 (1972), 163–81.

[3] [William Maginn], "Gallery of Illustrious Literary Characters. No. X. Mrs. Norton," *Fraser's*, 3 (1831), 222.

[4] [William Henry Smith], "Mrs. Hemans," *Blackwood's*, 64 (1848), 647; Sarah Josepha Hale, *Woman's Record* (New York, 1876), p. 347. Norton's essay is in the *Christian Examiner* for 1836; Peabody's, in the same periodical for 1845. In *The Feminization of American Culture*, Douglas argues that ministers who extolled Hemans were defending their own commitment to the emotions.

[5] Lydia Sigourney, "Essay on the Genius of Mrs. Hemans," in *The Works of Mrs. Hemans* (Philadelphia, 1840), pp. xiv, xix; [George Gilfillan], "Female Authors, No. I—Mrs. Hemans," *Tait's Edinburgh Magazine*, NS 14 (1847), 360–62 [359–63].

[6] In *Women Writers and Poetic Identity* (Princeton: Princeton Univ. Press, 1980), Margaret Homans argues that a woman trying to pattern herself after the major Romantic poets would discover that she had an entirely different relationship with her muse, whose gender would be a complicated matter; with "Mother Nature," who might call to her as daughter but destroy her as artist; and with language, which has been handed down from God to Adam, from Milton to Wordsworth.

[7] M[ary] A[nn] Stodart, *Female Writers: Thoughts on Their Proper Sphere, and on Their Powers of Usefulness* (London, 1842), pp. 86–88.

[8] Caroline May [Kirkland], *The American Female Poets* (Philadelphia, 1848), p. vi. Editor, critic, and domestic novelist, Kirkland also wrote under the pseudonym of Mrs. Mary Clavers. In 1845, she wrote the introduction for the American edition of Marion Reid's feminist tract, *A Plea for Woman*, which is discussed in Vol. I, Ch. 1.

[9] "Poetesses," *Saturday Review*, 25 (1868), 679 [678–79].

[10] [John Skelton], "Our Camp in the Woodland: A Day with the Gentle Poets," *Fraser's*, 70 (1864), 207.

[11] Rufus Griswold, *The Female Poets of America* (Philadelphia, 1848), p. 7.

[12] R.W. Crump provides an annotated bibliography of nineteenth- and twentieth-century criticism in *Christina Rossetti: A Reference Guide* (Boston: G.K. Hall, 1976). Relevant reviews are in *The Reader*, June 30, 1866, p. 613, and *Saturday Review*, 21 (1866), 761–62. For recent reassessments, consult Sandra Gilbert and Susan Gubar, *The Madwoman in the Attic* (New Haven: Yale Univ. Press, 1979), pp. 549–54 and 564–75; Jerome J. McGann, "Christina Rossetti's Poems: A New Edition and a Revaluation," *Victorian Studies*, 23 (1980), 237–54; and Delores Rosenblum, "Christina Rossetti: The Inward Pose," in *Shakespeare's Sisters*, ed. Sandra Gilbert and Susan Gubar (Bloomington: Indiana Univ. Press, 1979).

[13] H.B. Forman, "Christina Rossetti," in *Our Living Poets* (London, 1871), pp. 234–36, 239–40 [229–53]. The review was originally published in *Tinsley's Magazine* in 1869.

[14] Griswold, p. 93.

[15] Christina Rossetti, *Maude: Prose and Verse*, ed. R.W. Crump (Hamden, Conn.: Shoe String Press, 1976), p. 32.

[16] The process whereby Maude, Rossetti, and other women poets learn to efface themselves is cogently described in"The Aesthetics of Renunciation," which is Ch. 15 of *The Madwoman in the Attic*. On p. 548, Gilbert and Gubar are right in saying that it is the lyric poet's awareness of herself as subject that has so disturbed male critics; however, the point could have been better argued from nineteenth-century texts than from comments by Theodore Roethke and John Crowe Ransom.

[17] Quoted in Gardner B. Taplin, *The Life of Elizabeth Barrett Browning* (New Haven: Yale Univ. Press, 1957), p. 21.

[18] [James Ferrier], "Poems by Elizabeth B. Barrett," *Blackwood's*, 56 (1844), 621; Fuller is quoted in Taplin, p. 136. Taplin gives a detailed account of nineteenth-century responses to Browning's poetry.

[19] [William Stigand], "The Works of Elizabeth Barrett Browning," *Edinburgh Review*, 114 (1861), 529 [513–34]; later references will be incorporated into the text.

[20] Preface to *Poems of 1844*, in *The Poetical Works of Elizabeth Barrett Browning* (New York, 1897), p. xiv.

[21] See Mary Jane Lupton, *Elizabeth Barrett Browning* (Long Island, N.Y.: Feminist Press, 1972), pp. 32–41, and Susan Zimmerman, "Sonnets from the Portuguese: A Negative and a Positive Context," *Mary Wollstonecraft Newsletter*, 2 (1973), 7–20.

[22] Dedication to *Aurora Leigh*, in *The Poetical Works of Elizabeth Barrett Browning*, ed. Ruth M. Adams (Boston: Houghton Mifflin, 1974), p. 254; "To Mrs. Jameson," February 2, 1857, *The Letters of Elizabeth Barrett Browning*, ed. Frederic G. Kenyon (New York, 1897), II, 252; "Elizabeth Barrett Browning," *Athenaeum*, July 6, 1861, p. 20; [George Eliot], "Belles Lettres," *Westminster Review*, 67 (1857), 306; "Mrs. Browning," *Saturday Review*, 12 (1861), 41–42; "Last Poems," *Saturday Review*, 13 (1862), 472–74.

[23] *Aurora Leigh*, V. 200–22; for negative comments on this passage, see [W.E. Aytoun], *Blackwood's*, 81 (1857), 34–35, and [W.C. Roscoe], *National Review*, 4 (1857), 245.

[24] "Aurora Leigh," *Tablet*, November 29, 1856, p. 762 [762–63]. For Miss Bunion, Thackeray's caricature of an oafish, affected, and unloved poetess, refer to Ch. 1, n. 29. For recent reassessments, see Barbara Charlesworth Gelpi,

"*Aurora Leigh*: The Vocation of the Woman Poet," *Victorian Poetry*, 19 (1981), 35–48, and Cora Kaplan, Introduction, *Aurora Leigh and Other Poems* (New York: Horizon, 1978), pp. 5–36.

[25] "Aurora Leigh," *Saturday Review*, 2 (1856), 776–77 [776–78].

[26] In *Invisible Poets: Afro-Americans of the Nineteenth Century* (Urbana: Univ. of Illinois Press, 1974), Joan Sherman identifies Harper as the most popular black poet before Paul Laurence Dunbar. Her *Poems on Miscellaneous Subjects*, published in 1854 with a preface by William Lloyd Garrison, reached its twentieth edition in 1871. Other examples of women poets writing about social problems are cited in Watts and in Aaron Kramer's *The Prophetic Tradition in American Poetry, 1835–1900* (Rutherford, N.J.: Fairleigh Dickinson Univ. Press, 1968).

[27] Quoted in Lona M. Packer, *Christina Rossetti* (Berkeley: Univ. of California Press, 1963), p. 154.

[28] Helen Cooper traces Browning's increasing insight into her social responsibilities as a woman poet in "Working into Light: Elizabeth Barrett Browning," *Shakespeare's Sisters*, pp. 65–81. Her knowledge of and influence on other women writers have been discussed by Jack L. Capps, *Emily Dickinson's Reading, 1836–1886* (Cambridge, Mass.: Harvard Univ. Press, 1966), pp. 83–86; Gilbert and Gubar, pp. 575–80; Ellen Moers, *Literary Women* (Garden City, N.Y.: Doubleday, 1976), pp. 52–60; and Patricia Thomson, *George Sand and the Victorians* (New York: Columbia Univ. Press, 1977), pp. 43–60.

[29] "To Mrs. Jameson," April 12 [1853], *Letters* II, 110–11; "To Mrs. Martin," October, 1855, II, 213; "To Mrs. Martin," February, [1857], II, 254.

[30] [W.E. Aytoun], "Poetic Aberrations," *Blackwood's*, 87 (1860), 494 [490–94]. The review is consistent with his later attack on women lawyers and lecturers "cackling" about their rights; see "Rights of Woman," *Blackwood's*, 92 (1862), 183–201.

[31] [Kate Field], "Elizabeth Barrett Browning," *Atlantic*, 8 (1861), 368. Equally typical of the many pieces praising her as mother, wife, and poet are "Mrs. Browning," *Christian Examiner*, 72 (1862), 65–88, and Edward Hincks, "Elizabeth Barrett Browning," in *Eminent Women of the Age*, ed. James Parton (Hartford, Conn., 1868), pp. 221–37. For an account of Browning's changing attitudes toward motherhood, refer to Sandra Donaldson, "'Motherhood's Advent in Power': Elizabeth Barrett Browning's Poems About Motherhood," *Victorian Poetry*, 18 (1980), 51–60.

[32] Both letters are quoted in *The Letters and Private Papers of William Makepeace Thackeray*, ed. Gordon N. Ray, IV (Cambridge, Mass.: Harvard Univ. Press, 1946), pp. 226–29. Alethea Hayter analyzes the exchange in *Browning Society Notes*, 8, No. 3 (1978), 5–10.

[33] On Dickinson's knowledge of women writers, see Capps and Karl Keller, *The Only Kangaroo Among the Beauty: Emily Dickinson and America* (Baltimore, Md.: Johns Hopkins Univ. Press, 1979). On Dickinson's decision not to publish her poems, consult Thomas H. Johnson, *Emily Dickinson: An Interpretive Biography* (Cambridge, Mass.: Belknap Press of Harvard Univ., 1955), pp. 110–17; Jay Leyda, *The Years and Hours of Emily Dickinson*, 2 vols. (New Haven: Yale Univ. Press, 1960); and Richard B. Sewall, *The Life of Emily Dickinson*, 2 vols. (New York: Farrar, Straus, and Giroux, 1974), esp. Ch. 23. The following contain provocative analyses of Dickinson's sense of herself as a woman poet: Gilbert and Gubar, pp. 581–650; Moers, pp. 55–62, 168–70; and Rebecca Patterson, *Emily Dickinson's Imagery* (Amherst: Univ. of Massachusetts Press, 1979). In *Shakespeare's Sisters*, see

Terrence Diggory, "Armed Women, Naked Men: Dickinson, Whitman, and Their Successors"; Albert Gelpi, "Emily Dickinson and the Deerslayer: The Dilemma of the Woman Poet in America"; and Adrienne Rich, "Vesuvius at Home: The Power of Emily Dickinson."

³⁴ In addition to the essays excerpted here, the reader might consult the bibliographies of nineteenth-century texts in Elaine Showalter's influential *A Literature of Their Own: British Women Novelists from Brontë to Lessing* (Princeton: Princeton Univ. Press, 1977), and in Sally Mitchell's *The Fallen Angel: Chastity, Class and Women's Reading, 1835–1880* (Bowling Green, O.: Bowling Green Univ. Popular Press, 1981).

³⁵ Exact sales figures are hard to come by; see James D. Hart, *The Popular Book* (Berkeley: Univ. of California Press, 1963), and F.L. Mott, *Golden Multitudes: The Story of Best Sellers in the United States* (New York: Macmillan, 1947).

³⁶ Mitchell, p. 91.

³⁷ Elizabeth Strutt, *The Feminine Soul: Its Nature and Attributes* (London, 1857), p. 88.

³⁸ The best general study of these novelists is Vineta Colby's *Yesterday's Woman: Domestic Realism in the English Novel* (Princeton: Princeton Univ. Press, 1974). In "Dinah Mulock Craik and the Tactics of Sentiment: A Case Study in Victorian Female Authorship," *Feminist Studies*, 2 (1975), 5–23, Elaine Showalter shows how a domestic novelist could combine didacticism and subversive feminism.

³⁹ American novelists frequently associated with the sentimental tradition are Caroline Chesebro', Maria Cummins, Caroline Gilman, Sarah Josepha Hale, Caroline Lee Hentz, Mary Jane Holmes, Maria Jane McIntosh, Sarah Parton (Fanny Fern), Catharine Maria Sedgwick, Elizabeth Stuart Phelps, Emma Dorothy Eliza Nevitte Southworth, Ann Stephens, Harriet Beecher Stowe, Mary Hawes Terhune (Marion Harland), Anna Warner, Susan Warner, Augusta Evans Wilson. As a group, they have been the subject of considerable controversy during the twentieth century. In *The Sentimental Novel in America, 1789–1860* (Durham, N.C.: Duke Univ. Press, 1940), Herbert Ross Brown argued that the domestic novels upheld the joys of family life, the dignity of housewives' work, and the importance of submissive endurance. That view has been challenged by Helen Papashvily, who sees the novels as handbooks of feminine revolt motivated by women's anger against men; Dee Garrison, who discovers in the novels strong criticism of the clergy, the marriage laws, and the penal system; Ann Douglas, who treats the novelists and the clergy as disestablished groups seeking to become the self-appointed guardians of popular culture; Nina Baym, who argues that the novels are structured around a young girl's successful struggle to make her way in a hostile world; Mary Kelley, who shows that the women's efforts to forge a domestic ideal were consistently undercut by their own dissatisfaction and despair; and most recently by Jane Tompkins, who suggests that the sentimentalists used the central myth of their culture—the crucifixion—as the basis for a new myth that reflected their own interests. See Helen Papashvily, *All the Happy Endings* (New York: Harper, 1956); Dee Garrison, "Immoral Fiction in the Late Victorian Library," *American Quarterly*, 28 (1976), 71–89; Ann Douglas, *The Feminization of American Culture*; Nina Baym, *Women's Fiction: A Guide to Novels by and about Women in America, 1820–1870* (Ithaca, N.Y.: Cornell Univ. Press, 1978); Mary Kelley, "The Sentimentalists: Promise and Betrayal in the Home," *Signs*, 4 (1979), 434–46; Jane Tompkins, "Sentimental

Power: *Uncle Tom's Cabin* and the Politics of Literary History," *Glyph*, 8 (1981), 79-102.

40 Occasionally male writers adopted female pen names. As Papashvily notes, J.H. Ingraham published his last novel as Kate Conyngham.

41 [Margaret Oliphant], "Modern Novelists—Great and Small," *Blackwood's*, 77 (1855), 555, 557.

42 *Harriet Martineau's Autobiography*, ed. Maria Weston Chapman (Boston, 1877), I, 282; "Novels by the Author of *Two Old Men's Tales*," *Dublin University Magazine*, 34 (1849), 575-76, 590. According to Sally Mitchell, the promise of Marsh's first book, *The Admiral's Daughter*, was not fulfilled in her later works. Mitchell suggests that Marsh was typical of other minor female novelists who wrote more convincingly in isolation than they did after entering the literary world (p. 66).

43 Rev. of Emilia Wyndham, *Examiner*, April 11, 1846, pp. 227-29; [James Lorimer], "Noteworthy Novels," *North British Review*, 11 (1849), 479 [475-93]. Lorimer is not unique in identifying Sand as a notorious lady novelist. As Patricia Thomson has shown, English readers of the 1830s and 1840s saw Sand as an apostle of philosophical skepticism, a symbol of postrevolutionary writing in France, and a sexual libertine. See, for instance, reviews in *Foreign Quarterly Review*, 27 (1841), 118-41, and [H.F. Chorley], *Athenaeum*, May 22, 1847, pp. 543-44. On Sand's reputation in America, consult H.M. Jones, "American Comment on George Sand (1837-1848)," *American Literature*, 3 (1932), 389-407, and C.M. Lombard, "George Sand's Image in America, 1837-1876," *Revue de Littérature Comparée*, 40 (1966), 177-86. Moers shows Sand's importance to women writers.

44 [Caroline May Kirkland], "Novels and Novelists," *North American Review*, 76 (1853), 110 [104-23]; M.G. Van Rensselaer, "American Fiction," *Lippincott's*, 23 (1879), 753-61. Later references to Kirkland's article will be incorporated into the text. Although *The Wide, Wide World* was very popular in England, Margaret Oliphant dismissed the heroine as one of "those dreadful perfect little girls who come over from the other side of the Atlantic to do good to the Britishers," and Charlotte Yonge worried that Warner's novel would have "the really grave and really injurious effect of teaching little girls to expect a lover in any one who is good natured to them." See "Modern Novelists—Great and Small," p. 567, and "Children's Literature of the Last Century," *Macmillan's*, 20 (1869), 309. Edward Foster gives information on sales and reviews in *Susan and Anna Warner* (Boston: Twayne, 1978).

45 [Henry James], rev. of *The Schönberg-Cotta Family*, *Nation*, 1 (1865), 345 [344-45].

46 [R.H. Hutton], "Novels by the Authoress of John Halifax," *North British Review*, 29 (1858), 474 [466-481].

47 "Female Novelists," *London Review*, 1 (1860), 137 [137-38].

48 "On the Treatment of Love in Novels," *Fraser's*, 53 (1856), 414.

49 [W.R. Greg], "The False Morality of Lady Novelists," *National Review*, 8 (1859), 148-49 [144-67].

50 [J.M. Ludlow], "Ruth," *North British Review*, 19 (1853), 169-71 [151-74]. According to Nina Auerbach, the association between creativity and childbirth produced problems for "the century's greatest and most determinedly childless novelists": Jane Austen and George Eliot." See "Artists and Mothers: A False Alliance," *Women and Literature*, 6 (1978), 3-15.

51 [G.H. Lewes], "The Lady Novelists," *Westminster Review*, 58 (1852), 131-36

[129–41]. This essay shows greater tact than Lewes' 1850 review of Charlotte Brontë's *Shirley*, which is discussed later in this chapter.

52 [George Eliot], "Woman in France: Madame de Sablé," *Westminster Review*, 62 (1854), 448–53, 472–73 [448–73].

53 Gaskell used the name of Cotton Mather Mills for some of her earliest stories and published *Mary Barton* anonymously in 1848. But readers quickly identified her as a woman. On Gaskell's determination to reconcile writing and maternal responsibilities, see Ch. 1; for a discussion of *Ruth*, refer to Ch. 4. J.G. Sharps reports on a project which linked Gaskell to the American domestic novelist Maria Cummins in *Mrs. Gaskell's Observation and Invention* (Fontwell, Sussex: Linden Press, 1970), pp. 265–66. In 1857 Gaskell edited an annotated version of *Mabel Vaughan* for Sampson Low. Her preface emphasizes the importance of Anglo-American friendships and the usefulness of fiction in showing "the quiet domestic circle, into which the stranger is rarely admitted."

54 Quoted in *The Life of Harriet Beecher Stowe Compiled from Her Letters and Journals by Her Son* (Boston, 1889), p. 149.

55 "To Gamaliel Bailey," March 9, [1851], in Joseph S. Van Why, *Nook Farm*, ed. Earl H. French (Hartford, Conn.: Stowe-Day Foundation, 1975), pp. 16, 18.

56 Critics chastizing Stowe for her unwomanly presumption include James A. Waddell, *"Uncle Tom's Cabin" Reviewed* (Raleigh, N.C., 1852); George F. Holmes and John R. Thompson, both in *Southern Literary Messenger*, 18 (1852), 630–38 and 721–31. Several of the novels written in angry reaction to *Uncle Tom's Cabin* are by women, including Maria McIntosh's *The Lofty and the Lowly* (1853) and Caroline Lee Hentz's *The Planter's Northern Bride* (1854). For information on nineteenth-century responses to *Uncle Tom's Cabin*, refer to Jean W. Ashton, *Harriet Beecher Stowe: A Reference Guide* (Boston: G.K. Hall, 1977); Severn Duvall, *"Uncle Tom's Cabin*: The Sinister Side of the Patriarchy," *New England Quarterly*, 36 (1963), 3–22; and F.J. Klingberg, "Harriet Beecher Stowe and Social Reform in England," *American Historical Review*, 43 (1938), 542–52.

57 [Charles Beard], *"Uncle Tom's Cabin," Prospective Review*, 8 (1852), 490–513; [Anna Maria Fielding Hall], "American Opinions," *Sharpe's*, NS 1 (1852), 250–54.

58 George Sand, rev. of *Uncle Tom's Cabin, La Presse*, December 17, 1852; rpt. in *The Life and Letters of Harriet Beecher Stowe*, ed. Annie Fields (Boston, 1898), pp. 153–57 [151–57]. Stowe liked the Sand review so much that she included it in the 1889 edition of *Uncle Tom's Cabin*. Elizabeth Ammons discusses the domestic themes praised by Sand in "Heroines in *Uncle Tom's Cabin*," *American Literature*, 49 (1977), 161–79. Stowe's relationship with nineteenth-century women writers has been explored by Moers, pp. 14–18, 36–40; and by Gilbert and Gubar, pp. 481–83, 532–35.

59 See Showalter, *A Literature of Their Own*, Ch. 3, and Inga-Stina Ewbank, *Their Proper Sphere: A Study of the Brontë Sisters as Early Victorian Female Novelists* (Cambridge, Mass.: Harvard Univ. Press, 1968), Ch. 1.

60 "Recent Popular Novels," *Dublin University Magazine*, 57 (1861), 191–93 [192–208].

61 Elaine Showalter defined the "feminine phase" and compiled the list of male pseudonyms in *A Literature of Their Own*, esp. pp. 57–60. Consequences of male impersonation are also analyzed by Gilbert and Gubar, pp. 65–71.

62 On women's relationship with the press, see Showalter; Ann Douglas Wood, "'The Scribbling Women' and Fanny Fern: Why Women Wrote," *American*

Quarterly, 23 (1971), 3–24; and Glenda Gates Riley, "The Subtle Subversion: Changes in the Traditionalist Image of the American Woman," *Historian*, 32 (1969–70), 210–27.

⁶³ Showalter discusses the influence of the Eliot legend on pp. 107–10 and 150–52 of *A Literature of Their Own*, and in "The Greening of Sister George," *Nineteenth Century Fiction*, 35 (1980), 292–311.

⁶⁴ "To W.S. Williams," October 28, 1847, *The Brontës: Their Lives, Friendships and Correspondence*, ed. T.J. Wise and J.A. Symington (Oxford: Shakespeare Head, 1931–38), II, 151 [150–51].

⁶⁵ "To G.H. Lewes," November 6, 1847, *The Brontës*, II, 152–53; G.H. Lewes, "Recent Novels: French and English," *Fraser's*, 36 (1847), 690–94 [686–95]; "To G.H. Lewes," January 12, 1848, *The Brontës*, II, 178–79 [178–80].

⁶⁶ Franklin Gary makes this argument in "Charlotte Brontë and George Henry Lewes," *PMLA*, 51 (1939), 518–42.

⁶⁷ "To G.H. Lewes," November 1, 1849, *The Brontës*, III, 31; [G.H. Lewes], "Currer Bell's *Shirley*," *Edinburgh Review*, 91 (1850), 154–58, 164–66, 173 [153–73]; "To G.H. Lewes," [January, 1850], *The Brontës*, III, 67. In an 1857 letter to Elizabeth Gaskell claiming that he had not meant the article to be disrespectful to women, Lewes attributed some of the "offensive sentences" to Lord Francis Jeffrey of the *Edinburgh Review*; see *The George Eliot Letters*, ed. Gordon S. Haight (New Haven: Yale Univ. Press, 1954), II, 315–16.

⁶⁸ Note, for instance, his articles in *Westminster Review*, 59 (1853), 474–91, and *Leader*, February 12, 1853, pp. 163–64. Brontë's relationship with her critics has been studied by Winifred Gérin, *Charlotte Brontë: The Evolution of Genius* (New York: Oxford Univ. Press, 1967); Miriam Allott, *The Brontës: The Critical Heritage* (London: Routledge, 1974); and Tom Winnifrith, *The Brontës and Their Background: Romance and Reality* (London: Macmillan, 1973), esp. Ch. 7.

⁶⁹ [George Eliot], "Silly Novels by Lady Novelists," *Westminster Review*, 66 (1856), 459–61 [442–61]. Eliot's reading of Austen, the Brontës, Gaskell, Sand, and other women novelists is documented in Gordon Haight's *George Eliot: A Biography* (New York: Oxford Univ. Press, 1968). Questions of influence are addressed by Sandra Gilbert and Susan Gubar, Ellen Moers, Elaine Showalter, and Patricia Thomson.

⁷⁰ "To John Blackwood," [December 2, 1858], *Eliot Letters*, II, 506; "To Mme. Eugene Bodichon," [June 30, 1859], *Eliot Letters*, III, 106; quoted in J.W. Cross, *George Eliot's Life as Related in her Letters and Journals* (New York, 1885), I, 310. Haight describes the machinations surrounding the pseudonym in his biography; Alexander Welsh gives a fine analysis of the pen name in "The Secrets of George Eliot," *Yale Review*, 68 (1979), 589–97.

⁷¹ In *George Eliot: The Critical Heritage* (New York: Barnes and Noble, 1971), David Carroll notes that the third volume aroused "the most indignant and sustained opposition George Eliot had to face in her entire career" (p. 13). In addition to the reviews excerpted here, the following also take issue with Eliot's treatment of passion: [R.H. Hutton], *National Review*, 11 (1860), 191–219; *Guardian*, April 25, 1860, pp. 377–78; *Saturday Review*, 9 (1860), 470–71; [J.C. Robertson], *Quarterly Review*, 108 (1860), 469–99; A.C. Swinburne, *A Note on Charlotte Brontë* (1877), rpt. in *The Complete Works of A.C. Swinburne*, ed. Edmund Gosse and T.J. Wise (London: Heinemann, 1926), XIV, 14–17. For more information on nine-teenth-century criticism, consult Constance Fulmer, *George Eliot: A Reference Guide*

(Boston: G.K. Hall, 1977) and John Holstrom and Laurence Lerner, *George Eliot and Her Readers* (London: Bodley Head, 1966).

72 "Recent Popular Novels," *Dublin University Magazine*, 57 (1861), 198 [192–203]; "Novels and Novelists," *London Quarterly Review*, 16 (1861), 306–08 [301–310].

73 *Eliot Letters*, III, 56–57, 197–98, 198–99. Gaskell's love for George Eliot and her distress regarding the relationship with Lewes are documented in detail by Winifred Gérin in *Elisabeth Gaskell: A Biography* (Oxford: Clarendon Press, 1976), pp. 253–56.

74 [Margaret Oliphant], "The Life and Letters of George Eliot," *Edinburgh Review*, 161 (1885), 546. In *George Eliot: The Emergent Self* (New York: Knopf, 1975), Ruby V. Redinger shows how Eliot, her husband J.W. Cross, and some of her most devoted fans created the image of the novelist as sage and sybil.

75 Baym, Ch. 10. In America, the sentimentalists were succeeded by the generation of local colorists, including Kate Chopin, Mary Wilkins Freeman, Sarah Orne Jewett, and Constance Woolson; in England, attention shifted to the sensationalists and the militant "feminist" novelists, such as Mona Caird, Sarah Grand, Elizabeth Robins, and Olive Schreiner. On these phases of literary history, consult Ann Douglas Wood, "The Literature of Impoverishment: The Women Local Colorists in America, 1865–1914," *Women's Studies*, 1 (1972), 3–45, and Showalter, Chs. 7–8.

76 E.S. Dallas, *The Gay Science* (London, 1866), II, 296–99.

Chapter 3

1 [William Barnes], "Patmore's Poems," *Fraser's*, 68 (1863), 130, 131, 133 [130–34]. On the Victorian angel-heroine and her complicated cultural and literary functions, see also Alexander Welsh, *The City of Dickens* (Oxford: Clarendon Press, 1971), pp. 141–228; Carol Christ, "Victorian Masculinity and the Angel in the House," in *A Widening Sphere: Changing Roles of Victorian Women*, ed. Martha Vicinus (Bloomington: Indiana Univ. Press, 1977), pp. 146–62; Sandra Gilbert and Susan Gubar, *The Madwoman in the Attic: The Woman Writer and the Nineteenth Century Imagination* (New Haven: Yale Univ. Press, 1979); and Laurence Lerner, *Love and Marriage: Literature and Social Context* (New York: St. Martin's Press, 1979), pp. 130–53.

2 [Sarah Lewis], *Woman's Mission* (Boston, 1840), pp. 33, 36, 30.

3 Sarah Stickney Ellis, *The Women of England: Their Social Duties and Domestic Habits* (New York, 1839), pp. 22–23.

4 *Woman's Mission*, pp. 34–36.

5 [Abraham Hayward], "Thackeray's Writings," *Edinburgh Review*, 87 (1848), 54.

6 [John Forster], "*Vanity Fair*," *Examiner*, July 22, 1848, p. 468; [Henry F. Chorley], "*Vanity Fair*," *Athenaeum*, August 12, 1848, p. 795; "W.M. Thackeray and Arthur Pendennis, Esquires," *Fraser's*, 43 (1851), 76; "Contemporary Writers —Mr. Thackeray," *Dublin University Magazine*, 32 (1848), 448; "Novels and Novelists," *London Quarterly Review*, 16 (1861), 291; [Robert Bell], "*Vanity Fair*," *Fraser's*, 38 (1848), 321.

7 [David Masson], "*Pendennis* and *Copperfield*: Thackeray and Dickens," *North British Review* (Am. Ed.), 15 (1851), 42.

8 [Henry F. Chorley], "*Vanity Fair*," *Athenaeum*, July 24, 1847, p. 785.

9 "*David Copperfield*," *Examiner*, December 14, 1850, p. 798.

10 Nathanial Hawthorne, *English Note-Books*, ed. Randall Stewart (New York: Modern Language Association of America, 1941), p. 620; for Tennyson, see

Derek Patmore, *The Life and Times of Coventry Patmore* (London: Constable, 1949), p. 88; Caroline Norton, "*The Angel in the House* and *The Goblin Market*," *Macmillan's*, 8 (1863), 398–401.

[11] [R.K. Hutton], "*Poems* by Coventry Patmore," *North British Review* (Am. Ed.), 28 (1858), 292, 294.

[12] "Characters in *Bleak House*," *Putnam's*, 2 (1853), 561.

[13] [Henry F. Chorley], "*Bleak House*," *Athenaeum*, September 17, 1853, p. 1087.

[14] "A Gossip About New Books," *Bentley's Miscellany*, 34 (1853), 374.

[15] "Dickens' *Bleak House*," *Spectator*, 26 (1853), 924.

[16] [N.W. Senior], "Thackeray's *Works*," *Edinburgh Review*, 99 (1854), 197, 202–3 [196–243].

[17] "Mary L. Ware," *Putnam's*, 1 (1853), 371, 372–73 [370–82].

[18] "Thackeray's Women," *Knickerbocker*, 42 (1853), 156, 157–58 [155–59].

[19] [J.F. Kirk], "Thackeray as a Novelist," *North American Review*, 77 (1853), 213–14, 214–15 [199–219].

[20] See Christ, "Victorian Masculinity and the Angel in the House."

[21] Frances E. Willard, *Woman and Temperance, or The Work and the Workers of the Woman's Christian Temperance Union*, 3rd ed. (Hartford, Conn., 1883), p. 458.

[22] "Novels and Novelists," *London Quarterly Review*, 16 (1861), 292.

[23] See Gilbert and Gubar, pp. 3–94, for an imaginative discussion of the angel/witch polarity and its application to female authorship. Many of their observations with respect to the witch-as-author also describe the Victorian strong-minded-woman-as-author.

[24] "Feminine Wranglers," *Saturday Review*, 18 (1864), 112.

[25] Jane Austen, *Persuasion* (1818; rpt. London: J.M.Dent, 1906), pp. 51, 207, 99.

[26] [E.P. Whipple], "Novels of the Season," *North American Review*, 67 (1848), 356.

[27] [Coventry Patmore], "The Social Position of Women," *North British Review*, 14 (1851), 525–28 [515–40].

[28] *The George Eliot Letters*, Vol. II, ed. Gordon S. Haight (New Haven: Yale Univ. Press, 1954), 176n.

[29] [George Lewes], "The Lady Novelists," *Westminster Review*, 58 (1852), 129.

[30] "New Employments for Women," *Cassell's Family Magazine*, Ser. 3, no. 3 (1878), 331.

[31] Elizabeth Gaskell, *North and South* (London, 1855), II, 330.

[32] Caroline Norton, *Old Sir Douglas* (London, 1868), I, 160.

[33] Charlotte Yonge, *The Clever Woman of the Family* (1865; rpt. London, 1886), p. 357.

[34] Frances Power Cobbe, "What Shall We Do with Our Old Maids?" *Fraser's*, 66 (1862), 605.

[35] "*The Princess*; by Alfred Tennyson," *Gentleman's Magazine*, 183 (1848), 131.

[36] [?William Howitt], rev. of *The Princess*, *Howitt's Journal*, 3 (1848), 28–29.

[37] [Charles Kingsley], "Tennyson," *Fraser's*, 42 (1850), 250 [245–55].

[38] "Tennyson's *Princess*," *Eclectic*, 4th ser., 23 (1848), 423.

[39] Tennyson, *The Princess*, II. 154–64.

[40] *The Princess*, VII. 243–70. Quoted by [Dora Greenwell], "Our Single Women," *North British Review* (Am. Ed.), 36 (1862), 47; and R. Heber Newton, *Womanhood: Lectures on Woman's Work in the World* (New York, 1881), pp. 29–30.

[41] "New Novels by Lady G. Fullerton and Currer Bell," *Christian Remembrancer*, NS 25 (1853), 423.

[42] [E.P. Whipple], "Novels of the Season," *North American Review*, 67 (1848), 355.

[43] [James Lorimer], "Noteworthy Novels," *North British Review*, 11 (1849), 488.

[44] [George Lewes], "*Ruth* and *Villette*," *Westminster Review*, 59 (1853), 491 [474–91].

[45] [James Lorimer], "Noteworthy Novels," *North British Review*, 11 (1849), 476–77 [475–93].

[46] Rev. of *Jane Eyre*, *Christian Remembrancer*, 25 (1848), 396–409; [James Lorimer], "Noteworthy Novels," *North British Review*, 11 (1849), 487; [E.P. Whipple], "Novels of the Season," *North American Review*, 67 (1848), 356.

[47] "New Novels by Lady G. Fullerton and Currer Bell," *Christian Remembrancer*, NS 25 (1853), 442–43 [401–43].

[48] Rev. of *Jane Eyre*, *Christian Remembrancer*, 25 (1848), [396–409].

[49] [Elizabeth Rigby, Lady Eastlake], "*Vanity Fair* and *Jane Eyre*," *Quarterly Review*, 84 (1848), 173–74 [153–85].

[50] [Margaret Oliphant], "Modern Novelists—Great and Small," *Blackwood's*, 77 (1855), 557.

[51] [W.E. Aytoun], "Mrs. Barrett Browning—*Aurora Leigh*," *Blackwood's*, 81 (1857), 32, 33.

[52] [John Nichol], "*Aurora Leigh*," *Westminster Review*, 68 (1857), 406, 409.

[53] "*Aurora Leigh*," *Dublin University Magazine*, 49 (1857), 470.

[54] [Henry F. Chorley], "*Aurora Leigh*," *Athenaeum*, November 22, 1856, p. 1425 [1425–27].

[55] [Isaphene M. Luyster], "Mrs. Browning," *Christian Examiner*, 72 (1862), 88, 81 [65–88].

[56] [C.C. Everett], "Elizabeth Barrett Browning," *North American Review*, 85 (1857), 436 [415–41].

[57] "Mrs. Browning's New Poem," *Putnam's*, 9 (1857), 34, 29, 30, 31, 30, 32 [28–38].

[58] See Sally Mitchell, "Sentiment and Suffering: Women's Recreational Reading in the 1860s," *Victorian Studies*, 21 (1977), 29–45.

[59] "*Middlemarch*," *British Quarterly Review*, 57 (1873), 413 [407–29]. For a good account of recent responses to Dorothea, consult Elaine Showalter's "The Greening of Sister George," *Nineteenth Century Fiction*, 35 (1980), 292–311.

[60] Leslie Stephen, "George Eliot," *Cornhill*, 43 (1881), 167–68 [152–68].

[61] Edward Cook, *Life of Florence Nightingale* (London: Macmillan, 1913), I, 97.

[62] [Henry James], "*Middlemarch*," *Galaxy*, 15 (1873), 425–26 [422–28].

[63] Ibid., pp. 425, 428.

Chapter 4

[1] Mary Russell Mitford, *Recollections of a Literary Life* (London, 1852), III, 226; Henry Giles, *Illustrations of Genius* (Boston, 1854), pp. 80–81. A different type of division appears between reviewers who disagreed about the very propriety of Hawthorne's presenting a fallen woman in fiction. B. Bernard Cohen (*The Recognition of Nathaniel Hawthorne* [Ann Arbor: Univ. of Michigan Press, 1969]), Kenneth Walter Cameron (*Hawthorne Among His Contemporaries* [Hartford, Conn.: Transcendental Books, 1968]), and Joseph Donald Crowley (*Hawthorne: The Critical Heritage* [London: Routledge and Kegan Paul, 1970]) all present the humane,

complex evaluation of Hester by George Bailey Loring (*Massachusetts Quarterly Review*, 3 [1850], 484–500) and the hysterical diatribe by Rev. Arthur Cleveland Coxe (*Church Review*, 3 [1851], 489–511). Among other major American reviews, only *Brownson's Quarterly Review* (4 [1850], 528–32) agreed with Coxe that "it is the story that should not have been told" (p. 529). *Athenaeum* (1181 [1850], 634), *Graham's Magazine* (36 [1850], 345–46), and *The Literary World* (6 [1850], 323–25) expressly praised Hawthorne's moral and aesthetic handling of Hester; *North American Review* (71 [1850], 135–48) did not even raise the question of propriety. For recent work on the fallen woman, see Jean E. Kennard's *Victims of Convention* (Hamden, Conn.: Archon, 1978), pp. 63–79.

2 *The Letters of Mrs. Gaskell*, ed. J.A.V. Chapple and Arthur Pollard (Cambridge, Mass.: Harvard Univ. Press, 1967), p. 220. For Mrs. Gaskell and women, see Aina Rubenius' *The Woman Question in Mrs. Gaskell's Life and Works* (Upsala: Lundquist; Cambridge, Mass.: Harvard Univ. Press, 1950).

3 Margaret Oliphant, "Modern Novelists—Great and Small," *Blackwood's*, 77 (1855), 560 [554–68].

4 Gaskell, *Letters*, p. 223.

5 Ibid., p. 221.

6 Ibid., pp. 220–21.

7 For contemporary responses to *Ruth*, see Gaskell's *Letters* (pp. 220–27); Rubenius (pp. 188–216); A.B. Hopkins' *Elizabeth Gaskell, Her Life and Work* (London: Lehmann, 1952), pp. 128–32; Winifred Gérin's *Elizabeth Gaskell: A Biography* (Oxford: Clarendon, 1976), pp. 138–41; and Angus Easson's *Elizabeth Gaskell* (London: Routledge and Kegan Paul, 1979), pp. 110–12.

8 [G.H. Lewes] "Ruth and Villette," *Westminster Review*, 59 (1853), 479, 480 [474–91].

9 [J.M. Ludlow] "Ruth: A Novel," *North British Review*, 19 (1853), 154–55 [151–74]; later references will be incorporated into the text.

10 "Ruth and Villette," *Westminster Review*, p. 483.

11 "Contemporary Literature," *Bentley's Miscellany*, 33 (1853), 237–239 [233–40].

12 "The Lady Novelists of Great Britain," *Gentleman's Magazine*, 40 (1853), 22 [18–25].

13 "Ruth. A Novel," *The Literary Gazette and Journal* n.v. (1853), 79 [79–80].

14 *Letters Addressed to Mrs. Gaskell by Celebrated Contemporaries*, ed. Ross D. Waller (Manchester: John Rylands Library, 1935), p. 43.

15 *The Brontës: Life and Letters*, ed. Clement Shorter (New York: Scribner's, 1908), II, 264.

16 W.R. Greg, "The False Morality of Lady Novelists," *The National Review*, 8 (1859), 164, 165, 167 [144–67].

17 Most early reviews of *Adam Bede* were very positive (see *Blackwood's*, 85 [1859], 490–504; *Edinburgh Reivew*, 110 [1859], 223–46; *Dublin Review*, 47 [1859], 33–42; *Athenaeum*, 1635 [1859], 284). Only two journals subsequently attacked the presentation of Hetty as lurid and suggestive (*Quarterly Review*, 108 [1860], 476–77 and *North British Review*, 45 [1866], 118) and *Quarterly Review* later recanted (134 [1873], 342). In 1876 *Edinburgh Review* repeated its praise of *Adam Bede* and stressed the integrity of Eliot's presentation of Hetty (144 [1876], 445).

18 For these and many other laudatory comments, see Charles Wm. Wood's *Memorials of Mrs. Henry Wood* (London, 1894), pp. 241–42, 245–47, 249. Gail Cunningham relates *East Lynne* and *Ruth* to other portraits of women's problems

in the High Victorian period (*The New Woman and the Victorian Novel* [London: Macmillan, 1978], pp. 20–44).

[19] For attacks upon Norton's supposed moral failure, see "Our Female Sensation Novelists," *Living Age*, 78 (1863), 360–65 (originally published in *Christian Remembrancer* for 1863) and [Fitzjames Stephen] "Anti-Respectability," *Cornhill*, 8 (1863), 282–94. For aesthetic criticism of the novel, see *Saturday Review*, 15 (1863), 701–2.

[20] Rather than detailing Victorian essays on sensationalism, we will list recent works which both analyze the phenomenon and provide bibliography. Richard Stang, *The Theory of the Novel in England, 1850–1870* (New York: Columbia Univ. Press, 1959), pp. 58–59; Margaret Maison, "Adulteresses in Agony," *The Listener*, 65 (1961), 133–34; Kathleen Tillotson, "The Lighter Reading of the Eighteen-Sixties," introduction to *The Woman in White* (Boston: Houghton Mifflin, 1969), pp. ix–xxvi; P.D. Edwards, *Some Mid-Victorian Thrillers: The Sensation Novel, Its Friends and Its Foes* (St. Lucia, N.Z.: Univ. of Queensland, 1971); Harriet Adams Transue, "The Sensation Years: The Literary Character of England in the 1860's" (Ph.D. dissertation, Ohio State University, 1973); Randolph Woods Ivy, "The Victorian Sensation Novel: A Study in Formula Fiction" (Ph.D. dissertation, University of Chicago, 1974); Benjamin Franklin Fisher IV, "Sensation Fiction in a Minor Key: *The Ordeal of Richard Feverel*," in *Nineteenth-Century Literary Perspectives*, ed. Clyde de L. Ryals (Durham, N.C.: Duke Univ. Press, 1974), pp. 283–94; Elaine Showalter, *A Literature of Their Own* (Princeton: Princeton Univ. Press, 1977), pp. 153–81 (this chapter amplifies Showalter's earlier "Desperate Remedies: Sensation Novels of the 1860s" in *The Victorian Newsletter*, 49 [1976], 1–5); Winifred Hughes, *The Maniac in the Cellar* (Princeton: Princeton Univ. Press, 1980).

[21] For Collins, see Walter C. Phillips' *Dickens, Reade, and Collins, Sensation Novelists* (New York: Columbia Univ. Press, 1919); for Braddon, Robert Lee Wolff's *Sensational Victorian* (New York: Garland, 1979). The other side of women's reading interests in the 1860s is described by Sally Mitchell in "Sentiment and Suffering: Women's Recreational Reading in the 1860s," *Victorian Studies*, 21 (1977), 29–45.

[22] For Reade, see Phillips, and Wayne Burns's *Charles Reade: A Study in Victorian Authorship* (New York: Bookman, 1961); for Lawrence, Gordon Fleming's *George Alfred Lawrence and the Victorian Sensation Novel* (Tucson, Univ. of Arizona Bulletin, 23, 1952).

[23] For sensationalism in America, see Claudia Buckner's "The Origins and Early Development of the Sensation Novel in America: 1838–1870" (Ph.D. dissertation, Univ. of California, Berkeley, 1973). For the specific case of Alcott's sensationalism, see Madeleine Stern's introductions to *Behind a Mask: The Unknown Thrillers of Louisa May Alcott* and *Plots and Counterplots: More Unknown Thrillers of Louisa May Alcott* (New York: Morrow, 1975 and 1976).

[24] Margaret Oliphant, "Sensation Novels," *Blackwood's*, 91 (1862), 564, 564–65 [564–84]. For other indications of England's sense that America was "sensational," see "Sensation Journalism," *The London Review*, 2 (1861), 502–3, and "One Secret of American Bombast," *Spectator*, 39 (1866), 266–68.

[25] [John R. de C. Wise] "Belles Lettres," *Westminster Review*, 86 (1866), 269 [268–80]; "Recent Novels: Their Moral and Religious Teaching," *London Quarterly Review*, 27 (1866), 103 [100–24]. With its usually accurate sense of public sentiment, *Punch* parodied the influence of sensationalism in history and in religion

with its skit presenting Braddon as "Prof. of Modern History" in "Surprising to a Degree!" (44 [1863], 183) and with its "Sensation Sermons" (53 [1867], 17).

26 "Belles Lettres," *Westminster Review*, 1866, p. 270.

27 Mary S. Hartman, *Victorian Murderesses* (New York: Schocken, 1977), p. 251.

28 Eliza Lynn Linton, "Little Women," *Saturday Review*, 25 (1868), 545 [545-46].

29 [John R. de C. Wise] "Belles Lettres," *Westminster Review*, 84 (1865), 568 [568-84].

30 Hartman, p. 65.

31 "Tigresses in Novels," *Spectator*, 39 (1866), 275 [274-75].

32 "Sensation Novels," *Victoria*, 10 (1867), 460 [455-65].

33 W. Fraser Ray, "Sensation Novelists: Miss Braddon," *North British Review*, 43 (1865), 93, 96 [92-105]; later references will be incorporated into the text.

34 "Our Female Sensation Novelists," *Christian Remembrancer*, 46 (1863), 209-11, 228 [209-36].

35 "A Good Word for Sensation," *The Round Table*, 4 (1866), 152 [151-52].

36 Justin MacCarthy, "Novels with a Purpose," *Westminster Review*, 82 (1964), 41, 44, 45, 45, 46, 47, 48, 49 [24-49].

37 "Aurora Floyd," *Saturday Review*, 15 (1863), 149.

38 "Lady Audley's Secret," *The Times*, November 18, 1862, p. 4.

39 "HOW TO MAKE A NOVEL, a sensation song," *Blackwood's*, 95 (1864), 636-37. "Sense v. Sensation," *Punch*, 41 (1861), 31; "Mokeanna; or, The White Witness," *Punch*, 44 (1863), 71-72, 81-82, 93-94, 103-4, 115-16; "The Sensation Times," *Punch*, 44 (1863), 193; "Sensation Consensus," *Punch*, 6 (1864), 92. Francis Paget, *Lucretia; or The Heroine of the Nineteenth-Century* (London, 1868). Lewis Carroll, "Poeta Fit, Non Nascitur" (1861) in *The Complete Works of Lewis Carroll* (New York: Modern Library, 1936), pp. 880-83. W.S. Gilbert, "A Sensation Novel" in *Gilbert Before Sullivan*, ed. Jane W. Stedman (Chicago: Univ. of Chicago Press, 1967), pp. 129-66; "The Sensation Captain" in *The Bab Ballads*, ed. James Ellis (Cambridge, Mass.: Harvard Univ. Press, 1970), pp. 155-56. For other parodies, see "Daimona: The Dangerous Woman of the Period," *Southern Magazine*, 10 (1872), 331-41, plus at least half a dozen more items in *Punch*.

40 Bret Harte, "Selina Sedilia" in *Stories and Condensed Novels*, Vol. V of *The Collected Works of Bret Harte* (London, 1913), pp. 348, 348-49, 349-50, 350-51, 351, 352 [347-55].

41 For the most extended treatment of Oliphant, see Vineta and Robert A. Colby's *The Equivocal Virtue* (Hamden, Conn.: Archon, 1966).

42 For work on Jewsbury, see Jeanne Rosenmayer Fahnestock, "Geraldine Jewsbury: The Power of the Publisher's Reader," *Nineteenth Century Fiction*, 28 (1973), 253-72. Guinevere Griest also gives attention to Jewsbury in *Mudie's Circulating Library and the Victorian Novel* (Bloomington: Indiana Univ. Press, 1970).

43 "Recent Novels: Their Moral and Religious Teaching," *London Quarterly Review*, 27 (1866), 103 [100-24].

44 Margaret Oliphant, "Mr. Thackeray and his Novels," *Blackwood's*, 77 (1855), 95 [86-96].

45 Margaret Oliphant, "Novels by Sir Edward Bulwer Lytton," *Bentley's Quarterly Review*, 1 (1859), 91, 92, 93 [73-105]. In 1873 Oliphant repeated her strictures. In a review which praised Bulwer-Lytton's *My Novel* as "the most brilliant and perfect of contemporary works of fiction" (p. 376), she can still say that "he did not possess that [gift] of drawing women. It is rare among men. . . . A beautiful and sweet abstraction of womankind with hair, eyes, throat, &, nicely

put in, with smiles and tears handy, and a few pretty speeches, is all that is really necessary for a heroine of the good old-fashioned type . . . the abstraction is good enough for him" (p. 377) ("Lord Lytton," *Blackwood's*, 113 [1873], 356-78).

⁴⁶Margaret Oliphant, "Charles Reade's Novels," *Blackwood's*, 106 (1869), 501, 490 [488-514].

⁴⁷"Women's Heroines," *Saturday Review*, 23 (1867), 260 [259-61].

⁴⁸"Illustrated Sensations," *The Round Table*, 4 (1866), 35.

⁴⁹Fahnestock, p. 262.

⁵⁰"Sensation Novels," *Victoria*, p. 461.

⁵¹"Our Female Sensation Novelists," p. 233.

⁵²Margaret Oliphant, "Modern Novelists—Great and Small," *Blackwood's*, 77 (1855), 554-68; "Sensation Novels," 91 (1862), 564-84; "Novels," 94 (1863), 168-83; "Novels," 102 (1867), 257-80.

⁵³Oliphant (1855), pp. 557, 558; later references will be incorporated into the text.

⁵⁴Oliphant (1867), p. 263; later references will be incorporated into the text.

⁵⁵Wolff, *Sensational Victorian*, pp. 200-207, also quoted in Wolff's "Devoted Disciple: The Letters of Mary Elizabeth Braddon to Sir Edward Bulwer-Lytton, 1862-1873," *Harvard Library Bulletin*, 22 (1974), 5-35, 129-61.

⁵⁶Margaret Oliphant, *The Victorian Age of English Literature* (New York, 1892), pp. 494-95.

⁵⁷For example, [T.S. Baynes], "Swinburne's *Poems*," *Edinburgh Review*, 134 (1871), 93-95; and [Alfred Austin], "The Poetry of the Period: Mr. Swinburne," *Temple Bar*, 26 (1869), 468.

⁵⁸[Baynes], p. 93.

⁵⁹"Mr. George Meredith's 'Modern Love,'" *Spectator*, 35 (1862), 581; "Mr. George Meredith's Poems," *Saturday Review*, 16 (1863), 562, 563.

⁶⁰Mary Elizabeth Braddon, *Lady Audley's Secret* (1862; rpt. New York: Dover 1974, from the 1887 ed.), p. 47. Braddon's description is actually based on the severe Pre-Raphaelite style of the early 1850s, not on Rossetti's lush paintings of the 1860s (few of which had been exhibited by 1862). Rossetti's work of the 1860s fully justified the association Braddon drew, however.

⁶¹"Mr. George Meredith's 'Modern Love,'" p. 581.

⁶²[John Morley], "Mr. Swinburne's New Poems," *Saturday Review*, 22 (1866), 145-46.

⁶³[W.J. Courthope], "The Latest Development of Literary Poetry: Swinburne, Rossetti, Morris," *Quarterly Review*, 132 (1872), 71, 75, 71.

⁶⁴"Thomas Maitland" [Robert Buchanan], "The Fleshly School of Poetry: Mr. D.G. Rossetti," *Contemporary Review*, 18 (1871), 335-38, 343, 348 [334-50].

⁶⁵[John Skelton], "Mr. Swinburne and His Critics," *Fraser's*, 74 (1866), 639-40.

⁶⁶"Swinburne's Poems and Ballads," *Nation*, 3 (1866), 446.

⁶⁷Richard Grant White, "Mr. Swinburne's Poems," *Galaxy*, 2 (1866), 666, 667 [665-670].

⁶⁸A.C. Swinburne, *Notes on Poems and Reviews* (London, 1866; rpt. in *The Complete Works of Algernon Charles Swinburne*, ed. Edmund Gosse and T.J. Wise [London, 1926]), XVI, 369-70 and 372-73.

⁶⁹"Mr. Swinburne on His Critics," *Spectator*, 39 (1866), 1229.

⁷⁰[Alfred Austin], pp. 457-58, 459, 460-61, 461-62, 463, 464, 465, 467-68, 469 [457-74].

71 [Baynes], p. 95.

72 [Walter Pater], "Poems by William Morris," *Westminster Review*, 90 (1868), 303, 301, 309, 311-12 [300-12]. Reprinted, with some changes, as "Aesthetic Poetry" in Pater's *Appreciations* (London, 1889). The concluding part of the article, quoted here, was also used as the "Conclusion" to Pater's *Studies in the History of the Renaissance* (London, 1873).

73 Pater, *Studies in the History of the Renaissance* (London, 1873; rpt. in *Selected Writings of Walter Pater*, ed. Harold Bloom [New York: Signet/New American Library, 1974]), pp. 46-47.

74 [George Barnett Smith] "Mrs. Gaskell and Her Novels," *Cornhill*, 29 (1874), 191-212 [191-212].

75 For Collins' relations with Caroline Graves and Martha Rudd, see Kenneth Robinson, *Wilkie Collins; A Biography* (New York: Macmillan, 1952); for Reade and Mrs. Seymour, see Malcom Elwin, *Charles Reade: A Biography* (London: Cape, 1931); for the breakup of Meredith's marriage to Mary Ellen Peacock, see Diane Johnson, *The True History of the First Mrs. Meredith and Other Lesser Lives* (New York: Knopf, 1972); for Swinburne, see Jean Overton Fuller, *Swinburne: A Critical Biography* (London: Chatto & Windus, 1968). Wendell Stacy Johnson's *Living in Sin* (Chicago: Nelson-Hall, 1979) discusses the tangled lives of various eminent Victorians.

76 Kenneth Robinson, *Wilkie Collins* (New York: Macmillan, 1952), p. 119.

77 Wilkie Collins, *Armadale* (London, 1866).

78 "Daly's Broadway Theatre," *The New York Times*, November 11, 1873, p. 5.

79 "Olympic Theatre," *The Times*, May 21, 1873, p. 14.

80 "Broadway Theater—The New Magdalen," *Daily Tribune*, November 11, 1873, p. 4.

81 "The 'New Magdalen' and Its Lesson," *Daily Graphic*, November 17, 1873, p. 106.

82 "A Lady Critic Gives Her Views About Wilkie Collins' Great Play," *Daily Graphic*, November 11, 1873, p. 67.

83 "Daly's Broadway Theatre," p. 5.

84 "Broadway Theatre—The New Magdalen," p. 4.

85 Robert Ashley, *Wilkie Collins* (London: A. Barker, 1952), p. 126.

86 Nuel Pharr Davis, *The Life of Wilkie Collins* (Urbana: Univ. of Illinois Press, 1956), p. 274.

87 Davis, pp. 275-76.

Chapter 5

1 For histories of French, British, and American views of American women, see: Frank Monaghan's *French Travelers in the United States, 1765-1932* (New York: Antiquarian, 1961); Allan Nevins' *America Through British Eyes* (New York: Oxford Univ. Press, 1948); and Warren S. Tryon's *A Mirror for Americans* (Chicago: Univ. of Chicago Press, 1952). For some specifically feminist viewpoints by travelers not cited elsewhere in this chapter, see Fredrika Bremer's *The Homes of the New World; Impressions of America*, trans. by Mary Howitt (New York, 1853); Barbara Bodichon's *An American Diary, 1857-8*, ed. Joseph W. Reed, Jr. (London: Routledge & Kegan Paul, 1972); Emily Faithful's *Three Visits to America* (Edinburgh, 1884). Una Pope-Hennessy's *Three English Women in America* (London: Benn, 1929) studies Frances Trollope, Harriet Martineau, and Fanny Kemble. For studies of the American Girl, see Kate Gannett Wells's "The Transitional American Woman,"

Atlantic Monthly, 46 (1880), 817-23; "What the American Girl Has Lost: By an American Mother," *Ladies' Home Journal*, 17 (1900), 17; Howard Chandler Christy's *The American Girl* (New York: Moffat, 1906); Anne Morgan's *The American Girl: Her Education, Her Responsibility, Her Recreation, Her Future* (New York: Harper, 1915); William Wasserstrom's *Heiress of All the Ages* (Minneapolis: Univ. of Minnesota Press, 1959); Page Smith's *Daughters of the Promised Land* (Boston: Little, Brown, 1970); Ishbel Ross's "The Ladies Travel" in *The Expatriates* (New York: Crowell, 1970), pp. 120-41; Ernest Earnest's *The American Eve in Fact and Fiction, 1775-1914* (Urbana: Univ. of Illinois Press, 1974); Barbara Welter's "Coming of Age in America: The American Girl in the Nineteenth Century" in *Dimity Convictions* (Athens: Ohio Univ. Press, 1976), pp. 3-20; Susan Gregory Allison's "The American Girl, 1880-1900: Drawn from Fact and Fiction" (MA thesis, Univ. of Chicago, 1975); Paul John Eakin's *The New England Girl* (Athens, Ga.: Univ. of Georgia Press, 1976).

² The Marquis de Chastellux, *Travels in North America in the Years 1780, 1781, and 1782*, rev. trans. with introduction and notes by Howard C. Rice, Jr. (Chapel Hill: Univ. of North Carolina Press, 1963), pp. 615, 120.

³ Moreau de St. Méry, *Moreau de St. Méry's American Journey, 1793-1798*, trans. and ed. Kenneth Roberts and Anna M. Roberts (Garden City, N.Y.: Doubleday, 1947), pp. 284, 290, 286.

⁴ Frances Wright, *Views of Society and Manners in America* (London, 1821), pp. 30-31, 32.

⁵ Frances Trollope, *The Domestic Manners of the Americans* (London, 1832), pp. 413, 413-14, 267.

⁶ Harriet Martineau, *Society in America* (London, 1837), II, 106, 107-8, 108. For recent work on Martineau and American women, see Valerie Kossew Pichanick's "An Abominable Submission: Harriet Martineau's Views on the Role and Place of Woman," *Women's Studies*, 5 (1979), 13-32.

⁷ Alexis, Comte de Tocqueville, trans. Henry Reeve, *Democracy in America* (1835; rpt. New York: Schocken, 1961), vol. 2, pp. 237-42, 252.

⁸ Gustave de Beaumont (1802-66), lifelong friend, political associate, and literary executor of Tocqueville, produced from the American journey a novel about Indians and slavery, *Marie; ou, L'Esclavage aux États-Unis* (1835).

⁹ Quoted by George Wilson Pierson in *Tocqueville and Beaumont in America* (Oxford: Oxford Univ. Press, 1938), p. 144.

¹⁰ Ibid., p. 245.

¹¹ Among many works on James's women besides those listed in note 1, see: William Dean Howells' *Heroines of Fiction* (New York: Harper, 1901), II, 164-76; Cornelia P. Kelley's *The Early Development of Henry James* (Urbana: Univ. of Illinois Press, 1930, reissued 1965); Elizabeth F. Hoxie's "Mrs. Grundy Adopts Daisy Miller," *New England Quarterly*, 19 (1946), 474-84; Christof Wegelin's *The Image of Europe in Henry James* (Dallas: Southern Methodist Univ. Press, 1958); Ishbel Ross's "In the Shadow of Henry James," in *The Expatriates*, pp. 204-20; William Veeder's *Henry James: The Lessons of the Master* (Chicago: Univ. of Chicago Press, 1975), pp. 106-19, 150-83; Mary Doyle Springer's *A Rhetoric of Literary Character* (Chicago: Univ. of Chicago Press, 1978); Edward Wagenknecht's *Eve and Henry James* (Norman: Univ. of Oklahoma Press, 1978).

¹² James's "The Speech of American Women" and "The Manners of American Women" ran in *Harper's Bazaar* from November, 1906, through July, 1907; they have recently been collected under the title *The Speech and Manners of American*

Women, ed. E.S. Riggs, with intro. by Inez Martinez (Lancaster, Pa.: Lancaster House, 1973).

13 Henry James, *Portraits of Places* (Boston, 1884), p. 344.

14 Leon Edel, *Henry James: The Conquest of London* (Philadelphia: Lippincott, 1962), p. 359.

15 This and the next seven quotations from James and his heroines are taken from: "Poor Richard" (1867) in *The Complete Tales of Henry James*, ed. Leon Edel (Philadelphia: Lippincott, 1961 [hereafter referred to as *CT*]), I, 241. "New Novels," *The Nation*, 21 (1875), 202 [201–03]. "Opportunity," *The Nation*, 5 (1867), 450 [448–50]. "The Sweetheart of M. Briseux" (1873) *CT* III, 85. "An International Episode" (1878), *CT* IV, 290. "A Bundle of Letters" (1879), *CT* IV, 449, 450. "Madame de Mauves" (1874), *CT* III, 158. "The Pension Beaurepas" (1879), *CT* IV, 369.

16 Horace Scudder, "The Portrait of a Lady and Dr. Breen's Practice," *Atlantic Monthly*, 49 (1882), 127 [126–30].

17 *CT* IV, 385.

18 *Daisy Miller, A Study* appeared first in the June and July numbers of *Cornhill* for 1878; *An International Episode*, in the December and January *Cornhill* for 1878–79.

19 Edel, *Henry James: The Conquest of London*, p. 312.

20 *Life in Letters of William Dean Howells*, ed. Mildred Howells (Garden City, N.Y.: Doubleday, 1928), I, 271.

21 Edel, *Henry James: The Conquest of London*, p. 309.

22 "Editor's Literary Record," *Harper's*, 58 (1879), 310 [307–12].

23 For the reception of *Daisy Miller*, see Edmond L. Volpe's "The Reception of Daisy Miller," *Boston Public Library Quarterly*, 10 (1958), 55–59, and George Monteiro's "Henry James and His Reviewers: Some Identifications," *Papers of the Bibliographical Society of America*, 63 (1969), 300–304. For the best collection of Victorian and recent work on *Daisy Miller*, see *James's Daisy Miller*, ed. William T. Stafford (New York: Scribner's, 1963).

24 "Editor's Literary Record," p. 310.

25 Thomas Wentworth Higginson, "Henry James, Jr.," *The Literary World*, 10 (1879), 384 [383–84].

26 Richard Grant White, "Recent Fiction," *North American Review*, 128 (1879), 106 [97–110].

27 William Dean Howells, "The Contributor's Club," *Atlantic Monthly*, 43 (1879), 399–400 [392–404].

28 George Somes Layard, *Mrs. Lynn Linton, Her Life, Letters, and Opinions* (London: Methuen, 1901), pp. 232–33.

29 *Henry James Letters*, ed. Leon Edel (Cambridge, Mass.: Harvard Univ. Press, 1974), II, 303–4.

30 Henry James, *The Art of the Novel*, intro. by R.P. Blackmur (New York: Scribner's, 1934), pp. 269, 269–70, 270.

31 "American Mores and Daisy Miller," *The New York Times*, June 4, 1879, p. 4.

32 *Henry James Letters*, II, 209–10.

33 Mrs. Frank H. Hill, "Recent Novels," *Daily News*, March 21, 1879, p. 6.

34 *Henry James Letters*, II, 219–20, 220, 221.

35 Leon Edel, *Henry James: The Untried Years* (Philadelphia: Lippincott, 1953), p. 322.

Index

Acton, Dr. William, 111, 112
Adams, Clover Hooper, 194. *See also* American Girl, The
adultery, 50, 59, 125, 146, 150, 159
aestheticism, 146, 160, 162
"aesthetics of renunciation," 35, 200n16
Agnes Wickfield, xiv, 81, 83
Albert, 194
Alcott, Louisa May, 9, 65, 123, 125, 210n23
Allan, J. McGrigor, 123
amendments to U.S. Constitution: Nineteenth, 193
American Girl, The
  as literary type, 79
  foreign commentators upon: Chastellux and St. Mery find young women free and married women restricted, 171–72; British women emphasize restrictions—Wright, limited education, 172–73; Trollope, "beauty and insignificance" of, 173–74; Martineau, slavery of, 173, 174, 211n6; Tocqueville blends earlier views—sees young women as free and self-reliant, 175; as restricted by marriage, 175–76; denies slavery of, but insists upon severe restrictions upon, 177–78

American Girl, The (*continued*)

modern work on: Howitt, M., Monaghan, F., Nevins, A., Pope-Hennessy, U., Reed, J., Tryon, W., Wells, K., 213n1; Allison, S., Christy, H., Eakin, P., Earnest, E., Morgan, A., Ross, I., Smith, P., Wasserstrom, W., Welter, B., 214n1; Pichanick, V., 224n6; Pierson, G., 214nn9, 10

Henry James: forty years as commentator on The American Girl, 171, 178, 214n12; pre-*Daisy Miller* work—rejects extremes of angel and villainess, 178–79, 215n13; emphasizes freedom, 179; sees The American Girl as representative, 178–80; *Daisy Miller*—examines *two* roles, girl and wife, 180–81; the *Daisy Miller* controversy—uproar over and vogue of, 181; contrast with G.O.P. controversy, 181–82; men's response—no national chauvinism, 182–83; male chauvinism, 183; Howells, 183–85; women's responses—Americans disavow Daisy, 185; British question her morals, 185–86; expatriates find her idealized, 186–87; James's ultimate intent to show conflict between stereotyping and freedom, 80, 187–88; *New York Times* and "lady" question, 188–89; *An International Episode*—180, 215nn15, 18; Bessie Alden and free play of mind, 189–90; British thinskinned, 188, 190; James's response, 188, 190–92; the ultimate restriction upon The American Girl's freedom—Minnie Temple, Clover Hooper, and death, 192, 193

modern work on James: Hoxie, E., Kelley, C., Ross, I., Springer, M., Veeder, W., Wagenkneckt, E., Weglin, C., 214n11; Martinez, I., Riggs, E., 215n12; Edel, L., 215nn14, 19, 21, 29, 35; Montiero, G., Stafford, W., Volpe, E., 215n23; Blackmur, R., 215n30

American Wife, 171, 173, 192

American Woman, 172, 173, 175, 176, 177, 178, 186, 192, 210, 214n6

Angel in the House

as Victorian ideal, xiv, 48, 79, 80–82, 83, 84, 125, 127, 128, 132, 136, 185

as literary heroine: praised, 80, 82, 83; Amelia Osborne, 81, 82–83, 84–85, 87–88; Agnes Wickfield, 81, 83; Esther Summerson, 81, 83–84; Honoria, 81, 83, 84; criticized, 82–83, 84–88; intelligence in, 82, 84, 87; insipidity of, 83–85; combined with strong-minded woman, 101–110; as demon, 127; Isabel Archer, 194

modern work on: Welsh, A., Lerner, L., 206n1; Christ, C.,

206n1, 207n20; Gilbert, S. and Gubar, S., 206n1, 207n23; Mitchell, S., 208n18

Angel out of the House, xv, 48

Anthony, Susan B., xiv, 111

apocalyptic feminism, xv, 86, 169

Arnold, Matthew, 135

Austen, Jane, 12, 32, 56, 57–58, 68, 90, 93

Austin, Alfred, 146, 156–60, 212n57

Aytoun, W.E., 44, 208n51

Bailey, Gamaliel, 62

Barnes, William, 206n1

Baynes, T.S., 212nn57, 58

Beard, Charles, 63

Beatrice, 128

Beaumont, Gustave de, 176, 214n8

Bell, Currer, see Brontë, Charlotte

Bell, Robert, 206n6

Bentley, George, 168

Bible, 150

bigamy, 124, 125, 133

birth control, 194

Blondin, 123

Bodichon, Barbara, 75–76, 213n1

Boucicault, Dion, 123

Braddon, Mary Elizabeth, 122, 132, 210n21, 211n25; radical, 124, 170; conservative, 125, 126, 169; and Oliphant, 139, 140, 144, 145, 211n55; *Lady Audley's Secret*, 80, 112, 122, 123, 127, 131, 147, 156, 211n38, 212n60; *Aurora Floyd*, 123, 127, 131, 144, 211n37

Bremer, Fredrika, 213n1

Brontë, Charlotte, xi, 68–69, 78, 109, 132, 145, 190

nineteenth century images of: as successful, 4, 32, 66, 72, 103, 104; as dutiful daughter, 9, 12; as member of rebellious younger sisterhood, 49, 130, 190; as unwomanly, 54, 71

pseudonym: choice typical of a group of writers, 48, 65–66; Brontë's desire to protect, 68–69; Lewes' revelation, 70

relationship with G.H. Lewes: he recognizes originality of *Jane Eyre*, 66–67; she questions emphasis on experience, 67; she defends power of imagination, 67–68; she asks to be judged as a man, 69; her anger over review of *Shirley*, 71

works: *Jane Eyre*—sensational effect of, 48, 98–99; called unwomanly, 54, 98–99; Brontë's fear that it would be re-

Chorley, Henry F., 28, 83–84, 206n6, 208n54
Christianity: standard superior to conventional love, 115, 116, 117, 120, 164
Churchill, Winston, 192
Cigarette, 125
Cobbe, Frances Power, 93–94
Cobden, Richard, 114
Colleen Baun, The, 123
Collins, Wilkie, 111, 112, 122, 132, 139, 213nn75, 77, 85; *The New Magdalen*, 111, 112, 213nn78, 79, 80, 81, 82, 84; *Armadale*, 122, 164, 213n77; *No Name*, 122, 170; *The Woman in White*, 122, 138, 139, 210n20; *Basil*, 164. See also fallen woman, the
Comstock, Anthony, xi
Comstock, William A., 169
Contagious Diseases Acts, 193
Cornhill, 45–46, 181
Coxe, Rev. Arthur Cleveland, 209n1
Crowe, Catherine, 4
Cummins, Maria, 49, 202n39, 203n53
Cunningham, Gail, 209n18
Daisy Miller, *see* American Girl, The
Dall, Caroline, 95
Dallas, E.S., 78
Dante, 150
Darwin, Charles, 153
Davis, Rebecca Harding, 65, 121
Descartes, René, 59
De Staël, Madame, 71
Dickens, Charles, xiv, *David Copperfield*, 81, 83, 113; *Bleak House*, 81, 83–84, 93, 113; *Oliver Twist*, 113; and fallen woman, 113, 114; sensational, 132; Oliphant on, 135, 136, 137; and Collins, 164, 169, 170
Dickinson, Emily, 28, 41, 47, 198–99n33, 201n28, 201–02n33
Disraeli, Isaac, 6–7, 17
Dolly, 137
domestic novel
  as a woman's genre, 48
  uses of: to affirm conventional beliefs, 48–51; to awaken feelings and gain power, 60–61; to criticize a patriarchal society, 61–64
  its effects on critical controversies: sets standards for later

domestic novel (*continued*)

> fiction—everyday experiences, 48; emphasis on affections, 48, 51; belief in duty, 49–50; use of highminded girlish heroine, 50, 51; raises the question of realism, 51–53

Brontë's determination that *Jane Eyre* not be seen as a mere domestic novel, 66

modern work on: Colby, V., Showalter, E., 202n38; Brown, H., Papashvily, H., Garrison, D., Douglas, A., Baym, N., Kelley, M., Tompkins, J., 202n39

Dreiser, Theodore, 110, 111

Dryden, John, 129

Drysdale, Dr. George, xiv, 116

Duffey, Mrs. E.B., 126

economics, impact on women, 176

education, women's, 172–73, 174

egalitarianism, between the sexes, xiv, xvi

Egerton, George, 65

Eliot, George (Mary Anne Evans), 109, 123, 169

> as a novelist: reputation—generally high, 32, 48, 66, 78; among women, 47, 66, 75–77; use of pseudonym—as characteristic of a group of writers, 48, 65; her choice of names, 73; revelation of real identity, 74; Bodichon's disregard of, 76; decision to write fiction, 72; images of—as clergyman, 73; freethinker, 72, 74; free-lover, 74–75; eminent Victorian, 78; strong-minded, 92–93; sybil, 206n74

> as a critic of women's literature: admiration for women writers—E.B. Browning, 38; C. Brontë, 72; H. Martineau, 72; E. Gaskell, 72, 75, 77; belief that women's literature should be unique and influential, 58–60; problems with nineteenth-century women's literature—imitation of masculine style, 59; reviewers' false flattery, 72; lack of serious critical standards, 72–73; carelessness and vanity of aspiring authors, 72–73; calls for improvement—give women a wider range of experiences and ideas, 60; develop critical standards, 72–73; urge mediocre writers to abandon the field, 73

> life: liaison with Lewes, 72, 92

> works: *Adam Bede*, 48, 73–74, 75, 76, 107, 121, 122, 209n17; *The Mill on the Floss*, 48, 74–75, 78, 107, 194; "Woman in France," 58–60; *Scenes from Clerical Life*, 72, 73, 76, 77; "Silly Novels by Lady Novelists," 72–73; *Middlemarch*, 72, 89, 101, 105–09; *Romola*, 107

modern work on: Showalter, E., 205n63; Haight, G., Gilbert, S. and Gubar, S., Moers, E., Thomson, P., 205n69; Welsh A., 205n70; Carroll, D., Fulmer, C., Holstrom, J., Lerner, L., 205–06n71; Redinger, R., 206n74

Ellis, Sarah, xi, xiv, 81–82

An English Daisy Miller, 181

Evans, Augusta Wilson, 49, 78, 202n39

Evans, Mary Anne, *see* George Eliot

Everett, C.C., 208n56

Fairless, Michael, 65

Faithfull, Emily, 213n1

Falconer, Lanoe, 65

fallen woman, the

as character type, 79; and prostitution, 111; traditional figures, 113; radical potential first actualized in *The Scarlet Letter*, 113

Ruth: traditional and radical aspects, 113

Ruth controversy: Gaskell attacked personally, 114, 209nn4, 6; she admits subversive aspects, 114, 209n5; praised by important individuals, 114; by important periodicals, 115–16; her concern with all social outcasts, 116–17; reviewers disagree over her presentation of sexuality, 118–19; over need for Ruth dying, 119; Greg's charge of righteousness, 120–21; *Cornhill* retrospective, 163

novels between 1853 and 1873: titles and authors, 121; critical responses, 122

Collins: as subversive—life, 163–64; attacks conventional morality, 164; defies Mudie, 168; prefers anonymity to humbug, 170; as conservative—about women, 169–70

The New Magdalen: plot, 163; controversy—critics focusing on formal aspects, 164–65; on formal and moral, 165; on moral, 165–67; interpretation of the controversy, 167–69

modern work on: Cameron, W., Cohen, B., Crowley, J., 208n1; Kennard, J., 209n1

modern work on Gaskell: Chapple, J. and Pollard, A., 209n2; Rubenius, A., and Easson A., Gérin, W., Hopkins, A., 209n7; Ludlow, J., 209n9; Waller, R., 209n14; Shorter, C., 209n15; Phillips, W., 210nn21, 22; Robinson, K., 213n76; Ashley, R., 213n83; Davis, N., 213nn86, 87. *See also* prostitution

Fallen Woman Question, 116

Farnham, Eliza, xv

fathers and daughters, 113, 131, 139, 141

feminism, "women's rights," 89, 90, 95, 104. *See also* apocalyptic feminism

Fern, Fanny (née Sarah Willis): financial success, 4; sees writing rooted in woman's anger and frustration, 9, 14–16, 22; modern work on—Wood, A., 197n20, 202n39

Flaubert, Gustave, 52

"fleshly": poetry, 146, 148, 151–53, 156, 160, 162; heroines, 112, 146, 147. *See also* Pre-Raphaelite, aestheticism, Meredith, Swinburne, D.G. Rossetti, sexuality

Forman, H.B., 33–35

Forster, John, 206n6

Fox, Eliza, 13, 114

freedom, *see* American Girl, The

Fuller, Margaret, 36, 193; and apocalyptic feminism, xv

Gaskell, Elizabeth

nineteenth-century images of: as successful, 4, 72; as respectable domestic novelist, 9, 55, 61, 204n53; as rebellious member of younger generation, 49

sense of self as woman writer: determination to reconcile writing and domestic responsibility, 12–14; determination to invoke maternal power against social evil, 61; relationships with other women writers: admiration for George Eliot, 76–77

works of: *Life of Charlotte Brontë*, 12–13, 197n17; *Mary Barton*, 48, 55, 77, 111; *Ruth*, 48, 61, 62, 111, 112; *North and South*, 93; *A Dark Night's Work*, 123

and strong-minded heroine, 93, 109

modern work on: Gérin, W., 197n17, 206n73; Sharps, J., 204n53. *See also* fallen woman, the

Gérôme, Jean-Léon, 55

Gessner, Salomon, 6–7

Gilbert, W.S., 132, 211n39

Giles, Henry, 208n1

Gilfillan, George, 28–29, 30

Girl of the Period, 79, 89, 156, 181, 182

Gissing, George, 109

Goëthe, Johann Wolfgang von, 23, 58

Gore, Catherine, 48, 49

Grace, Roseberry, 166, 167

Graham, Ennis, 65

Graves, Caroline, 213n75

Greenwell, Dora, 96
Greenwood, Grace, 62
Greg, W.R., 54, 111, 119, 120, 209n16
Grey, Maria, 18–19, 26–27
Griswold, Rufus, 33, 35
Grundy, Mrs., 126, 168, 169, 170
Guizot, François, 114
Hale, Sarah Josepha, xv, 4, 28, 202n39
Hall, Anna Maria, 63
Hardy, Thomas, 109, 111
Harper, Frances Ellen Watkins, 40
Harte, Bret, 126, 132–34, 211n40
Hartman, Mary S., 126, 210n27, 211n30
Hawthorne, Nathaniel, 4, 47, 50, 83; *The Scarlet Letter*, 113, 208n1, 209n1
Hayward, Abraham, 206n5
Hemans, Felicia, xiv, 27, 28–29, 32, 35, 36, 46, 64
heroines, literary: and cultural images of woman, 79–80; changes in, 81
    passionate: society's concern with woman's sexual purity, 111; liberalization of mid-Victorian attitudes, 111; distinguishing among strong-minded, fallen, sensational, and fleshly types, 112; major controversies between 1853 and 1873. *See also* American Girl, Angel in the House, domestic novel, fallen woman, "fleshly," "new woman" fiction, Pre-Raphaelite, sensation heroine
Hentz, Caroline, 49, 202n39, 204n56
Hidden Fire, 125
Higginson, Thomas Wentworth, 47
Hobbes, John Oliver, 65
home, ideal of, 125
Homer, 28, 30
Hooper, Clover, *see* Clover Hooper Adams
Hope, Lawrence, 65
Hewitt, William, 207n36
Hunt, Holman, 146
Hutton, R.H., 52–53, 203n46, 207n11; "Novels by the Authoress of John Halifax," 203n46
Isabel Archer, 179, 192, 194
Jackson, Helen Hunt, 40
James, Henry: on Yonge and Warner, 51–52; on *Middlemarch*, 108–09; *Portrait of a Lady*, 109, 110, 179, 188, 192; *The*

James, Henry (*continued*)
    Bostonians, 178; "Julia Bride," 178; "The Pension Beaure-
    pas," 179, 180, 215n15; *The American,* 187; "The Speech of
    American Women," 214n12; "The Manners of American
    Women," 214n12; *The Speech and Manners of American Women,*
    214n12; *Portraits of Places,* 215n13; "Poor Richard," 215n15;
    "The Sweetheart of M. Briseux," 215n15; "Opportunity,"
    215n15; "New Novels," 215n15; "Madame de Mauves,"
    215n15; "A Bundle of Letters," 215n15; *The Art of the
    Novel,* 215n30. *See also* American Girl, The
Jameson, Anna, 9, 22–24, 41, 95, 198n32
Jewsbury, Geraldine, 4, 22, 24–25, 135, 137, 211n42
Johnson, Virginia, 181
Kemble, Fanny, 213n1
Kingsley, Charles, 95, 101, 114, 124
Kirk, J.F., 207n19
Kirkland, Caroline May, 31, 50–51, 60–61, 199n8
Kotzebue, August von, 165
La Fontaine, Jean de, 73
Lake, Claude, 55
Land at Last, 126
Landon, Letitia, 27, 36
Lawrence, G.A., 123, 132, 210n22
Leclercq, Miss, 167
Lee, Holme, 65
Lee, Vernon, 65
Leotard, 123
Lewes, George Henry
  satire of male writers and their fears about women writers: as
    economic competitors, 4; as irresponsible wives and
    mothers, 5–6; as angry women, 5–6
  theories of literature: originates in suffering, 21, 67; as tran-
    scription of experience, 56, 58, 67
  theories of women's art: origins of—thwarted domestic or
    maternal affections, 21; hereditary organic tendency, 21–
    22; fiction as a woman's genre, 57; achievements limited
    by maternal function, 69
  ideas about women: different organization of, 56, 69; domi-
    nance of emotions over intellect, 56; their experiences
    primarily domestic, 56–57; maternity their grand func-
    tion, 69–70
  as a critic of women novelists: their strengths—insight into

emotions, 56–57; depiction of woman's experience, 56–58; use of details, 57; their weaknesses—imitation of men, 56–57; construction of plots, 57; treatment of male characters, 57

recognition of Jane Austen: her place in the history of women's literature, 56; praise for—her artistic superiority, 57; her sense of life, 57; her womanly point of view, 58

recognition of George Sand: praise for womanly point of view, eloquence, life of passionate experience, 58; criticism of philosophy and failure wth male characters, 58

relationship with Charlotte Brontë: praises *Jane Eyre*, 66–67, 97, 99; urges her to write from experience, 67; reveals female identity of, 68, 70; faults *Shirley* for depiction of unnatural female characters, 70–71; attributes weaknesses to Brontë's lack of maternal experience, 70; consequences of their relationship, 71; on *Villette*, 209n8

relationship with George Eliot: begins liaison, 72; encourages her to write fiction, 72; acts as literary husband, 72; advises her to adopt psuedonym, 73

works of: "A Gentle Hint to Writing Women," 3–6; "The Lady Novelists," 21–22, 56–58, 92; "Currer Bell's *Shirley*," 69–71, 205n67; *Rose, Blanche, and Violet*, 196n5

Lewis, Sarah, 81–82, 101

Linton, Eliza Lynn, 4, 135; *The Girl of the Period*, 79, 89, 156, 181–82; and sensationalism, 123, 125, 180, 211n28; and *Daisy Miller*, 185, 186, 188, 189, 190, 215n28

Lorimer, James, 49–50, 208nn45, 46

Loring, George Bailey, 209n1

Lowell, James Russell, 181

Ludlow, J.M., 55, 62

Luyster, Isaphene, 208n55

Macarthur, Mary, xiii

MacCarthy, Justin, 126, 129, 131, 135, 211n36

Madaleine, 170

Magdalen, 113, 121

Malet, Lucas, 65

man: defective training of, 85–86; and double standard, 113; as woman's standard of conduct, 137–38. *See also* sexuality, male

Margaret Dacre, 126

Marie; ou, L'Esclavage aux Etats-Unis, 214n8

Marsh, Anne, 4, 48, 49–50, 51, 97, 211n42

marriage: and woman writers 5–16; wife's role—as angel, 80–82, 84; as partner, 84; as complementary to husband's 96; strong-minded women and, 93, 98–99, 101; and sensationism, 125; in Pre-Raphaelite poetry, 146, 148, 152; Trollope, James, Eliot on, 159, 194; as slavery, 172, 175–78

Married Women's Property Act (1882), 193

Martineau, Harriet, 4, 48, 72, 122, 172, 176, 215n1. *See also* American Girl, The

Masson, David, 82

Maurice, J.F.D., 114

Mephistopheles, 127

Mercy Merrick, 163, 164, 165, 166, 168, 170

Meredith, George, 164, 212nn59, 61, 213n75; *Rhoda Fleming,* 121; *Emelia in England,* 130; *The Ordeal of Richard Feverel,* 130; *Modern Love,* 146, 147, 148, 150, 162

Mill, John Stuart, xi, xiv, 9, 143, 156

Millais, J.E., 146

Milton, John, 28, 31

Mitford, Mary Russell, 208n1

Morley, John, 150

motherhood: and women's writing, 13–14, 55, 62, 69–70; Lewes on Brontë's Mrs. Pryor, 70; maternal love, 88; strong-minded women and, 93, 94, 95, 98–99, 101; as way to reclaim fallen woman, 116; as restricting, 172, 173; woman's inability to cope with, 180, 184, 186

Mrs. Miller, 180

Mudie, Charles Edward, 126, 168, 169

muse, female, 7, 198n33

muse, male, 196n7

McIntosh, Maria, 49, 202n39, 204n56

Neal, John, 17–18

Neil, Ross, 65

New Magdalen, The, see fallen woman, the

"new woman" fiction, 109–110

Newton, R. Heber, 96

Nichol, John, 205n52

Nightingale, Florence, 44, 108, 114

Norton, Andrews, 28

Norton, Caroline, 27–28, 36, 40, 83, 93; illustration 3; *Lost and Saved,* 121, 122, 128, 129, 130, 210n19

novel

as a woman's genre: can be written within confines of ordinary life (Schreiner), 22; its material drawn from their experience—of human life (Schreiner), 22; of domestic life (Lewes), 57; requires no training or education, (Schreiner) 22, (Eliot) 73; is consistent with woman's emotional nature (Lewes), 57

religious, 123

control over by Mudie and Grundy, 168–70

Oliphant, Margaret, 78, 123, 126, 209n3, 210n24, 212n52; on reconciling writing and domesticity, 9, 11–12; on American heroines, 203n44; *Chronicles of Carlingford*, 136. *See also* sensation heroine

orphans, 113, 141

Ouida (Marie Louise de la Ramée), 123, 125

Paget, Rev. Francis, 132, 211n39

passionate heroine, the, *see* fallen woman, fleshly heroine, Pre-Raphaelite, sensation heroine

Parkes, Bessie Rayner, 3

Pater, Walter, 146, 160, 161–62

Patmore, Coventry: *The Angel in the House*, 80, 81, 83; on emancipated women, 90–92

Peabody, Andrew, 28

Petrarch, Francis, 80

Phelps, Elizabeth Stuart, 121, 190, 202n38

poetry: epic, 30–31; lyric, 30–31, 33; comic/satiric, 132. *See also* "fleshly," Pre-Raphaelite, women poets

Pre-Raphaelite, 34; poetry, 34, 147–49, 151, 160; painting, 146–47, 150; women, 146, 147, 150, 156

Proctor, Edna, 40

prostitution, 111, 115, 137, 166, 167; in Pre-Raphaelite poetry, 156. *See also* fallen woman

pseudonyms: female, 49, 203n40, 204n61, 205n70; neutral, 65; male; *see* women novelists

Putnam, G.P., 47

Raine, Allen, 65

Ray, W. Fraser, 126, 127, 128, 211n33

Reade, Charles, 132, 144, 164, 213n75; as sensational, 123, 210n22; heroines of, 136, 137, 212n46; and prurient prudes, 165, 166

Recommended to Mercy, 129, 130

religion, 123, 137, 166, 176

Rigby, Elizabeth (Lady Eastlake), 4, 99–101

Ross, Martin, 65

1867 essay—praise for and criticism of Braddon, 139; examines woman's portrayal of woman, 140; Broughton's Nelly as forward, 141; as isolated from women, 142; woman's role in society's moral life, 143–44, 212n54; Braddon's response, 144–45; Oliphant's retrospective, 145, 212n56

compared with fleshly heroine, 147

modern work on sensationism: Buckner, C., Edwards, P., Fisher, B., Hughes, W., Ivy, R., Maison, M., Mitchell, S., Showalter, E., Stang, R., Tillotson, K., Transue, H., 210n20; Wolff, R., 210n21, 212n55; Burns, W., Fleming, G., 210n22; Stern, M., 210n23; Wise, J., 210n25, 211n29; Stedman, J., 211n39; Colby, R. and V., 211n41; Griest, J., 211n42; Fahnestock, J., 211n42, 212n49; Smith, G., 213n74; Elwin, M., Fuller, J., Johnson, D., Peacock, M., 213n75

sentimentalists, *see* domestic fiction

sexuality, female: and women's writing, 16–20, 21, 22, 23–24, 69, 198n24, 203n50; in *Ruth*, 118–19; in Pre-Raphaelite painting, 146–47, illustration 7; in Pre-Raphaelite poetry —Meredith, 146, 147, 148, 150; D.G. Rossetti, 146, 148–49, 150–53; Swinburne, 146, 149–50, 152–60; attacked, 146, 150–53, 155–60; defended, 153–55, 160–62; prudery, 154–55, 172; promiscuity of American young women, 172; of Daisy Miller, 185–86. *See also* fallen woman, "fleshly," prostitution, sensation heroine, woman, nature of

sexuality, male, 146, 147–54, 156, 157, 159, 160–61

Seymour, Mrs. Laura, 213n75

Shakespeare, 128, 157

Shelley, Percy Bysshe, 21

Sheridan, Richard Brinsley, 27

Shirreff, Emily, 18–19, 26–27

Sigourney, Lydia, 22, 27–29, 30, 32, 35, 36, 198n30

single woman, as writer, 21, 23–24, 55

sisterhood, 49, 115, 142–44

slavery: women and blacks, 41, 42–44, 62, 63; women enslaved by husbands, 172, 174, 177–78; by society, 173–74, 176, 187–88

Smith, Madeleine, 126

Social Purity Reform, 86, 169, 193

social science, 108

Southworth, E.D.E.N., 4, 49, 202n39; illustration 1

suffrage, 89, 103, 106, 193
Taylor, Bayard, 121
Taylor, Harriet, 9
Temple, Minnie, 192, 194
Tennyson, Alfred Lord, 83, 150, 151, 156–60; *Maud*, 41; *The Princess*, 89, 94–97, 101, 103, 109, 159
Thackeray, W.M., 39, 45–46, 76, 169 illustration 2; heroines of, 81, 82–88, 136, 137, 211n44; *Vanity Fair*, 81, 82–88
Thompson, William, 116; as advocate of egalitarianism between the sexes, xiv
Tocqueville, Alexis Comte de, 174, 179; *Democracy in America*, 214n7. *See also* American Girl, The
Trafford, F.G., 65
Treason at Home, 125
Trollope, Anthony, 121, 123, 156, 158, 159, 169
Trollope, Frances, 49, 172, 173, 176, 213n1, 214n5
Van Rensselaer, M.G., 50
Victoria, Queen, 115, 194–95
Warner, Anna, 49, 202n39
Warner, Susan: as successful domestic novelist, 4, 47, 48, 49, 60–61; responses to *The Wide, Wide World*—C.M. Kirkland, 50–51; H. James, 51–52; M. Oliphant and C. Yonge, 203n44; modern work on, 202n39, Foster, E., 203n44
Which Should It Be?, 125
Whipple, E.P., 207n26, 208nn42, 46
White, Richard Grant, 153–54, 182, 183, 215n26
wife, properly disobedient, 113. *See also* American Girl
Wigan, Alfred, 164
Willard, Frances, 88–89, 111
Williams, W.S., 66
Willis, Sarah, *see*, Fern, Fanny
Wills, W.H., 164
Winkworth, Catherine, 114
Winter, John Strange, 65
Wollstonecraft, Mary, xiii, xv, 95
woman
   changing attitudes toward, 125
   duties of, 194
   health of, 174, 192
   nature of: sensitive and artistic, 8, 17–18; imaginative, 19; emotional, 56; instinctive, 63; True Womanhood, 79, 80, 85; pure, 80, 81, 86, 111, 130, 137–38, 140–43, 144–45;

nation, 52–53; associated with their gifts for observation and expression, 53, 57

controversy over experience: debate—their fiction limited by triviality and necessary constraints of their lives, 53–54; fiction enriched by their experiences of motherhood, marriage, and sex, 55, 56–58; call to enlarge their range of experiences and ideas in order to improve their art, 59–60; practical consequences—C. Brontë criticized for too little experience of love, 69–71; G. Eliot reprimanded for having too much, 74–75

use of male pseudonym: as characteristic of a group of British writers, 48, 65; motives for, 64–65; described as—sign of divided life, 12; a ludicrous disguise, 64–65; a way to escape critics' bias, 69, 73; C. Brontë's desire for, 68–69; G. Eliot's need for, 73–74

relationships among: severe judgments of one another's work, 66, 72–73; friendship, 75–77

modern work on: Showalter, E., 197n14, 202n34, 204n61, 206n75; Mitchell, S., 202nn34, 36, 203n42; Auerbach, N., 203n50; Moers, E., 204n58, 205n69; Gilbert, S., and Gubar, S., 204nn58, 61, 205n69; Ewbank, I., 204n59; Wood, A., 204n62, 206n75; Riley, G., 205n62. See also domestic fiction, sensation novel, women writers, entries under individual authors

women poets

images of: idealizations—as lady, 27–28, 29; as wife and mother, 45; caricatures—by W. Thackeray, 39, 198n29; by G.H. Lewes, 196n5

critical expectations for the "poetesses": merits—gentility, 27, 29, 30; humility, 29; modesty, 29, 33, 35, 45; spontaneity, 29, 30; lack of self-consciousness, 29, 30, 35; emotional control, 29, 30, 33–34; seclusion, 30, 31; happiness, 33, 34–35; faults—lack of thought, 29, 32; limited scope, 32–33; subjectivity, 32; dependence on other women, 33; emotional excess, 33, 35; lack of workmanship, 34; self-consciousness, 37, 39–40; knowledge of evil, 40, 45; anger, 44

emotions: as source and subject of women's poetry, 30–31, 32; disagreement concerning their value and proper artistic treatment, 30–35

experiments: the poetry of self-definition, 36–40; the poetry of social protest, 40, 41–46

modern work on: Diehl, J., Faderman, L., Bernikow, L., 196n7;

women poets (*continued*)

> Booth, B., Wood, A., 198n30; Watts, E., Douglas, A., 199n2; Homans, M., 199n6; Gilbert, S. and Gubar, S., 200n11; Sherman, J., Kramer, A., 201n26. *See also* individual authors, especially E.B. Browning, F. Hemans, C. Rossetti

women writers

> success of, 3–4, 26
>
> men's fears about: professional, 4; personal, 5–6
>
> as deviants from proper female roles, 5–6, 9, 20–22
>
> and domesticity: conflicts between duty and art—fear that household will be chaotic, 4–6; fear that duties will drain artistic energies, 9, 14; responses—endorsement of domestic ideal (Oliphant and others), 9–12; uneasy reconciliation (Gaskell), 12–14, 197n14; anger regarding household monotony (Fern), 14–16
>
> motives for writing: anger, 5–6, 14–16; obligation to develop God-given talents: 9, 10, 12, 14; noble ideal, 9, 10; to find shelter from everyday afflictions, 13, 24; to avoid madness, 15–16; to find outlet for energies, 15, 22–24; to develop sympathy for others, 24, 29; to establish bonds with other women, 24–25; to attack social evils, esp. those pertinent to women, 41–42, 46, 62
>
> and motherhood: a source of tension—children a distraction (Gaskell), 13–14; pregnancy an inevitable limitation (Lewes), 69–70; a source of strength—expands sympathy and experience (Gaskell), 14; provides courage to speak against social evils (E.B. Browning and Stowe), 46, 62; increases "womanly perfection" (Ludlow), 55
>
> sexuality of: writing a result of emotional and sexual frustration, 16–17, 21–24; writing a sign of sexual energy or even promiscuity, 16, 18, 20–21
>
> friendships of: G. Jewsbury and J. Carlyle, 24–25; E. Gaskell and G. Eliot, 75, 76–77
>
> eighteenth-century, 48, 198n24
>
> as strong-minded, 89, 93–94, 98
>
> modern work on: Moers, E., Olsen, T., Showalter, E., Hill, M., 197n14; Gérin, W., 197n17; Wood, A., 197n20; Gilbert, S., and Gubar, S., 197n23; Taylor, W., Lasch, C., Bernikow, L., Davidson, C., Broner, E. M., 198n33; Spacks, P., 198n24; Auerbach, N., 203n50. *See also* women poets, women novelists, entries for individual authors

women's imagination

dangers of: associated with seduction, 11, 18; distraction from duty, 14; volatile erotic force, 16; animal sensibility, 17–18; raging fire, 18, 20

legitimate uses of: shelter from daily trials, 13; way to reach the ideal, 14

contradictory theories about: as a faculty particularly active in women, 17–18, 19, 20; as a faculty lacking in women, 16, 52–53

women's defense of: C. Rossetti, 40–41; C. Brontë, 67, 68

women's literary tradition, 33, 56

Women's Movement, 192

women's reading

effect on publishing, 8, 52

novels: a source of danger, 20, 27; sensation novels, 137–38, 143–44

poetry: appropriate reading for women, 26–27; depicts an ideal world, 27; elevates the thoughts, 27

modern work on: Mitchell, S., 202n34

women's rights, 138, 143

Wood, Charles William, 209n18

Wood, Mrs. Henry, 126, 169, 209n18; *East Lynn*, 121, 122, 123, 130

Woolf, Virginia, 110

Wordsworth, William, 82

work, literary, 3, 4–6, 47

Wright, Frances, 172, 173, 214n4

Yates, Edmund, 126

Yonge, Charlotte, 47, 48, 51–52, 93, 198n33, 203n44